architectyourhome

architectyourhome

Hugo Tugman

COLLINS & BROWN

This book is dedicated, with love, to Jude.

First published in the UK in 2010 by
Collins & Brown
10 Southcombe Street
London
W14 0RA

An imprint of Anova Books Company Ltd

All information is correct at time of going
to press.

ISBN 978-1-84340-474-3

A CIP catalogue for this book is available
from the British Library.

10 9 8 7 6 5 4 3 2 1

Reproduction by Dot Gradations Ltd, UK
Printed and bound by Imago, Singapore

This book can be ordered direct from the
publisher at www.anovabooks.com

contents

Introduction

Architect Your Home is about bringing the skills, experience and creativity of architects to home owners in a way that is **friendly** *and useful. Typically (understandably)* **people** *are daunted by the prospect of building works, unclear as to what an* **architect** *actually does, and frightened by the prospect of* **cowboy** *builders.*

Since it was formed in 2001 Architect Your Home has grown into many things. It has become a network of like-minded architects, a reference point for home owners and a bench mark for innovative customer service, but most of all Architect Your Home is a process.

This process was conceived in order to bring two bodies together in a new and effective way: architects and home owners. The unique Architect Your Home process has proved so popular with both parties that, within only a very few years, it has become by far the largest supplier of architectural services to home owners in the UK.

But why did this coming together need to happen at all? From the architect's side, it was necessary because the traditional way in which architects were offering their expertise to the public was daunting, poorly communicated and out of step with customer expectations. From the public's point of view, there has been a huge surge of interest in home design and people wanted a service that they could understand and control.

There are many factors behind this surge of interest that has been seen in home design over the last fifteen years or so. TV shows and magazines have both fuelled and fed upon the public appetite for beautiful and innovative interiors, but this alone cannot be responsible.

Marketeers of products, from kitchens to curtains, home-cinemas to home-workshops, have turned things we previously thought of as functionally necessary into expressions of status and design awareness.

Probably, more than any other single factor, the rise and rise of the property market has given an investment dimension to home improvement. At the time of writing, the basis of this is very much in question as confidence in the market has dissolved. How long will this last? Everyone seems to have an opinion, but in truth, no-one knows.

Whatever upheavals the market has in store for us in years to come, and at whatever levels they sit, market values are relative and we are beginning to reassess what we mean by value itself.

Investment opportunity may have fuelled our interest in home design as a means of climbing the greasy property ladder, but now that we have seen, touched and lived in beautiful homes and interiors, we are hooked. The joy of living with good design is difficult to put a monetary value against, and difficult to express to someone who has not been lucky enough to do so, but unmistakable nonetheless.

One of the characteristics of good design – whatever 'style' is adopted – is that of effortless ease. Good design always feels natural and somehow *right* – as if the scheme adopted was clear and obvious, as if it should *always* have been like this.

However, people often mistakenly think that the simplicity of good design, which is easy on the eye, is simple to produce. They could not be more wrong. To achieve this easy, natural simplicity the designer needs to control and co-ordinate literally thousands of different elements, any one of which can throw the whole design off course.

⋀ Light and space. *The last decade has seen a surge of interest in the possibilities of more open, spacious design, and in respect of how home improvements can enrich lives. This kitchen space is a great example of how simple, inexpensive materials and fittings can function beautifully if the space and light are arranged and guided with sensitivity.*

Architects are the professionals trained and best equipped to take on this task. They are not specialists, but experts across a wide field of subjects within the world of building design. From the technical and technological construction details, to the aesthetic, economic, environmental and political aspects of a project, everything can be guided and orchestrated by an architect.

The way in which an architect's services have traditionally been offered to the consumer has become out of step with the public's expectations. People are no longer willing to be patronised by a paternalistic professional who shrouds what he does in mystery so that he may simply be allowed to get on with it. People are now *interested* and want to be *involved*.

Architect Your Home provides home owners with the expertise, creativity, experience and professionalism of an architect and clearly explains the architectural process for them to use as they wish from a position of knowledge and control.

This book attempts to explain the entire process, illustrating the necessary sequential stages that an architect will go through in designing a project and the constant streams of thought that must be carried through the process from beginning to end. Of course, many projects are built without any involvement from an architect, but one way or another all of these stages will need consideration by someone at some point.

< *Design in detail.* Architects' skills extend far beyond the ability to design the outsides of buildings. This fabulous storage unit is also a giant door that provides access to a larder.

∨ *Maximising space.* The cost of housing is such that making the most of every available space – and enlarging where possible – makes much more sense than moving house. This bedroom was previously a dusty loft used for storing suitcases.

If you are considering a project, you may or may not choose to use an architect to help you, and if you do, you may choose to use one only sparingly for key elements of what you are doing.

This book is intended to help you gain an understanding of the best way of getting from the germ of an idea to a finished project: what stages to follow, how to avoid pitfalls and missed opportunities and how to use an architect to help you achieve the best possible result.

‹ **Beautiful bathrooms.** *This bathroom is a good example of where the breadth of an architect's expertise can really help. To get such a project successfully designed, the water pressure, spacial arrangement, shower fittings, lighting, tile choice, drainage and ambient temperature all need to be taken into consideration.*

› **Case study (see p.27).** *While this book features many projects, it only follows one (illustrated opposite) all the way through from the initial ideas, through the design development and build to completion. The chapters describe the main stages of the design process in turn, and each chapter finishes with illustrations of how far this project had evolved at each stage.*

1 Starting point

It may seem obvious, but working out your objectives before launching into design is of fundamental importance. I meet so many people who are often well down the path of building work, without even having agreed why they want to change their home.

People are influenced by television, advertisements, books, magazine articles and friends. If this is you, then take three steps back. Ask yourself: why are you doing this? What are your underlying objectives? At what level will the cost not be worthwhile? How much of this is about investment and resale – and how much is about what you want for yourself?

practicality

aesthetic

environment

cost/value

regulations

communication

Preconceptions and decisions

Having helped thousands of people improve their homes by **alteration**, **extension** *or* **refurbishment**, *Architect Your Home has developed a system that provides home owners with just the level of* **support**, **creative input** *and* **experience** *that each customer needs.*

Working with customers across many projects of different sizes, budgets and styles has been very revealing and interesting. There are common themes in people's expectations and preconceptions, and we developed Architect Your Home to help customers work through these in a logical, straightforward way. Many commonly held preconceptions are often the root cause of many of the problems that occur in projects. My hope, with this book, is to realign your expectations and provide you with a better understanding of the process necessary for a successful project.

Untangle the process

The single, most common and dangerous preconception that people tend to hold is to underestimate the complexity of any sort of a building project. I do not mean the technical complexity (which, in many instances, is imagined as more difficult than it really is), more the huge number of interlocking decisions that will need to be made on even the most straightforward project.

It is very easy to focus on solving the problems posed by, for example, planning permission, and in doing so forget the question of budget, or the aesthetic ambitions of the project. Similarly, it is easy to get carried away with the specification of the kitchen, only to find that the amount of daylight has not been considered and everything has to change at the last minute.

Many people jump into a project with both feet and find themselves in the middle of a great tangle of questions that they never imagined and that need instant decisions. Conflicting issues, cost problems, regulations that have not been considered in advance, delays, arguments with builders and many more such problems can arise, leading to time overruns, unsatisfactory results, wasted money and unnecessary stress.

It is important to go through an orderly, step-by-step design process that will deal with all aspects of your proposal. This book aims to encapsulate the main ideas behind Architect Your Home and outlines a range of factors that you will need to consider to help make your development project a success.

Untangle your questions

No-one, however experienced, can make every necessary decision about a project at the outset. The most **effective** *way to prepare for a* **successful** *project is to follow a* **logical process** *that looks at each issue in detail beforehand and while it progresses.*

Architect Your Home was developed to help customers untangle the many questions, issues and decisions a project will involve. Their approach is followed in this book and, in the same way, you can make informed decisions about what you want to achieve, how much you hope it will cost and how feasible it will be.

This book focuses on the issues that need to be considered in your project. For simplicity these are grouped into six categories:

As you progress through the book, from design and specification to preparation for building, these six categories will appear on each page, acting as a reminder that you need to continuously reappraise and crosscheck to keep your project on track.

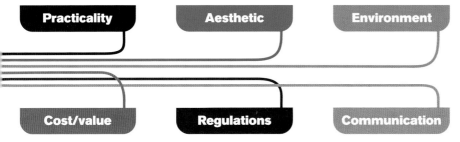

| Practicality | Aesthetic | Environment |
| Cost/value | Regulations | Communication |

Using an architect from the start

The experience and creativity that an architect will bring to a project can be a great help at the outset, and enable you to focus on the pertinent options at each stage of the process. An architect can help you to find solutions that you never imagined, guide you through the choices available – and keep you in budget.

The building industry is packed with people trying to foist 'free' advice or 'free' design services onto home owners. Don't be fooled – this advice or service is never free, they are sales devices and will be skewed towards selling a particular product or system. An architect, however, can provide independent advice that is focused on helping you to find the best project solution for you and your home.

DOORS &
WINDOWS

planning
permission

VISUALISATION

ELEVATIONS

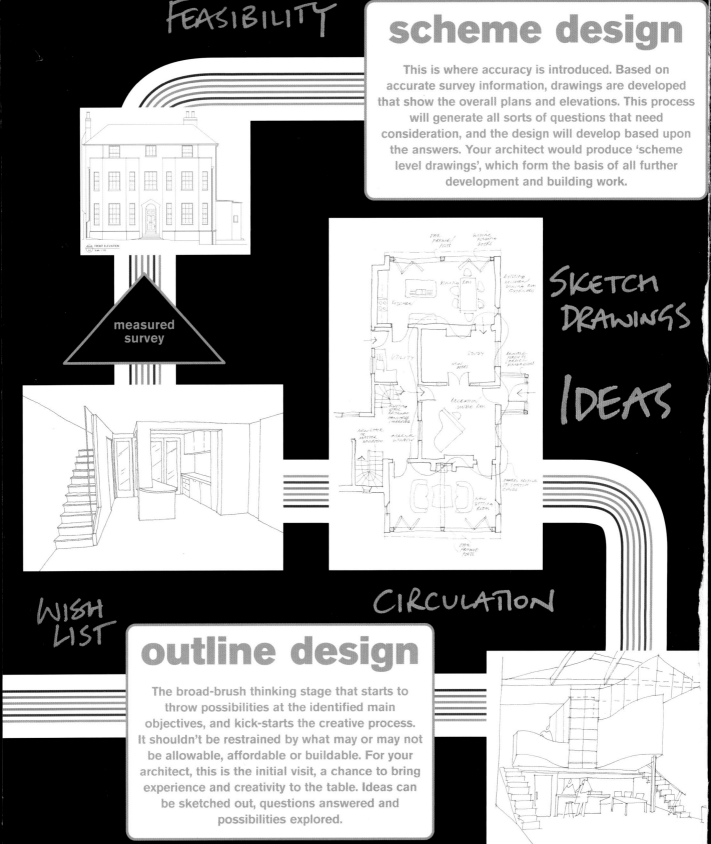

FEASIBILITY

scheme design

This is where accuracy is introduced. Based on accuracy survey information, drawings are developed that show the overall plans and elevations. This process will generate all sorts of questions that need consideration, and the design will develop based upon the answers. Your architect would produce 'scheme level drawings', which form the basis of all further development and building work.

measured survey

SKETCH DRAWINGS

IDEAS

WISH LIST

CIRCULATION

outline design

The broad-brush thinking stage that starts to throw possibilities at the identified main objectives, and kick-starts the creative process. It shouldn't be restrained by what may or may not be allowable, affordable or buildable. For your architect, this is the initial visit, a chance to bring experience and creativity to the table. Ideas can be sketched out, questions answered and possibilities explored.

OBJECTIVES

Design process

Every building, refurbishment or extension will have undergone a design process. Take, for example, a building we all know, St Paul's Cathedral in London. Christopher Wren did not design the building in every detail in one go.

It probably started as a sketch, an idea of a cross-shaped building with a large central dome. As the design developed, he worked up more detail, what stone he would use, how many windows would fit along each side, and so on. Wren would have had to present the preliminary designs to his customer (who we know had ideological pressures that conflicted with some of his ideas), in order to get their consent. He would not have been able to answer detailed questions at the early stages because the details were yet to come.

As he progressed through the design process, decisions would be made and ever greater detail would receive focus. He would have had to double back on many occasions as costs became clearer and problems became evident, working over ground that he had already covered. Eventually he would have had the design developed in detail, all the materials chosen and everything costed. Only then would the building be ready to start.

It may seem ridiculous to compare your own home improvement to St Paul's Cathedral, but the process is exactly the same. Here, I have identified five stages of progression, from outline design (where ideas are sketched out and broad-brush thinking dominates), through scheme and detail design and specification, to preparation for the building work.

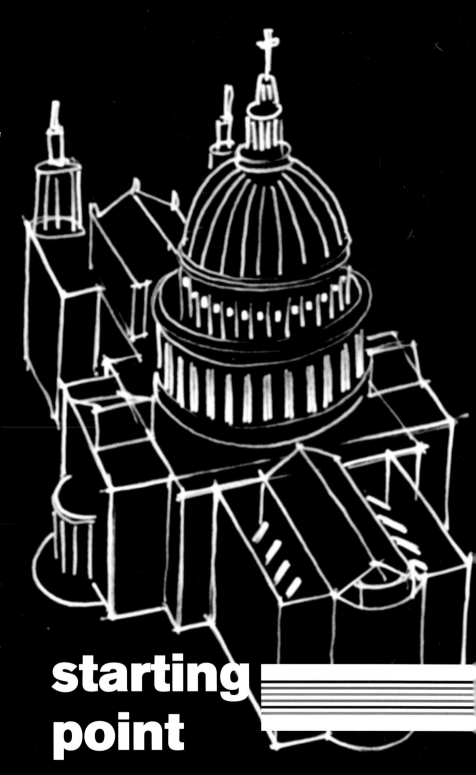

starting point

finished project

DECORATION

snagging
and
finishing

SITE MEETINGS

building your design

Choosing the right builder, negotiating a good price and sealing the
deal in a suitable contract are vital if your project is to be successful.
The timescale for the building works needs careful planning, and what
if you cannot find someone prepared to do the work for the right
price? This is the most expensive and disruptive stage of all.

SCHEDULE
OF WORKS

SUB-CONTRACTORS

tender
and building
contract

final cost
check

INSURANCES

CONSTRUCTION

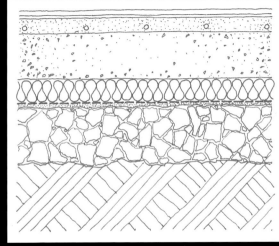

detail design

Any project involves a myriad of detail that needs to be addressed. Whether it is structural calculations, building regulations or construction details, it is important to decide how much you are going to define with detail drawings. Balance the cost of working these details out in advance against the need to control what your builder is going to build. Anything not defined exactly will be left for him to make up as he goes along.

INSULATION

STRUCTURE

building regulations

BRICKWORK

PARTY WALL CONSENT

specification

At this point, consider which materials, finishes, fittings, appliances, tiles, sanitary ware, bricks, lights, and so on, are to be incorporated in the design. The choice of materials makes a vast difference to the finish and cost of a project. If simple, this information can be added as notes to the drawings, but more often it is contained in an outline schedule of works or even a full specification document.

VENTILATION   FINISHES

Starting point

Defining your starting point, aims and objectives is vital because it will be your point of reference as you go forward. Even with the help of architects and other specialist consultants, you will need to take literally thousands of decisions.

Building projects have a way of spiralling into a much bigger deal than was originally intended. Unforeseen problems arise and the phrase, 'well, we're spending all this money anyway' can carry you right off track. Having defined and recorded your aims and objectives at the outset will allow you to focus on the reason that you started the project.

At this stage you simply need to define 'why'. I am not talking about an idea of a building form, materials or technology; that will all come in due course. The four main reasons for undertaking home improvements that I see are:

1 More space

By far, the most common objective is the desire for more space. More often than not, this is driven by a function that your home cannot fulfil satisfactorily. If this is your key objective, try to distil exactly how you would use the space. You might be struggling in a small kitchen, or be expecting a child and need an extra bedroom. You might want extra space in order to work from home, or need somewhere for guests to stay.

> You are setting out your wish list here, so don't hold back. Think about how you actually use your home, and which rooms you spend the most time in. Think how this could be improved.

2 Better space

Even if your home is big enough, it may well be that you can improve the space to suit your lifestyle. Perhaps the circulation is poor, or you feel cut off from the family when in the kitchen. You might want to improve the view of the garden or bring in more natural light. As the way we live changes, the way our homes are arranged can become outmoded; it is now common to want a computer and work space in the heart of the home, especially if the whole family need to use it.

> If you want a certain style of home, try to identify that feel using magazines and books.

3 Increased value

The huge growth in property prices over the past decade has meant that our homes are the backbone of financial stability for most of us. The desire to climb the property ladder by improving a home and moving on is widespread. The recent credit crunch has cast doubt over such enterprise, but so many people still have so much money tied up in their homes that property will continue to hold value. Today, more and more people are planning to stay in their property and are keen to know that any money they spend on their home will increase the value by at least as much as the improvements have cost. If this is a main motivator for your project, it is good to identify it now, as it will shape many of the decisions to come.

> Most of our homes were not built with environmental concerns in mind. This could be a good time to improve energy efficiency or add solar technology, for example.

> What are your aims and objectives worth to you? Can you put a price on it? If you are looking to improve and sell, you can easily set a budget based on the perceived uplift in value. If this is purely for you, try to put a value on the benefit.

4 Change of use

Identify how well the current space and arrangement of rooms suits your lifestyle. Can certain areas be more effective if used differently? Can you redevelop a carport into a comfortable living room, or turn a small bedroom into an *en-suite* bathroom? If you are lucky enough to have outbuildings or a cellar, can they be converted into a bright games room or a self-contained guest suite?

> The reality of various regulations will come crashing in soon. For now, think freely about what you want to achieve and don't dwell on what may not be allowed.

> We often meet couples who both want to be involved in the project, but only realise that they have very different objectives to each other once things get started. Early communication is vital.

Putting your brief together

The design process needs to be collaborative to be successful, so it is important to be able to communicate what you are trying to achieve to whoever you are going to work with, be it a builder, planner, interior designer, heating engineer or architect.

Furthermore, it is useful to record your starting point for your own benefit. People can get so involved with the progress of their project that they cannot accurately remember their objectives. Setting your 'brief' need not be an onerous task, but it does require clarity and balance. Setting out your brief is essentially about clarifying and recording three things:

1. Background information

This includes copies of any existing drawings of the property, surveyor's reports, previous correspondence with the planning department, or notes about restrictive covenants in your deeds. This will save research time and may avert unforeseen problems. However, don't include reams of barely relevant material, as this will bring cost without benefit.

2. Key objectives

This is where you list the main reasons for your development. For example, you may need one more bedroom, you may have an absolute completion date in mind, or you simply must have good hot water pressure. These absolutes must be clarified as such and this section should only contain those things that you regard as fundamental.

This section is best presented as a written list, although you may want to attach photographs and drawings that illustrate the point. Set the context for your budget simply by stating, for example, that you don't want to over capitalise for the location.

3. Wish list

This can be any combination of written items, sketches, tear-outs from magazines, downloaded images, and so on, to communicate what you are after. For example, you may like the idea of creating somewhere to work from home, but have no idea where this might be. An architect will be able to come up with all sorts of ideas, so don't be too prescriptive at this point.

Getting the most from your brief

Unrealised expectations, insufficient creative input and wasted time are often down to a misunderstanding at the briefing stage. Getting the right balance between the key objectives and wish list is vital. If, for example, you set out a rigid list that spells out a strong vision of what you want, your architect may feel that he/she is there principally to assist you in pulling that vision together, rather than exploring alternative options. If you want creative input, leave room for it even if you cannot imagine what sort of an answer may ensue. However, if you do have a clear picture of what you want, then make this clear.

An architect can, of course, help with this clarification and should question your brief thoroughly to ensure that he/she understands your expectations. When working with Architect Your Home, this would typically happen at the beginning of your 'initial visit' ➤ see also **Design process** pp.18–23.

Try to be very clear in the key objectives section of your brief as to your specific practical needs.

Have you been inspired by the style of something you have seen? Maybe a magazine article or a hotel room? Be clear if you have an aesthetic aversion to roof tiles, or a soft spot for traditional sash windows.

How strongly do you feel about environmental issues? Are you hoping to invest in solar heating, for example?

Do you have a specific budget ceiling, or is it more about getting value for money? Where do you want your money to be focused?

Check your lease or deeds to see if there are any restrictive covenants or if a landlord's consent is required for any works. Your architect will probably not be able to check this for you.

Communicate your brief in whatever way gets the message across most effectively. Tear pictures from magazines, write lists of objectives and cite all the kinds of things you want to avoid.

Case study

The photographs and drawings of the many and various projects throughout the book are used to illustrate a host of different aspects of the design process. Some are there to demonstrate the broad thinking of the outline design stage, some to show use of finishes or materials or how thoughtful detail design can transform the drab into the electric.

Alongside these examples this book singles out one project as a case study to follow through all of the stages, from the starting point and wish list, through outline design, scheme design, detail design, specification and construction to the finished home.

1. Starting point
The starting point is illustrated overleaf ➤ **see pp.28–9** and shows the ambitions and aspirations that were laid on to a very ordinary 1965 detached house.

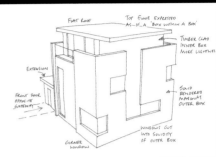

2. Outline design
The concept sketch drawings of the outline design stage ➤ **see pp.94–7** show how the ideas of a contemporary re-modelling of the house are germinated and the broad flow of spaces is explored.

3. Scheme design
The gatefold section ➤ **see pp.138–143** illustrates some of the scheme level plans and elevations that harden up the rather soft sketch drawings into something dimensioned and accurate. Here the form is also explored in 3D.

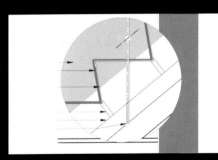

4. Detail design
Here you can see examples of some of the detailed design drawings alongside photographs of the finished built details for purposes of comparison ➤ **see pp.202–7**.

5. Specification
This is all about specification and a selection of the specification choices made for this case study project are shown at the end of the chapter ➤ **see pp.244–7**.

6. The built design
Finally, the finished home is illustrated inside and out in the final gatefold section ➤ **see pp.258–63**. It is quite a transformation from the rather ordinary house that we started with and shows what is possible with a little imagination and a fully considered sequential design process.

Case study

1. Starting point

Whilst a quick profit was not the objective, not spending more than the value of the property was nonetheless important. Financially the house had plenty of scope for growth. The average house prices in the area were considerably higher than the purchase price of this one, largely due to the 1960s style and poor condition of the house. So one important objective was to optimise the value of the property.

In straightforward terms we wanted to convert three bedrooms (one of which was very small) and one bathroom into four decent sized bedrooms and two bathrooms (one en-suite to the master bedroom). On the ground floor we were looking for an open, but sub-dividable space that would give us kitchen, dining, living and study spaces. In addition, we wanted a downstairs WC, a laundry/utility room, and an entrance space for greeting guests with adjacent storage for coats and shoes.

One of the great things about the property is that it is detached and has quite generous outside space. We wanted to make the most of the garden and to create a strong connection between the interior and the exterior space. The positioning of the house on the site was slightly strange with the front door out of line, so we decided to rectify this to help both the inside and outside spaces work more naturally.

However the ambition for the house was not simply practical and financial. We wanted to create a contemporary piece of residential architecture that we could be proud of, something aesthetically exciting and ecologically responsible. The focus of much contemporary architecture is so much on 'lightness' that often it ends up looking quite flimsy. One of the great things about classical architecture is it's ability to convey solidity and significance. We hoped to combine a contemporary approach with the visual 'weight' of such buildings.

WISH LIST

- 4 Beds / 2 Baths
- Open Ground floor
- Connect to garden
- Lots of daylight

- Kitchen – Dining – Living
- Study Area
- Utility / WC / Coats
- STORAGE IMPORTANT

- Energy efficient & WARM

- Lots of Storage
- Recycling Area
- Contemporary but not flimsy
- DURABLE
- REAL & HONEST

existing

existing

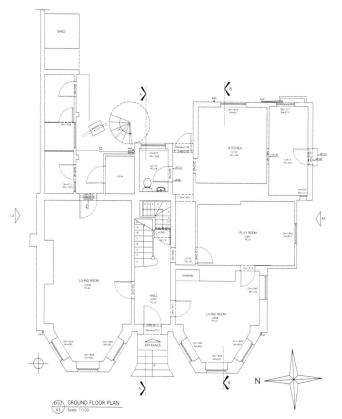

▽ Measured survey. *These drawings of the front elevation and ground floor of a large double-fronted house will give the architect accurate dimensional information about the house so that new works can be correctly incorporated.*

The survey stage

The term 'survey' can be the cause of a great deal of confusion for many people as there seem to be so many different types of survey – and so many different types of surveyor. What you need for developing your property is a 'measured' survey.

In many cases, the initial design can be done from rough measurements and an accurate survey will only be needed at scheme design stage ➤ see also **Chapter 3: Scheme design** pp.100–45. If you are sure that you are going to proceed with building works, I recommend that you get a measured survey done as soon as possible so it is available from the outset. If you want to explore feasibility before deciding whether or not to go ahead with your project, I would suggest that the survey waits until accuracy becomes important.

Measured surveys

Valuation surveys (often required by mortgage companies) estimate the current market value of your home, condition surveys report on the general condition of a property, and structural surveys look at the structural integrity of a building. A measured survey does not cover any of the above. The purpose of a measured survey is quite simply to get an accurate set of drawings that show the building (or site) as it is.

A proper measured survey can take a surveyor a day to take the measurements (these are taken by laser and entered directly into a computer) and a further day in the office to draw up (using drawing software). Expect a measured survey to cost several hundred pounds for a three-bedroomed house.

Different levels of information may (or may not) be required. A listed building might need a great deal of information showing internal elevations of old panelling, for example, and a curved plan, or an old building with bent walls will be more time consuming (and, therefore, expensive) to measure than a simple square one.

So why is a measured survey so necessary? The convention within the building industry is that design proposals are communicated, more than anything, with technical drawings. Increasingly, these are computerised and can be reproduced at different scales, allowing certain elements to be blown up for close inspection. You will need drawings for many reasons, including planning applications, and to illustrate to your builder what he/she is supposed to do.

The measured survey gives you an accurate starting point. If you are extending an existing house, you will have the precise dimensions of the house, so the plans can be properly prepared. If you are building new, you will have the size and levels of the land. Even if you are simply knocking through two rooms within a house, the survey will give accurate information on the thickness and span of the wall so that suitable structures can be designed. Without an accurate starting point, what chance is there of accurate proposals?

In one example that I came across, a space was found for a shower-room as a result of a measured survey. A space between two bedrooms had been walled in and was not obvious while walking around the house. The survey revealed the spare space and, following redevelopment, it was used to great effect.

Architects often undertake measured surveys themselves, but generally it is advisable to use a specialist. This is mainly because an architect is over-qualified to do this task and may charge more than you need to pay. An architect will usually be able to introduce you to a suitable surveyor instead.

A measured survey will give you accurate drawings of the existing building. Using old plans or sketch plans can cause confusion and problems may arise further down the line.

Getting the proportions right for an extension (for example) will make a huge difference to the look of your project. If the drawings of the original house are wrong, the design may not work as intended.

Flooding is a matter of increasing awareness and importance. Understanding the slopes and levels of the land around your property might be crucial.

While a proper survey will cost several hundred pounds, it is almost always well worth the money, given the potential for problems when proceeding without accurate information.

If your drawings prove to be inaccurate, planning approvals and listed building applications can be nullified, causing long delays and extra expense.

Even for such things as ordering carpets and washing machines, a measured drawing communicates the dimensions needed to ensure everything will fit.

2 Outline design

It is impossible to conceive of a project in every detail from the word go. If you try to you will certainly miss all sorts of very important factors and opportunities.

Outline design is the free, broad-brush conceptual stage where you think only of the big picture, playing with all sorts of possibilities and sweeping aside the detail for a later day. Working with a pencil and plenty of sheets of tracing paper, just draw, draw, draw – testing even the most unpromising ideas on paper – unravelling the puzzle until all the main parts hang together in a harmonious arrangement.

practicality

aesthetic

environment

cost/value

regulations

communication

What is outline design?

Software experts often **enthuse** *about how computer modelling can enable you to design in* **three-dimensions** *on screen, but they miss the point of* **outline** *design. The freedom of a* **pencil** *and paper means that details can be kept* **rough** *and imprecise while* **focusing** *on the big issues.*

An outline design is intended to explore possible design solutions in enough detail to be able to appraise feasibility at a very basic level, without spending too much money and time. If the initial indications stack up then you can develop the detail a bit further to get a slightly better idea, and so on until the design, strategy, timescale and predicted costs are highly detailed.

It is vital during this stage of the process to keep the overall picture in mind, rather than get bogged down in detail. The experience and expertise of an architect are a great help in undertaking this work, partly because architects are used to visualising how a space might be if extended or rearranged, but also because an architect can avoid distractions of whether or not this or that can be done.

The Architect Your Home 'initial visit' to the location is the ideal medium to kick-start this process as it involves a very thorough session with the architect and home owner developing ideas together. Rough measurements are taken, possibilities are discussed and sketch layouts and options can be prepared, usually while sitting around the kitchen table.

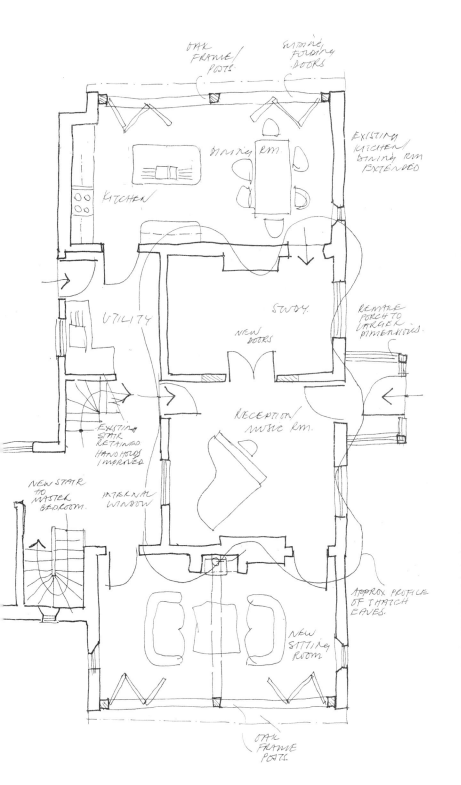

OAK FRAME/ POSTS.

SLIDING/ FOLDING DOORS

EXISTING KITCHEN/ DINING RM EXTENDED

DINING RM.

KITCHEN

UTILITY

STUDY.

NEW DOORS

REMAKE PORCH TO LARGER DIMENSIONS.

EXISTING STAIR RETAINED HANDHOLDS IMPROVED

RECEPTION/ MUSIC RM.

NEW STAIR TO MASTER BEDROOM.

INTERNAL WINDOW

APPROX PROFILE OF THATCH EAVES.

NEW SITTING ROOM

OAK FRAME POSTS.

Outline design drawings. This floor plan and the accompanying sketch (opposite) illustrate proposed changes to a country cottage, including a sitting room extension, enlarged kitchen-dining room and new access to the first floor, allowing improved circulation.

To get the most from the outline design stage, you need to be really open-minded, but this does not mean that practicality should be ignored. Just be prepared to see that there may be more than one way of meeting the practical considerations.

Don't let a style that you may have in mind cloud your view of what is possible. Visual style is not fundamental to layout or circulation and can distract the necessary focus on the basics.

If you are considering renewable energy devices, such as solar panels and heat pumps, their locations need to be taken into account even at this early stage.

Some people see this stage as a frivolous and unnecessary expense, but the most costly mistake that one can make is to build something, only to realise afterwards that it could have been completed better, cheaper or quicker.

The art of this stage is to bear in mind the fundamental issues that planning, building regulations, and so on, will impose, without getting bogged down in the detail and losing momentum.

Don't be shy about your drawing ability; there is no substitute for a pencil and paper to get your ideas across quickly. Be patient and keep drawing and drawing and drawing until you have it right.

Going in

It is **possible** *to categorise the ways to add space to a home into four segments:* **in, up, out** *and* **down**. *The sequence here is important as it follows what is generally the* **most** *cost-effective solution through to the* **least** *cost-effective.*

Adding space by rearranging internally (IN) is almost always the most cost-effective solution, and it is amazing how often it is possible to make a layout work in a much more efficient way so that the required space can be found. Of course, the art here is to find opportunities for additional, useful space within the existing footprint. Many people start an initial visit with the pre-conception that they need an extension, but it is always worth taking a step back to see if the required space can be found within the confines of the existing home. If such a solution can be found, it will be likely to save a great deal of time and money.

Further on in this chapter we are going to explore the opportunities for going UP with a converted and/or extended loft (usually the next most cost-effective option) and OUT with an extension to the side or rear of a property. We will also look at the possibilities and pitfalls of going DOWN by excavating a basement extension, which can be complex and therefore, more costly.

Changing the way we live

Often, there are opportunities for finding more space simply by rearranging the layout and way you use a property. This is because the way we typically live these days has become far less formal than when most properties were built. Even homes that were built relatively recently follow the old conventions that were established in Victorian and Edwardian houses, with separate kitchens, dining and sitting rooms.

Nowadays our lives have become more multi-dimensional and our daily routines tend to overlap. For example, we might want to prepare a meal while overseeing a child's homework, browsing the Internet or watching television. This has meant that separate rooms are often less appropriate and that blurring the boundary between kitchen and eating space, or between the dining and soft-seating spaces, can work well.

While many people feel uncomfortable with a fully open-plan space, the technique of 'zoning' the living spaces of a home, so that they are open to each other and yet each is identifiable, is one that is tremendously popular and successful.

The great thing about this is that by combining two spaces (for example, a dining and living room) and blurring the boundary between the two zones, each zone not only feels larger, but also actually *is* larger because the overlapping space counts twice ➤ see also **Overlapping living spaces** p.39. The dining space is larger as it occupies part of what used to be the living room, but the living room is also larger because it flows into part of the original dining room.

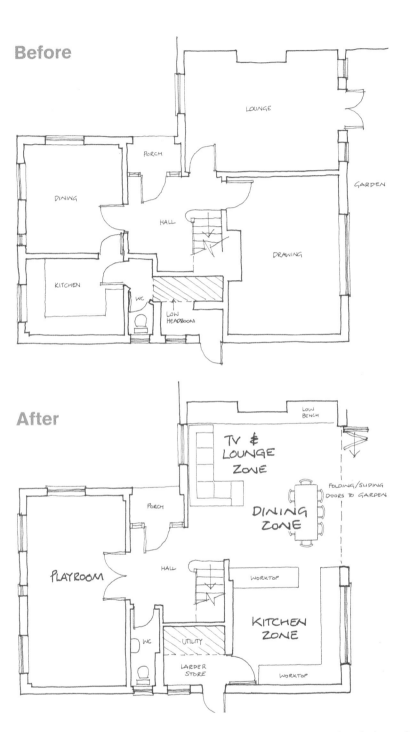

Before

LOUNGE

PORCH

DINING

GARDEN

HALL

DRAWING

KITCHEN

WC

LOW HEADROOM

After

LOW BENCH

TV & LOUNGE ZONE

FOLDING/SLIDING DOORS TO GARDEN

DINING ZONE

PORCH

PLAYROOM

HALL

WORKTOP

WC

UTILITY

KITCHEN ZONE

LARDER STORE

WORKTOP

∧ **Finding more space inside.** *The top diagram shows the floor plan of a house built between the wars. The rooms are separate and poorly connected, and there is no relationship between the kitchen and garden. The lower diagram shows the internal layout completely rearranged, giving a large playroom for the children which can be shut off or opened up with double doors and well defined zones for kitchen, dining and living, which all have an open relationship with each other and with the garden via folding/sliding glass doors.*

Knocking out or making openings in internal walls is more straightforward than people imagine, whether structural, load bearing or otherwise. However, you should know the structural implications of removing any wall before doing so.

Complete open-plan is not the only answer; try to imagine the zones you want and identify how independent or combined you want them to feel.

Clever rearrangement of existing spaces within a home is usually far more efficient in terms of energy and resources expended, compared to building an extension.

Finding the additional space required without extensive building works is always going to be the most cost-effective solution. It is worth investing at outline design stage, as the potential savings on build costs will dwarf such expenditure.

With notable exceptions (for example, listed buildings), internal remodelling will not require consent from the planning department, which can save a great deal of time and money. You still need to follow building regulations.

When working with an architect or designer, it is important to convey your feelings on how comfortable you are with the idea of open-plan. Some people are keen, others less so.

‹ Sharing light and space. *Daylight from the front of the house (south) is allowed to fill the length of the space with the staircase offering the minimum visual block.*

⌄ Kitchen break-out. *The kitchen, previously contained in a box room at the back, now expands to a great length overlapping with the dining area.*

Project

Overlapping living spaces

This project shows how the grand sweep of an outline design idea to clear internal walls, overlap spaces and share light has been carried through to create more space with no additional square feet.

Originally, the ground floor of this house was divided into small rooms, with a very steep staircase and a gloomy north-facing kitchen and dining room.

The design solution

It was decided to remove the three walls that divided the house across its width. The design was based on drawing the eye down the length of the house and everything was set to enhance this linear arrangement.

The staircase was replaced and the direction reversed. By building a low half-landing and two steps, it did not need to be so steep, and circulation improved upstairs. The new staircase was designed to be as visually lightweight as possible so that it allowed the eye to see through it down the length of the house.

The kitchen worktop and the storage units above were deliberately designed to be impressively long. The worktop drew the kitchen into the dining room, creating a spacious kitchen. The dining area flowed in to overlap with the kitchen, and to use the previously wasted circulation space around the foot of the stairs.

Finally, a wonderful, tall new window in the front bay brought in gallons of south-facing daylight, which now could flow beyond the open staircase and bring a complete change of character to the whole arrangement.

Look for solutions that serve several purposes, such as the landing that allowed the staircase to be set less steeply, while creating great storage beneath.

The staircase is the visual 'hero' of this design, but note how the floorboards, worktop and lighting are all arranged to draw the eye down the length of the space.

The tall new front window used here allows much better use of natural light, which is not only more pleasant, but also more energy efficient than in a gloomy house where the lights are always needed.

By avoiding the cost of an extension, you are able to focus the available budget on quality finishes and interesting features within the house.

No planning permission was needed for this project. Even the installation of the tall front window was dealt with under permitted development **> see pp.106–7.**

< **More space with no additional square feet.** *The plan on the far left shows how the original floor plan is chopped up, with several doorways into small separate rooms. After the internal walls have been removed (left) the space available to each zone is magnified as they overlap.*

Sketching the floor plan out over and over again allowed the arrangement of space to be tested and shown to the home owners in various different configurations.

Kitchen/eating space

Much is currently being made of the importance of family interaction within the home. With computer games and television threatening to isolate and separate us, design can play an important role in bringing families together and there is no better medium for this interaction than a meal around a table.

Breakfast and early evening times can be complicated with many activities needing to coincide. A combined kitchen/eating space can allow breakfast to be consumed, packed lunches to be prepared and conversation to take place all in the same space. With a separate kitchen this is more difficult.

There are different ways to arrange a space, which give different levels of interaction between kitchen and eating area. Clearly the solution will depend to a great extent upon what kind of space is available. A good starting point is to think about the two zones and where the movement of people will take place.

Track your circulation

On some rough layouts, draw circulation lines, using thicker lines for the ones that constantly take place and thinner lines for the less frequent movements. Don't hold back: it is well worth the time and trouble to take lots of photocopies of layouts and go over and over these, exploring variations. Diagrams like this are a great help in playing with different arrangements, as you will be able to see patterns begin to emerge.

Imagine a large square room with kitchen units arranged around the walls and a table in the middle (top left of the diagrams opposite). It sounds reasonable enough, but as soon as you start to draw movement flows over the layout, the problems become apparent (top right). People coming in and out, and to the table area are going to be in the way of whoever is moving between the work stations of the kitchen.

A better arrangement zones the room into two, so that the circulation flows do not interrupt each other (bottom left). An alternative, which is also very popular, is to use a kitchen island as a divider between the two zones and to provide an extra worktop and a place to sit and eat (bottom right). In some instances, an island can take the place of a table. The great thing about an island is that people cooking and people sitting will be more likely to face each other, encouraging interaction.

There is a well-known principle of an ideal triangle of movement within a kitchen between fridge, cooker and sink. The triangle is a somewhat simplistic version of the flow diagrams described above, but it is at the core of kitchen design. When working on a more multi-functional space such as a kitchen/eating space, the flows are more complex, but the principle is the same.

Simple style

Another important principle, no matter what 'style' of kitchen you prefer, is that of simplicity. Whether you want a country-style or an urban minimalist kitchen, simplicity of layout is vital. There are so many complexities involved in the essential functions of a kitchen/eating space that the very last thing you should do is make things more complex with fussy layouts and stop-start units. Keep to the longest, cleanest runs of worktop, try to group all of your full height units together, and allow appropriate space both to sit and circulate around a table.

A common difficulty with town houses is that kitchens are often located on the lower-ground or basement level, while dining and living spaces are usually on the

Well-defined zones. *This small kitchen works well because the food preparation zone is distinct from the dining area, and kept apart from the route out to the garden by a very practical island.*

Dear George + Jenny,

Thank you so much for your delicious lunch last Saturday. We thoroughly enjoyed ourselves and it was lovely to see the "séjour" completed and what a nice job you have done.

Ursula + Guillaume had a good time in Berlin and the cats a good time with us!

Eurostar came up trumps yet again, 1h 20 minutes late for no particular reason we could see, Mark now has a free return ticket if the goal posts have not been moved. Have a great time in "Vienna". Lots of love Angela

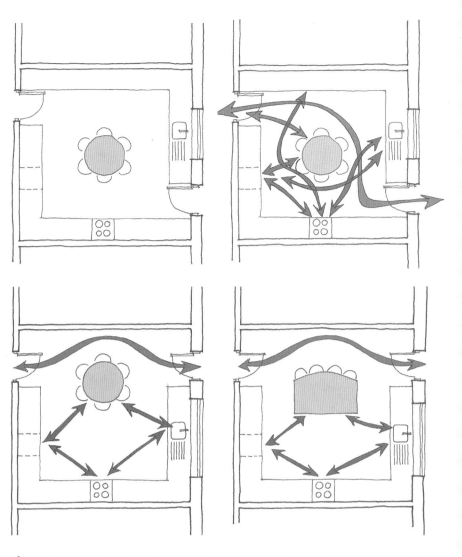

∧ *Flow diagrams help you to arrange kitchen space.* *A table in a square room with kitchen units wrapped around (top left) might seem alright until you study the circulation flows (top right). By moving the position of the door and rearranging the units the flows work better, either with a table (bottom left) or a kitchen island (bottom right).*

ground or raised-ground floor. To create a really effective kitchen/eating space can, therefore, cause dilemmas.

In some cases, the lower level is turned into an informal family/kitchen/eating space. This can work well, but often it means that the very heart of the home is squeezed in where there is a low ceiling height and little daylight. It also means that the upper level rooms, which typically will have lovely light and generous ceilings, tend to be wasted.

On the other hand, bringing the kitchen up into the high ceiling rooms on the upper level does not maximise the use of space and the lower level often becomes little more than a television den and/or utility room. The project illustrated on the next four pages shows a great solution to this problem.

The functions of kitchen/eating spaces are so important that they *must* be practical. Analysis of the movement flows involved in the various activities will help you arrive at a practical arrangement.

Whatever style you want the kitchen to evoke, keep the layout simple. It is easy to add visual complexity to break up something bland, but much harder to simplify the look of a messy layout.

Aim for natural, sustainable materials that are durable. For example, if you want a timber worktop, avoid tropical hardwood, as it is not sustainable, but also avoid softwoods that will not last.

It is really worth investing in getting the design right. An effective design will avoid lots of money being wasted further down the line. 'Free' design services provided by kitchen shops will usually not properly look at the bigger picture, so beware.

Be aware that opening up a hallway can compromise the means of fire escape from the upstairs bedrooms. Discuss with your architect and local building regulations department.

Don't restrict your flow diagrams to the kitchen only; try this technique as a way of discussing and exploring the effective circulation around the whole floor level. It is often amazing what you'll discover.

Illuminating family space

This house had a very gloomy semi-basement that was disconnected from the upper-ground floor rooms, which themselves failed to make best use of beautiful garden views. The essence of the project was to open up views, bring the various living spaces together and unify them with gallons of natural light.

The kitchen zone was moved to the front part of the lower level of the house. A bay window admitted light to this area, and a lobby from the lower front entrance dealt with incoming muddy footwear. The adjacent space became a large pantry/larder, leaving the main kitchen space clear and simple. The use of an island, combined with wall units to one side, kept the kitchen movements clear of the doors to the lobby and the pantry.

The space opened up allowing a family dining table in the centre, with enough space at the side for desks. This extra width was achieved by the removal of the original staircase.

< **Bringing daylight into a basement kitchen.** *Moving the kitchen down to the basement of this house would have created a claustrophobic and gloomy space if the rear of the property had not been opened up.*

∨ **Indoor balcony.** *The lovely rooms on the upper-ground floor connect to the less formal family spaces downstairs via a dramatic floor void, which creates an indoor balcony as well as allowing light to pour down to basement level.*

Using pale and reflective surfaces in the basement, such as these cream floor tiles and shiny white kitchen units, significantly affects the amount of light bouncing around on this floor.

People are sometimes wary of including modern features – for instance, the rear glazing here – in a house with classical details and proportions. In this case the mix works wonderfully well.

High-performance glazing means that this design has all the energy benefits of good daylight, while heat-loss is suppressed. The specification of the glazing system is very important to energy efficiency.

Rebuilding the back of this house was a major project and cost a great deal of money, but these changes transformed the value of the property.

Despite the extensive building work, this project did not need planning permission as the proposed alterations added no volume to the original house and fell within the bounds of 'permitted development'.

Explaining the idea of the floor void and indoor balcony to the customer at outline design stage was made much easier by making a small, rough cardboard model of the house so that they could see the idea in three dimensions.

∧ **Connected up.** *The light well/void means that games can be played on the upper-ground floor without the rest of the family being completely cut off.*

< **Inside-out.** *This exterior view shows how the new glass enclosure relates to the garden. The external shape of the house has not changed or been enlarged, but the sense of space inside is transformed.*

\> **Visual link.** *A staircase makes use of the double-height space, providing a direct connection between the different levels and visually emphasising the link in quite a sculptural way.*

The main structural work was at the rear of the house, where the upper floor was cut back to create a double-height space. This allows light to pour into the lower level through huge new windows. Adding a sculptural spiral staircase provides more width in the basement, access to the upper level and a visual delight.

The lovely living spaces on the upper level are no longer cut off from the lower level as the internal balcony allows vertical integration. The combined living areas are unified in a way that allows great interaction for the family.

Sacrificing some of the upper floor area was deemed a small price to pay for the benefits gained in connecting the spaces. Sometimes you can create more space while actually losing floor area.

Maximising daylight penetration, keeping the layout simple and highlighting the design with a sculptural staircase were the keys to making this a beautiful and impressive space.

The staircase treads, handrails and flooring on the upper floor in this project are all made from oak. A beautiful and versatile timber, oak forests in Europe and North America are generally well managed, making this a very sustainable material.

The structure of this staircase was made from mild steel off site in a workshop. Forming the curved sides of the stairs would have been very expensive in most other materials.

Basements need to be separated with fire doors and fire resisting construction to comply with building regulations. **\>see p.152** This house had basement level exits both front and back, allowing a more relaxed approach.

To properly explain this project with drawings requires a 'section' as well as plans and elevations. A section is drawn as if the house has been cut apart vertically, and shows the floor thicknesses.

Work space

Home working falls into two categories, each requiring a differently designed space. The first kind is work that needs to be done in the heart of the home, such as school homework or Internet shopping for groceries. The second is work that needs to be free from distractions, such as employed work or report writing.

Linked to living space

Architect Your Home recently designed a kitchen/eating space with an adjacent work station (see top diagram opposite). The customer runs a small business and needed a desk and space for a computer, phone and filing. She wanted to be near the kitchen during the working day, but to be able to close her work station down when everyone came home. Our solution was to form an alcove with a roller (or 'tambour') door that could be opened up to reveal the space or rolled down to close it off. The option to 'close' the work space is often desirable with a home working environment.

Another project involved the design of a special desk that opened up to form an L-shaped work station, with drawers for filing and a worktop for a computer keyboard (see lower diagram opposite). One leg was hinged to allow the desk to close like a book. When closed, all the drawers and papers were contained and concealed.

⌄ *Cupboard love.* *Work stations are not always tidy, but it is a pain to have to constantly clear up before the rest of the household returns and everything gets lost. This clever home office is concealed simply by shutting the cupboard doors.*

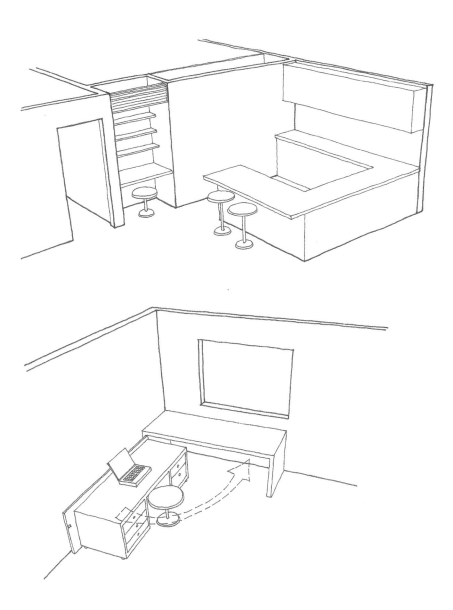

⟨ *Hideaway home-working.*
The alcove work station (top) and the
L-shaped closable desk (below) both as
described opposite.

Most people want work and home life to
be kept separate. This can be achieved
if the home work space is designed
according to the working needs.

Motivation can be a problem when
working from home as all the distractions
of the home are there. If your work space
is inspiring, comfortable and inviting, it is
easier to focus on the task in hand.

Environmentalists champion home
working as it reduces road congestion. In
addition, energy that would have been
used to heat a home all day while the
occupants were at work is not wasted.

Avoiding the commute to work not only
benefits the environment but also saves a
great deal of money. The price of a train
season ticket alone can justify the cost of
setting up an office at home.

If your business grows and your home
becomes more an office building than a
dwelling, there may well be issues over a
'change of use'.

Tell your architect just how you like to work,
how self-contained you need to be and
how much storage you will need. A well
designed home office can be invaluable
if designed to meet your needs correctly.

Space to concentrate

The design of a separate work space is hugely dependent upon the nature of the
work to be undertaken. For example, a home photographic studio that requires
blackout would lend itself to a basement, whereas craft work might well be able to
be undertaken in an attic, with lots of suitably orientated roof windows.

The one common agenda for this second category of home working is the need for
separation and privacy. A very popular solution is to convert a garage or outbuilding.
In some cases, where there is nothing suitable, one can be built.

When designing a work space, think about your movements, in the same way as
described on pages 40–1, but this time on a more detailed scale. Think about your
movement between phone, computer, papers and files (if these are the tools of
your trade). You may be surprised to find how a very compact space can be hugely
efficient, if well planned in relation to the tasks that you actually need to do.

Storage and ancillary spaces

Home owners often want cleaner, more open and lighter spaces, and part of that is being clutter free. More than anything, the key to being clutter free is having suitable space in which to put a whole range of items.

You can spend a lot of money on cupboards and wardrobes, but while offering somewhere to put things, if they don't work with the internal geography of your home, they can end up as clutter in their own right. You need to consider storage as part of your outline design stage.

Storage design clearly depends on what you are hoping to store. Whether you are thinking of coats and shoes, laundry equipment and drying space, hi-fi equipment and DVDs, or mops and ironing boards, consider the following:

- what size and shape of storage you need
- how often you will need access
- where you will need it to be situated for easy access
- what scope for growth you will need.

Design and function

It may well be that a lovely piece of furniture can suit both your space and your storage requirements; this possibility should be a part of your thinking. However, often the most successful storage is that which does not attract the eye. Look for opportunities to incorporate storage at the outline stage while the design is fluid.

Full-height cupboards can form a wall, and this can be a useful device for high-density storage where you can afford to lose some width in a room. Try to keep the lines simple. If you are going to build large cupboards, aim to fill a whole wall to full height and full width. Empty space beside and above storage will feel more cumbersome in the room (as well as reducing storage space).

Using small ancillary spaces will keep your main areas free. Wasted spaces below staircases, beside chimney breasts, cellars, and the ends of odd-shaped kitchens can be converted to efficient use. For example, finding a neat space for a utility room where a washing machine and hanging clothes can be dealt with away from the kitchen or bathroom is a great way to keep down the inevitable clutter of daily life.

Finding these spaces once a design is advanced can prove impossible, or else ruin a settled arrangement. When the design is at the outline stage, work over the plan looking for recesses. Focus in the areas of the home where they will be required.

The storage you create must be suitable for your needs or it will be inefficient. Wardrobes need to be wide enough to hang clothes sideways (55cm/22in min).

Storage should play either a starring or a quiet role in your interior. If it is not a feature of the room, blend it with the natural lines of the room.

Enthusiasm for recycling can be eroded if you end up with lots of untidy piles of bottles, cardboard and plastics. Design functional storage for these items.

Building fitted wardrobes and cupboards can cost much more than you think. It may be possible to create spaces that are just the right size for inexpensive, flat-pack storage. This can save a lot of money.

If you are housing appliances, particularly those that use gas or risk overheating, you may need to meet regulations with regards to outdoor ventilation.

Make a list of all the things that you need to store so that you can incorporate suitable storage into your design from the start. Trying to shoehorn such things in after the event can ruin a well-designed space.

◁ **Lift-up bench.** *In this exciting space storage is cleverly concealed either side of the steps below lift-up bench tops* ➤ *see p.280.*

▷ **Living room storage.** *People often overlook the amount of stuff they tend to have in their living rooms. This low unit hides away hi-fi, DVDs and other equipment. Suitable holes in the timber top allow cables to discreetly connect the phone and TV, which can sit on the unit.*

Combining functions in an open-plan space

Particularly in small properties, combining different living functions in an open-plan space can be an effective way to make the most of the space available, share daylight, overlap zones and facilitate better family interaction.

Most people tend to be more comfortable with 'zoned' spaces rather than complete open-plan living. A zoned area provides a strong sense of where you are, whether it be in the kitchen or dining zone. There are many ways to fine-tune the power of zones to give each a greater or lesser sense of being self-contained.

Structural starting point

In existing buildings, particularly older houses, the structural beams that are installed when walls are removed can create natural indicators of moving from one zone to another. If these breaks happen where you want to indicate a different zone they can be emphasised by setting the bottom of the beam below the ceiling level, creating a lowered ridge across the ceiling (generally known as a 'down stand'). Sometimes the beams do not coincide with zone changes and it is often possible (although it involves more tricky construction) to lose them within the thickness of the floor above, allowing a flat ceiling beneath.

All sorts of devices can be used to enhance flow between zones or emphasise the move from one zone to another. Changes in ceiling level are very effective, and adding two or three steps to change floor level is also a good technique. In the example (see opposite and below), a dining area is zoned from the living area by a change in floor level as well as the double height space above the living area.

Zoned flooring

Floor finishes also can be used to define or combine zones. For instance, a timber floor can be used to enhance the connection between three separate zones in a house > see also **Overlapping living spaces** p.39. In the example opposite, a slate floor gives way to a timber floor in the softer seating zone two steps below.

❮ Depth of field. *Views in an open-plan space can be enhanced and given greater depth. Here you can look from the kitchen zone, through the hallway space to the dining and living areas beyond.*

❯ Separating devices.
A midnight blue curved wall with an opening defines the hallway from the dining area. The change in ceiling level and the way the timber beam stands down from the ceiling level indicate the boundary of the dining zone without the need for a wall.

Think carefully how self-contained you want your zones to be. Over-zealous use of level changes can cause all sorts of trip hazards.

The more continuous and connected your zones are, the larger a small space will feel. Having more than one finish in a fairly small space can look messy.

Large open-plan spaces require lots of energy for heating. If part of the home is used infrequently, it may be worth separating the power supply so that you can adjust the heating when not in use.

The removal of a structural element or wall is not necessarily expensive. The basic cost of structural works is often overshadowed by the associated costs of plastering, joinery, finishes and making everything good.

When there is a basement > **see pp.52–3**, be careful to include fire doors as necessary to comply with the need for a direct means of fire escape.

Architecture gives us all sorts of visual communication devices without the need to put signs on everything. Many of these will not be consciously noticeable in themselves since the effect is what is important.

Before

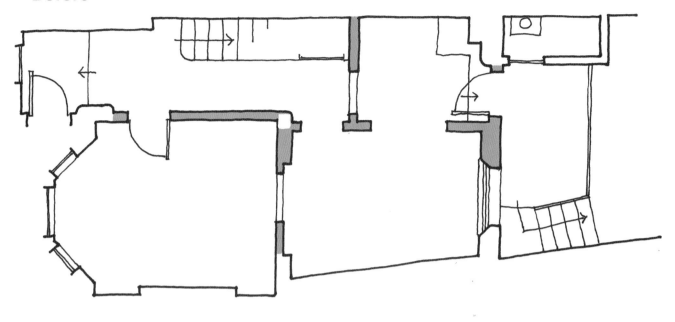

After

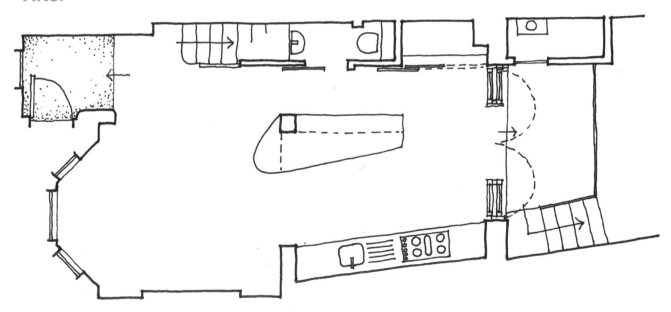

⌃ *Three small rooms and a wasted hallway. By removing the internal walls of the original basement space (before) a new zoned space (after) with a much larger kitchen, open dining area, good access and views of the garden, a separate WC and a home-work space has been fitted in without anything feeling cramped or crowded.*

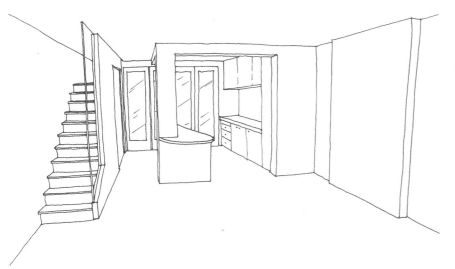

⋀ Sketch 'visual'. *In order to help the home owner visualise how the space might feel, the architect prepared a perspective sketch during the initial visit, looking from the front towards the stairs and kitchen through to the garden beyond.*

Opening up a pokey basement

Project

This project is a good example of how small separate spaces can be combined to function much more openly and satisfactorily. Looking at the original plan of the basement of the small house illustrated in the drawing opposite, you can see that there was a doorway at the front which opened from a small light-well into an even smaller hallway. Inside there were three rather tight spaces, which were poorly served by daylight and quite restrictive.

The solution was to open up the whole area to provide a spacious but zoned kitchen/family space. The kitchen island is a really useful device that works well to give more worktop space, but also both anchors the structural column and indicates the separation of the kitchen zone from the family zone.

In this case the island has been proposed as a sensitively curved shape to soften its impact and provide a little highlight to the design. A small home office space and a downstairs WC have been incorporated into the design too.

Although the garden is small, it is quite charming and only half a level above the basement floor. The original door to the garden was small and allowed very little light or access. The enlarged doorway to the garden is predominantly glass to bring in as much daylight as possible, and in the summer the doors can be thrown open to enhance the sense of space even more.

For a young family, having the dining table in a connected space to the kitchen allows Mum to prepare the supper while overseeing homework.

The fold-back glass doors to the garden will help flood the room with daylight and limit the feeling of being in a basement.

Reusing the basement space so effectively avoided the need for a ground floor extension to this house, which would have required far more energy and resources to build.

Keeping the kitchen sink and WC near to the rear of the house meant that no money was wasted re-directing drainage below ground level.

In order to open the space to the stairs, a fire-separating doorway was needed at the top of the stairs, so as not to compromise the 'means of escape' **> see pp.92–3 and p.197**.

In order to open the space to the stairs, a fire-separating doorway was needed at the top of the stairs, so as not to compromise the 'means of escape' **> see pp.92–3 and p.197**.

A sketch 'visual' such as the one shown above can really help people get a sense of how their modified space will appear. Many people have great difficulty visualising just from plans.

Bedroom and bathroom space

In contrast to living, kitchen or eating spaces, finding more space for bedrooms and bathrooms cannot generally be achieved by combining functions in an open-plan space. For most people, the functions of bedrooms and bathrooms dictate that they are separated.

Some Manhattan-style loft apartments have open-plan bedrooms, separated by curtains or blinds from the rest of the space, but most of us would not be happy with this. A more popular phenomenon that has grown partly as a result of the popularity of designer boutique hotels is an open-plan bedroom/*en-suite* bathroom. You can also see stand-alone baths appearing in the bedroom space.

Using circulation space

As combining spaces in an open-plan area is not the way to go for many people, how can extra space be found for bedrooms and bathrooms? The answer lies, more often than not, in the use of circulation space.

Looking at the position and orientation of a staircase is often a good place to start. The example below shows the middle floor of a house with three levels. The staircase to the second floor takes up a great deal of space. By setting this staircase directly above the lower staircase, a whole new space is made available to accommodate a bathroom.

Another good way of gaining bedroom/bathroom space is to replace old-fashioned heating systems that require bulky hot and cold water tanks and large boilers. New boilers are much more space efficient and pressurised hot water systems can be located in more convenient positions than their predecessors. It may be that you are only gaining the space of an airing cupboard, but very often the circulation of the whole floor can be freed up by such a move, creating much better space for bedrooms and bathrooms.

∧ *Free-standing headboard. In this simple bedroom a high, beech-veneered headboard conceals wardrobe storage in an elegant way. Bedside lights are mounted on the headboard too and a large mirror bounces daylight back into the room.*

Before

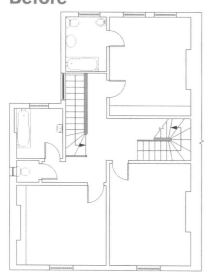

After

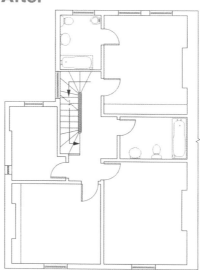

< *Stairs wasting space. The plan on the far left shows two staircases (one going up to the second floor and one going downstairs) taking up a great deal of the first floor space in this house. The plan on the left shows how the staircase up to the second floor has been relocated, a new bathroom made and a fourth bedroom found.*

> *Wall coverings. A generously sized double bedroom is given a fun feel with this funky wall-covering. In a small bedroom such a strong pattern could be oppressive, but here the room is large enough to carry it off.*

◁ **Working with the space available.**
This bathroom maximises the sense of space by opening up an area that is partly under the sloping roof. Note how the maximum headroom has been utilised for the area around the basin and in the shower.

Unlike kitchen/dining/living spaces, open-plan bedrooms are not practical for most people. Reworking inefficient circulation and services to find a better layout is often the most practical solution.

When the proposed layout is much more simple and natural than the existing layout, and it feels as if it should always have been that way, you know that you are doing the right thing.

New condensing gas boilers are significantly more efficient than their predecessors. If combined with a solar-thermal panel these can significantly reduce energy consumption.

Houses in the UK are valued as much as anything by the number of bedrooms they have. If internal rearrangement can generate an additional bedroom, the uplift in value will be likely to far exceed the cost of the work.

In flats it is particularly important to abide by the fire regulations for escape from bedrooms to a place of safety without passing through other habitable rooms.

Talk to your architect about how your bedroom spaces can be most effectively used. Who needs an *en-suite* bathroom? Do the kids have other spaces in which to play or is their bedroom their den too?

Simplifying a barn conversion

Originally a barn set in beautiful rolling countryside, this property was badly converted into a dwelling in the 1970s. Much of the ground floor was charming, but the entrance hall was compressed and the upstairs was a complete mess.

The original roof trusses cut across the upper-floor space so that it was impossible to move along the length of the building at first floor level. To access the bedrooms, three separate staircases were needed, taking up huge amounts of floor space on both levels.

To get to one of the bedrooms, you needed to clamber between the roof structures. Some people might think this quaint, but it severely affected the practicality of living in the house as well as its market value.

∧ **Cotswold stone.** *It was once a farm outbuilding, but now it is a beautiful rural home. The thick stone walls, slate roof and iron wall ties all add to the rustic charm.*

> **Bedrooms should be simple.** *Getting to the bedrooms of this house used to require clambering through roof trusses. By modifying the structure and opening up the hallway access, the bedrooms are now laid out in a way that is both natural and modern.*

Restructuring made the first floor layout much more practical than the previous arrangement.

The double-height hallway with sculptural staircase set against a large picture window (see overleaf) changed a cramped and disappointing entrance into an uplifting and exciting space.

A large proportion of the materials (stone, flooring and slates) used in the remodelling of this building were reclaimed and recycled from other old buildings. The spare oak beams were sold for another barn project.

While the restructuring of this old roof was an expensive task, the additional value to the property was much more significant.

Structural alterations fall within Section A of the building regulations **> see pp.196–7** and a structural engineer was needed to do the necessary calculations for approval.

A detailed measured survey was needed before the architects were able to unlock the puzzle that this house represented. There is no substitute for good drawings.

The design solution was to restructure the roof from within. While the original trusses were charming, they made a sensible first floor layout impossible.

The original structure was retained where it did not impede circulation, so that there was plenty of original oak in evidence, but we replaced three truss members with steel members within the thickness of the roof itself.

This modification allowed a complete reorganisation of the first floor level and the replacement of the two separate staircases with one central staircase.

The space saved on the ground floor allowed us to include a magnificent double-height hallway with a big window to capture a key view of the countryside. Into this double-height space we added a stone spiral staircase that went up to a 'bridge' across the space to the bedrooms.

This key central space became the link to unify the house, not only allowing direct and natural access but also providing an inspiring space, with a sculptural staircase that made the most of the beautiful stone walls.

The rooms felt as if they had always meant to work in this way. Access became very natural as all of the awkward spaces had been removed and the sense of additional space was palpable.

If an accountant were to analyse the house, overall, he or she would find a net reduction of floor area in the house due to the double-height hallway. However, the house actually feels more spacious, which comes from the fact that all of the available space is now being used effectively.

◁ **Open hallway space.** *A double-height space, with a sculptural staircase, became the central link within the house.*

▽ **Access 'bridge' with glass panels.** *A new 'bridge' with a timber floor and glass panels either side links the spiral staircase to the bedrooms.*

Due to the restricted headroom, it was most practical to serve each bedroom with its own *en-suite* bathroom.

The materials used in this project have a great visual 'softness' – the beautiful old stone walls and oak beams blend in with the new staircase, stone floor and timber boards. The glass gives a modern accent or highlight.

There is much debate as to the worth of old buildings as homes, due to their poor energy efficiency. This house is admittedly less well insulated than a new build, but insulation has been added where possible and beauty has to count for something.

The reconstituted stone staircase is a proprietary product that can be bought 'off the shelf'. This is much cheaper than having a bespoke version.

The glass sides to the bridge look simple, but the detailed design of concealed fixings and the structural calculations necessary to prove that they are strong enough can be quite complex.

The architect needs to be able to properly convey the spirit of what is proposed to the home owner. Enlightened customers can understand the beauty of mixing modern and rustic elements.

Adding a bathroom

As glamorous bathrooms become more and more desirable, their inclusion in a home inevitably adds to the value of the property. It was not long ago that the idea of an *en-suite* bathroom to a master bedroom was exceptional and decadent. Nowadays it is a requirement for many.

Conversely, when viewing a prospective property to purchase, the sight of a dirty bathroom with stains under the taps and mould in the grout lines is a real turn-off.

One nice trick that can be learned from the boutique hotel is the 'giant headboard'. Where a bedroom is large enough to move the bed away from the wall, it is possible to build a freestanding wall that can act as a headboard (often containing reading lights and recesses for books or a glass of water). In the space behind, fit a small *en-suite* bathroom, possibly with a walk-in shower entered from one side and a WC and basin from the other.

Simple arrangements

The first, and most fundamental thing to get right once you have found your space is the arrangement of elements within. Bathrooms do not have to be large (although more space can certainly add to the sense of luxury), but even if space is restricted it is vital to keep the lines simple and to maximise the sense of unity. A common mistake is to try to cram too much into a small bathroom.

If you cannot choose between a bath and a shower, don't try to squash in both, but find an elegant way (there are many) of using the bath as the shower tray. Resist the temptation to squeeze in a bidet between the basin and WC unless there is genuinely plenty of room. Twin basins are great, unless they have to be small and close together – much better to include one large basin and everything will feel larger.

⋀ *Dramatic timber veneer. In this project, the bed-head device to separate out an en-suite bathroom has been formed with a dramatic dark timber veneer, with the grain arranged vertically. Lighting is built in for clutter-free convenience.*

Before

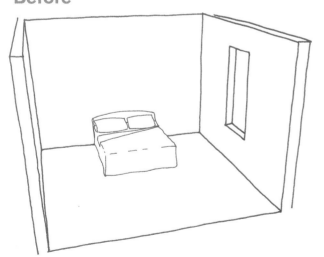

⋀ *Large bedrooms in old houses. Many older houses have very large bedrooms, often with great high ceilings, but most will not have an en-suite bathroom as this was not a common feature of the day.*

After

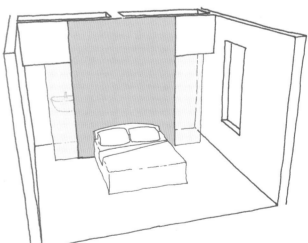

⋀ *Headboard wall. By building a wall that can act as a headboard, a cool shower-room/bathroom can be accommodated elegantly within the room space. Sliding frosted glass doors add privacy if required.*

Saving bathroom space

One inventive solution that Architect Your Home proposed involved a really tiny house. The upper floor had just enough room for two tiny bedrooms, but the bathroom was located in an awkward box beside the kitchen on the ground floor.

The size and shape of the bathroom greatly reduced the kitchen space and prevented any view through to the garden.

The solution was to position the bath (with a shower over the top), washbasin and WC in a line as if in a corridor.

The whole bathroom wall – including the sliding doorway – was designed to swing like a giant gate, and then be fixed adjacent to the door frame. This way, when in bathroom mode, the wall could move across, stealing space from the kitchen.

When the kitchen is being used, the wall is moved back and the bath/ shower is inaccessible, but access remains to the WC and washbasin.

Clearly, in a family house this sort of arrangement would not be practical, but this little house had only one occupant and the occasional guest, so the arrangement worked very well.

This is a great example of using available space creatively and efficiently. It would not work in many instances, but in this tiny house, the hinged wall provided one solution to several design problems.

Builders will often say that you can't put a bathroom here or there because of the plumbing. There is always a way to solve the plumbing; work out where the bathroom will work best and stick to your guns.

Lovely bathrooms sparkle, so the lighting has to be right. Simple recessed low-voltage halogen down-lighters are yet to be matched for their light quality in bathrooms. Select the enclosed type suitable for bathroom use.

Wastewater from basins, baths and showers is called 'grey' water and it can be recycled for use in toilet cisterns or for watering the garden.

The complexity of the plumbing and the variation in specifications mean that the cost of a bathroom is hugely variable. Bathroom details are probably the most noticeable of all. The best quality looks fantastic, lasts well and costs the most.

While pumped macerators can give a great deal of flexibility in how you arrange the waste plumbing, regulations require that at least one WC in a property is gravity drained.

The idea of the moving wall in this example was so unusual that it was vital for the architect to sit down with the home owner and fully explain how it would work.

Before　**After A**　**After B**

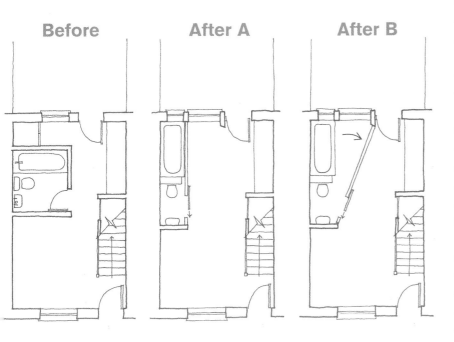

⌃ **Using the space twice.** *The plan on the left shows the bathroom in this tiny house, which leaves little space for the kitchen. The middle plan shows the rearranged bathroom and larger kitchen area, and by swinging the bathroom wall like a gate (right) space is stolen from the kitchen for use in the bathroom.*

Project

Going up

*It is generally easier and, therefore, more **cost-effective**, to develop the **top** of a building than to extend sideways or downwards. **Regulations** will generally mean that adding **height** to the roof externally is not possible, but there are still lots of opportunities for **adding space**.*

If it is not possible to find the additional space that you need by reconfiguring the internal arrangement, then the next most cost-effective way to add space is to go UP. For most buildings, this means converting and possibly extending the loft space within the roof to make it habitable. This opens up all sorts of possibilities and the space can be used for many different functions.

⌃ Staircase in the room. *In this loft conversion the doorway that separates the loft from the rest of the house is at the foot of the stairs. This allows a much greater sense of open space in the loft room. Here, the high space above the door has been used for storage and to house a TV.*

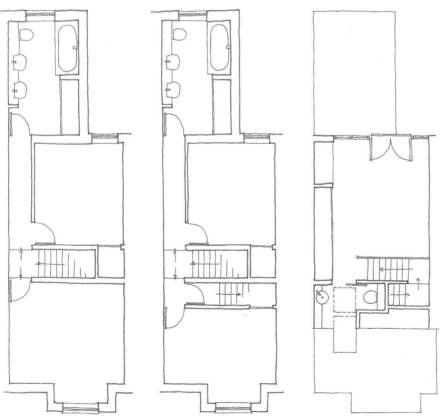

Before 1st floor   After 1st floor   After 2nd floor

⌃ Staircase arrangements. *The original first floor plan (far left) has two bedrooms. The middle plan shows that a stair-wide slice has been taken from the front bedroom, and the door to the new loft room positioned on this floor. The necessary landing space at the foot of the staircase has been allowed and the staircase is positioned partly over the stairs below. The stairhead is completely open as it arrives into the new room (near left and as illustrated opposite) at a convenient position, which maximises the sense of space.*

Lofts

There are three main types of loft room: The simple conversion (often with roof windows); lofts with dormer windows; and box dormer lofts. The following pages deal with each of these in turn, but before you turn to these pages, it is important to consider the stairs. Just how are you going to get up to this new loft accommodation?

Stairs

The reason that stairs should be considered at an early stage is that they are the one element that has a very significant, if not controlling, influence on both the existing floor below and the new floor above. In many cases, the positioning of a staircase might seem obvious, but there are many factors that must be considered. Often the ideal staircase position for the new floor is the worst position for the floor below and vice versa.

Spiral staircases are often thought of as space-saving, but the reality is that they rarely are the most space-efficient solution for a loft. While spiral stairs do not take up as much length as a standard stair, they take up twice as much width. It is unusual for there to be enough space on the existing floor to accommodate them.

Ceiling heights and doors

To many people's surprise there is no minimum ceiling height for a loft room. However, there are important, minimum ceiling heights above staircases and this tends to control loft ceiling heights. While there are various exceptions, the basic aim should be to achieve a minimum of 2m (6½ft) height above a stair.

In lofts where ceiling heights are sloping and often restricted, this can mean making sure that the stairs bring you up near to the highest point of the available space. However, if the stair occupies part of the highest part of the loft, then the space left for the room that you are trying to create can be largely wiped out. Another easy mistake to make is to place your new staircase so that it impedes the headroom over the stair below; again this would contravene the regulations.

Choose the ideal position to depart the floor below and the ideal place to arrive at the top. Can your staircase link these points? > see p.186.

A staircase exists in double-height space and can often be a sculptural and interesting form, as well as being a way of accessing another level.

Windows over a staircase void will add daylight and naturally expel hot air, if cool air can be drawn in through lower level windows. This natural ventilation is known as a 'stack effect'.

A staircase is essentially a piece of joinery and need not be an expensive item. Do not skimp on getting the design right as this can have a huge influence on the success and eventual value of the finished project.

It is very easy to fall foul of the many regulations that relate to staircases. Be particularly careful of head heights, steepness, tapered treads (or 'winders'), handrails and guardings.

Loft-build companies very often have only one way of doing a loft. The fact is that there are many alternatives and an architect will illustrate the range of possibilities with no vested interest.

Bookcase balustrade. This is another example of the loft bedroom door being set at the foot of the staircase – in this case to the left of the landing at the bottom. The required barrier beside the staircase opening at the top has been formed as bookshelving so as to make the most of every storage opportunity.

1. Loft conversion

The simplest way to use a loft space is to convert it from a dusty storage area into a habitable room. You need to factor in whether there is enough space without extending the roof, or if you will need to build out in some way.

In a typical pitched roof space, it is common that there is only sufficient headroom to stand in the central zone beneath the ridge of the roof. The higher the ridge (depending on the angle of the roof) the wider this zone will be.

Before you can start moving into your loft space there are two important structural factors to solve. Firstly, there will probably be a number of angled timber members crossing the loft space ('trusses'). These need to be removed, but as they perform an important function, the structural support for the roof will need to be changed to allow their removal ➤ see also **Roof structure** pp.134–5. This need not be a major task, but it is vital that it is designed and executed correctly.

Secondly, the floor of a typical loft space is simply the ceiling joists of the room below. These will not have been designed to carry the weight of a floor, so it is usual to install new floor joists. Make sure that the new floor joists do not touch the ceiling joists below, as this will form a good acoustic break between the separate rooms ➤ see also **Using roof space** pp.136–7.

When working out how much space there will be in your loft, make allowances to lose some height due to adding a thicker floor (typically 150mm/6in) and insulation in the roof thickness (usually 75–100mm/3–4in).

Bedroom and *en-suite* bathroom

In this project, the roof space of a listed building was converted into a bedroom with an *en-suite* bathroom. It was clear from the start that there would be no chance of getting permission to extend this loft. The task, therefore, was to make the most of the available space.

The central zone was fairly narrow so the staircase was positioned against one of the sidewalls, rising parallel to the pitch of the roof above. The door to the loft room was set at the base of the staircase so that the space at the top could be maximised.

At the far end of the room there was enough space for a small, but beautiful, shower-room. Conservation-grade roof windows brought in masses of daylight and were high enough to allow a desk to be set beneath.

The great thing about loft spaces is that, with a little imagination, you can use all of the space, even that which is too low to stand up in. There are a number of clever storage solutions for the eaves (low part) of a loft room. Here, a specially designed angled wardrobe pulled out like a drawer from beside the shower-room.

It is very unusual that planning permission is granted to make a roof higher. If there is not enough space to stand, before you start, usually the only option will be to lower the ceilings below.

While there may only be a limited zone that is high enough to stand in, setting the sidewalls low to the eaves gives a much greater sense of space.

Loft rooms need a lot of insulation and there are many different types to choose from. Sheep's wool is becoming increasingly popular. It is a high performance insulation, entirely natural and produced in the UK.

A loft space is likely to be the largest unused space within a house, so utilising it is usually one of the most cost-effective ways to enlarge your home.

Most roof constructions will need an air gap for ventilation between the insulation and roofing felt to prevent the build up of condensation (typically 50mm/2in).

In a listed building such as this, the need for clear and detailed drawings to fully explain and communicate the proposals to the conservation officer is vital. Any lack of clarity can lead to a refusal.

∨ Maximising storage. *These angled cupboards pull out like giant drawers from the lower part of the roof space to the side of the shower-room.*

∨ Central spine. *This loft allows good standing height only under the centre of the roof. This means that the top of the stairs, bathroom door and shower all needed to be in the middle.*

2. Loft dormers

A great way to create more internal space when converting a loft is to add a 'dormer' window. A dormer is where a small roof form is built out from the slope of the main roof.

A dormer window achieves two things. Firstly, it creates a vertical surface into which a standard window can be set (before roof windows, this was the only way to put a window into a roof slope). Secondly, a dormer window can create much greater internal volume, often in a part of the roof that otherwise would be too low to stand in.

Structurally, forming a dormer window is more complicated than simply converting an existing roof space. The work will usually require scaffolding to the building and a significant amount of new external roofing work will be required. Some building companies make their dormer structures away from the building site, bring them on a truck and crane them into position. This means that work on site can be done more quickly and with a cost saving, even taking the crane into account.

A dormer window can be formed in a pitched roof with a pitched roof itself, or with triangle-shaped 'cheeks' and a flat roof. The flat roof dormer creates a flat ceiling inside and a wider volume with the extra height. However, flat-roofed dormers are usually not as visually appealing as their pitched roof cousins, in particular from the outside. It is usual for planning departments only to allow dormer roof extensions to roofs facing away from roads.

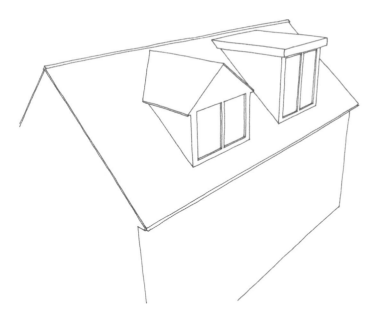

⌃ Flat and pitched roof dormers. *This diagram shows the difference between a flat roofed dormer (right), which will give larger windows and more internal volume, and a pitched roof dormer (left), which will often give a more attractive appearance externally.*

⟨ Headroom and daylight. *This charming example of a girl's loft bedroom with generous height shows how much extra headroom and volume has been created with a pitched roof dormer. In lower roof spaces a pitched roof dormer may not have as great an effect.*

In many instances, dormer windows are the most practical way of creating the necessary additional headroom within a loft space.

Pitched-roof dormers tend to look more charming externally but do not create as much internal volume as flat-roofed dormers.

Solar panels are most effective facing south. A dormer on an east/west-facing roof can provide a south-facing pitch to which solar panels can be mounted.

Decide whether or not the value added by the additional internal volume that the dormer provides is worth the extra building cost.

A dormer window is considered as a roof extension. Where not facing a highway, it will often fall within permitted development **> see pp.108–9**, but when on the front of a house it will usually need a planning application.

A sketch or photo-montage that shows how a house will look with the addition of dormer windows is relatively easy for an architect to prepare, and will help you get a feel for what the outcome will look like.

3. Loft box dormers

When the scale of a flat-roofed dormer is increased so that it takes up most or even all of a roof slope, it is commonly known as a 'box' dormer.

Box dormers are very common on terraced houses, where the rules of permitted development **>** see also **Permitted development** pp.108–9 allow the extension of a roof slope as long as it does not face a highway. Typically, a flat (or very slightly sloping) roof is run from the ridge of the roof backwards, the party walls are built up to form the triangular sides of the box, and the back wall of the house is built up, with windows facing out to the gardens below.

The popularity of box dormers is due to the fact that they create the maximum internal space within the regulations and they can be built for a relatively low cost. Like many other things, there is a range of solutions from the cheap and nasty to the well designed. There is a horde of specialist loft companies who are well versed in the construction of these dormers, but while many of them claim to offer a free 'design' service, they often only have one design that they try to apply to each and every house.

These cheap box dormers tend to be timber-framed and clad with vertically hung roof tiles, typically concrete or faux slate. The flat roof is usually finished with a cheap mineral felt and the windows are more often than not uPVC.

∨ Glass doors can enhance a space.
The use of full-height, timber-framed glass doors across the new rear wall creates an elegant and spacious feeling. The photograph below shows how this effect has been taken even further with the addition of a 'Juliet balcony'.

Room in the roof. *If done well, box dormers can look handsome as well as enhancing the value of the house. The recent change in regulations means that – as built – this example, which met permitted development criteria at the time, would now require planning approval.*

A box dormer can be a very practical way to add usable space to your house. You need to have enough height in your loft to start with.

Box dormers are much maligned because there are so many ugly examples out there. However, it is possible to design them attractively. Choose quality materials and avoid concrete roof tiles and uPVC windows.

Timber cladding, such as overlapping weatherboarding, is an increasingly popular exterior finish to box dormers. Softwood cladding is sustainable and can be treated to be weather resistant and flame retardant.

If your loft is small, a box dormer is likely to be the most cost-effective way of increasing the internal space.

However, box dormers do not have to be like this as it is quite possible to design them attractively using sympathetic materials. Building up the side walls in brick (rather than tile-hung timber frame) is solid and ensures that the extension feels part of the house, rather than something plonked on top. Including generously proportioned windows or even French doors adds to the impression that this is a significant and important part of the house.

As mentioned earlier, outside of conservation areas, box dormers can usually avoid a planning application and be built under permitted development. However, the 2008 changes to the permitted development rules have meant that to avoid a full planning application, dormers must now be set back from the eaves of the roof by at least 200mm (8in) and that balconies are excluded. Such rules make it harder now to achieve the sense of continuity illustrated above.

The building regulations on escape routes from loft bedrooms have been updated and, in some ways, relaxed recently. Rules that your neighbours may have had to follow will not necessarily apply now.

The wording of the legislation for permitted development can be confusing and it is important before going forward to be absolutely sure that you are within the various rules.

Loft in an 'M'-shaped roof

While it is true that most houses in the UK have front-to-back pitched roofs, there are many exceptions. Here is one example of a loft extension for a different roof form.

This recent project offers an interesting twist on the box dormer. The house had a roof shaped like a capital 'M', with two ridges running across and a V-shaped valley in the middle. The front half of the roof rose to a ridge that was about 300mm (12in) lower than the ridge on the rear half. The customer originally imagined a box dormer to the rear half of the roof to create better headroom.

This project illustrates the many facets of an outline design task. The brief required new accommodation in the loft and so we explored various loft forms. We had to work within the permitted development regulations to find roof forms that would avoid a full planning application.

The focus of attention at this point was entirely on the external size and shape. During the outline design process we thought again about the internal layout, and the best overall solution became apparent.

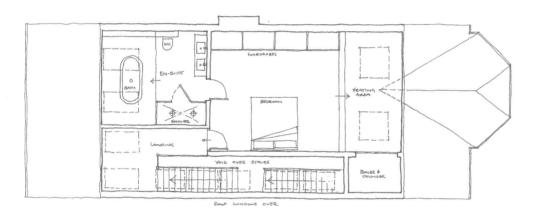

◀ **Space where space is needed.** *The flat roof area was concentrated exactly where it was needed, over the second floor rooms. Roof windows in the sloping roof over the staircase allowed daylight to pour down the stairwells to the hallways below.*

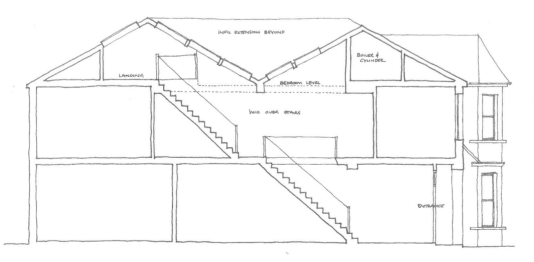

Filling in the middle. Rather than building a box dormer to the rear, this project shows how a tremendous amount of new internal space has been created in a way that has virtually no impact when viewed from the ground.

With limits on the extent of what can be done, it is important to prioritise. Here, the new loft room was considered more important than a high ceiling above the staircase.

Infilling the central valley of an M-shaped roof gave the best internal space and was the least visible option externally.

The new flat roof reduces the external surface area of the roof overall. Combined with efficient insulation, this roof should offer better thermal efficiency than the one it replaced.

This new roof space adds approximately 25 per cent to the overall floor area, increasing the value of the property as a whole.

In order to take advantage of your permitted development rights, it is important to know exactly what the limits are **> see pp.106–9.**

Architects frequently need to manage the expectations of their clients because home owners often find that the need to jump through various hoops in order to meet the planning rules can be quite daunting.

The design solution

It was decided to join up the two ridges by raising the front ridge to the same level as the one at the rear. This would create maximum space inside while being mostly invisible from the ground.

Two elements were critical in getting this proposal through the permitted development criteria **> see also Permitted development** pp.108–9 and so avoiding the delays involved when seeking full planning permission. The first issue was the maximum height. It was possible to raise the front ridge, but the regulations state that it should be no higher than the highest point of the roof (the rear ridge in this case). We had to be very careful that no other elements, such as brick parapets or roof windows, peeked over this maximum height.

The second issue was to stay within the maximum volume limit. To do this we would not be able to infill the whole of the central valley all the way across. The first thought was to reduce the width of this infill on the free side of the house, but this would have made the new bedroom smaller. We opted instead to reduce the width of the infill in the area over the stairs on the party wall side of the house. The original slope of the roof remained in place here with the stair beneath.

This is, of course, slightly absurd. The reduction in volume was now to be set in a place that could only be seen from the air. Nonetheless, if this is what needed to be done to keep within the letter of the law, this was the best solution.

Loft bathrooms

The main aim of the majority of loft conversions and extensions is to create an additional bedroom, but many people try to squeeze in an *en-suite* bathroom or shower-room as well.

More often than not, the bedroom has already taken the best of the loft space and loft bathrooms are often squeezed into difficult spaces. The first thing to be sacrificed when it becomes apparent that a bathroom is going to be tiny is usually a bath. Baths take up a great deal of floor area compared to showers, and so showers tend to lend themselves more readily to small loft spaces. Increasingly, stand-alone baths can be found in bedrooms, with a shower, basin and WC in the *en-suite* bathroom.

The important thing to remember about showers is that the showerhead needs to be high enough for someone to stand under it. Many lofts have sloping ceilings, so when planning your space remember that the shower must have sufficient height.

Just because a loft shower-room is small, does not mean that it cannot be luxurious. In fact, in a small bathroom, you may be able to justify more expensive materials and tiles because you will not need as many.

Mirror, mirror on the wall. *The shower takes the highest possible part of this space, with the basin adjacent to the door, and the WC in the lower area. The two roof windows, one above the other, help the feeling of space tremendously, and the mirror helps the light bounce around. Extending the flooring right through to the lowest part of the roof also enhances the sense of spaciousness.*

Free-standing bath. *In this loft conversion, the symmetry of a free-standing bath with central taps, and an original round window make a tight space feel quite generous. There is not enough height to stand up in at either end of the bath, but extending the floor into the eaves of the roof helps create an illusion of greater space.*

⌃ Small and simple is beautiful.
This shower-room is fitted out with a very beautiful and reflective veined marble, which gives a luxurious effect, even though the room is small. The fitted mirror and cantilevered washbasin have deliberately simple lines and do not crowd the space.

⟩ Maximum height for the shower.
The shower is fitted in the central apex of the loft, as this is the only place where the ceiling is high enough.

⟨ Clean lines. The room really uses the space to the maximum, with the floor outside the shower doubling as standing space in front of the washbasin and access to the WC.

When planning a shower in a tight space, make sure that there is enough height to stand below the showerhead.

Keeping the lines of a small bathroom clean and simple is vital to generate the feeling of space.

Good ventilation of a bathroom is essential to dissipate steam and avoid condensation. However, over-zealous ventilation can allow heat to escape and reduce the efficiency of the roof insulation.

If you are creating a master bedroom in your loft, an en-suite bathroom will usually add more value than it costs to install, so, if it is feasible, it is a good idea.

A bathroom is not classified within the regulations as a 'habitable' room and, therefore, a direct means of fire escape is not required.

Are you a shower person or a bath person – or both? It is important that your architect understands how you want to live before designing in features that you may not use.

Going out

Expanding your home **sideways** *means enlarging the 'footprint' of your house on the ground.* **Ground works** *such as* **foundations**, *moving manholes and building floor slabs can be expensive, particularly considering that the* **result** *will be* **invisible**.

If the additional space that is needed for your home cannot be found by rearranging things internally, and the option of converting or extending the loft space is not feasible, the next option to consider is an extension: going OUT.

Extensions

The reason that extensions are usually next in the cost-effective pecking order is that, unlike loft conversions, they require work to be done on the ground. Ground works are not necessarily complicated, but they can be fairly expensive and the cost is commonly known as 'invisible' money. This means that the work, and the cost of the work, although necessary, is all invisible in the end, as there is nothing directly to show for it. These works include digging and laying foundations, moving or diverting drains or other services in the ground, and laying floor slabs.

Nonetheless, if you need to add space, in particular to the ground floor of your home, an extension is often the most straightforward way to create what you need. Extensions are many and various depending upon the aims of the project, the nature of the existing building and the space available outside.

Side return

A common form of extension is known as the 'side return' (for reasons that I cannot fathom!). One of the most usual layouts for terraced and semi-detached houses in the UK is to have a slightly narrower kitchen at the rear of the house, with outdoor space at the side and a window or door in the back of the main block of the house. Extending the kitchen sideways to the full width of the house creates extra space.

Side return extensions can be very successful. The two main structural changes will be the removal of the original side wall of the kitchen and the need for a foundation (usually a strip or trench foundation) for the new external wall. This new external side wall is more often than not on the boundary line and can become a 'party wall' > see also **Party wall legislation** pp.144–5.

Even if the extra width generated is as little as 1.5m (5ft), it can make a tremendous difference to the internal space. As the example opposite illustrates, the extra space has meant that this kitchen now has room for a table and seating.

One important issue to consider is daylight, in particular to the middle of the house. Side return extensions block the windows or doors that the space was left for in the first place, and the danger is that the middle room becomes landlocked and gloomy. There are two common solutions to this problem. Glazing part, or all, of the new roof can bring good daylight right into the depth of the house, and knocking through the front and middle rooms can bring daylight from the front into the middle room.

Side return extensions are generally very practical as they add space exactly where it is needed and take away an external space that often adds little to a garden.

Both pitched (sloping) and flat-roofed side returns can be very pleasing forms. It is generally more attractive to set a flat roof below a parapet or up-stand.

The total glazed area is inefficient in terms of heat loss compared to insulated constructions. A balance between the minimum glazed area and the maximum daylight penetration will save energy used for artificial lighting.

So long as the ground work is straightforward, the construction cost of a side return should be modest. Don't underestimate the cost of the fit-out. New kitchens can be very expensive and there will be lots of 'making good' to the building.

As long as they are single storey, most side return extensions can be built under permitted development > see pp.106–7 and do not need a planning application.

It is sometimes difficult to explain to customers just how much more spacious a room will be when made wider by as little as 1.5m (5ft). Examples like this illustrate the effect nicely.

Daylight into the heart of the house. *This side return was built before the recent changes to part L of the building regulations > see p.199, which effectively limit the amount of glazed area that an extension can contain. To be energy efficient, architects must utilise glass as effectively as possible.*

Simple construction. *Once the original side wall of the kitchen has been removed and the new party wall built, the rest of the work is relatively lightweight.*

Living rooms

Living rooms are extended for a number of reasons. It may simply be that a larger room is wanted, or because other internal arrangements have taken over some of the original space. A customer may also want to separate living room functions.

Project

Extending an old farmhouse

When extending a property you need to consider how the extension works with the original building. We were asked to design an extension for an old and very charming farmhouse. The brief was for a new modern living space, for use as a home cinema and a place to work or browse the Internet ➤ see also **Technology** pp.240–1.

The brief contained some interesting and potentially conflicting criteria. The customer required a modern space, but it was also necessary to design something that would work well with the exterior of the existing house. The garden was going to be redeveloped to create a new external area and the new extension would need to sit happily with all of these different elements.

The design solution

The solution was to use reclaimed bricks and roof tiles so that the new walls and extended roof matched the original house. The extended area is the lower part of the roof, beside the dormer window (see the centre of the photograph below), and includes the wall below with the three tall windows.

Many people feel that contemporary and classic design are incompatible, yet I think this project illustrates that a clean modern interior can co-exist very happily with a farmhouse-style exterior. Note that the new landscaped terrace is also styled in a very modern, almost Japanese way, but is perfectly in keeping with the house.

➤ *Clean, modern living. This light and airy living room doubles as a home cinema ➤ see pp.240–1 and also provides work stations for home working and browsing the Internet.*

˅ *Joinery can keep it simple.* The desk was specially designed so that cable runs and computer equipment were hidden away to give an uncluttered look, leaving only the screen, keyboard and mouse on display. The knee space below the desk was kept clear to enhance the effect of the tall windows.

Technology is moving ahead so fast that it is important to try to 'future-proof' a project such as this. We included cable routes, which may be needed in the future, with wires to draw cables to key points within the room.

In a clean interior it is vital to keep the lines simple. All mechanisms need to be concealed, so it is important to allow enough space at the outline stage, although details can come later.

A true home-cinema experience requires a big surround-sound effect. Good acoustic insulation in walls and ceilings and well-sealed doors can contain potential noise.

While this project was a simple structure, all the materials used were of the highest quality and were carefully sourced, making this a relatively expensive build.

This house is situated in land designated as 'green belt'. Development is resisted so that rural separation from towns is retained. Each area establishes limitations on where new and extended houses are allowed.

Originally these customers wanted an extension that was expressively modernist on the outside, but once the collaborative design process started they leaned towards a more traditional style.

Adding a modern extension

In contrast to the previous example, this extension to a Victorian detached house is deliberately expressed externally as a new addition to the original.

The house was laid out in a classic fashion, with a strong central hallway and staircase dividing the house in two. The function of this extension was to connect the rooms across the back of the house and, in so doing, create an informal space with great views of a lovely garden.

This project shows how the house was designed for a modern family wanting to live in a less formal way than the lifestyle for which the house was designed. Previously, rooms were isolated from each other and did not promote family interaction. The new living room flows directly from the kitchen space, where a family table forms the hub of the home. It also connects with the large living rooms that were cut off from the action.

The proportions of the original house are large scale and strong, and the design of this extension matches that strength in a very contemporary style. While the shape of the extension is modern, the materials used were chosen to be natural and visually soft. Weathered stone steps from the garden level form a base for walls in cedar wood and glass, beneath a 'reversed pitch' roof, clad in weathered zinc. Strategically placed roof windows bring daylight into the depth of the room, but the largest expanse of glass faces the garden, making the most of the view.

While quite small in terms of the amount of additional floor area it created, this extension brings more of the house into use.

A striking contemporary form can be softened with natural and weathered materials. Cedar wood weathers beautifully over time to a silvery grey, and the zinc is visually crisp and soft at the same time.

Western Red Cedar is a sustainable material. It grows in many parts of the world and is particularly common in Canada, where its growth is managed responsibly.

The budget here has been directed where it will have the most effect. The giant double-glazed window was very expensive, but creates a strong feature for the project.

Before achieving planning permission for this project, it was necessary to produce diagrams with sight lines that demonstrated that the scheme would not overlook the neighbours or undermine their privacy.

Architects cannot just expect their clients to blindly trust their judgement. Drawings, models and visualisations will all help the architect communicate the vision. Only then can a decision be made.

⌃ 'Soft' materials.
While the form of the building is distinctly modern, the materials, which include pale stone, red cedar and weathered zinc, were chosen for their visual softness.

⌃ Garden views.
Most of the available glass area was reserved for a huge picture window that gave lovely views down the long garden of this Victorian house.

⌃ 'Butterfly' roof.
Inside, the reverse pitch roof (sometimes referred to as a 'butterfly' form roof) is more apparent and the strategic roof windows bring light into the depth of the room.

‹ Strong base, floating roof. *Getting the right hierarchy in the weight of materials used is important so as to create harmonious feeling. Here the base – or 'plinth' – is expressed in heavy stone and concrete, the lighter timber-framed walls sit on the base, and the roof is designed to visually 'float', with a deep shadow between the top of the timber and zinc-clad overhang.*

Extensions on two floors

If you are looking to add space in different places – for example, a larger kitchen and an extra bedroom – you can extend a house on two or more storeys. Given that ground works are relatively expensive, putting two levels of additional floor space on the same foundations provides value for money.

The addition of a bedroom to a house generally adds a great deal of additional property value and I struggle to think of many people who would not like the option of one extra bedroom, even if it is utilised as a study or home office.

More often than not, the reasons not to build an extension on two storeys are because the upper level simply will not fit (blocking windows or preventing light coming into the space below), or because planning permission would not be forthcoming.

A planning application is much more likely to be required for a two-storey extension ➤ see also **Feasibility appraisal** pp.98–9. Accommodation at first floor level can be the cause of loss of privacy to neighbours, due to 'overlooking', or be deemed to be 'overbearing'. These are very common reasons for planning permission to be withheld.

As a result, when designing an extension on more than one level it is important to be very mindful of the potential reasons for refusal. The distance between your house and neighbouring properties, the extent to which your proposals project further than the rear building line of a neighbour's house, and the relative position of windows on each building all need to be given careful consideration.

While planning and/or permitted development considerations can be key, there are many other factors to consider, in particular, how the extension will affect the overall appearance of a house. Simply broadening the front elevation of a house can work in some cases ➤ see also **Traditional front, modern back** p.83 and sometimes can significantly enhance a building, but if it is done without sensitivity, it can ruin the proportions or make a house feel lop-sided.

Extensions over a garage

If you have a garage adjoining your house, a very efficient way of finding more space is to extend the first floor over the top of it. Building over a garage makes sense in construction terms, and it can also enhance the appearance of the building as a whole.

Often, an adjoining garage can look rather secondary alongside a house. Connecting the buildings at first floor level and putting a substantial roof over the extension can have the effect of unifying the building so that it all appears more impressive.

One common doubt is whether the existing foundations of the garage will be strong enough to carry an extra storey. In the majority of cases, the foundations are more than strong enough, but it is always important to have it checked out. A 'trial hole' approximately 600mm (23in) square is usually dug against the side wall, deep enough to expose the foundation and to see how far down it goes. A structural engineer will be able to make an assessment from this. A good way to keep down the costs of the engineer is to dig the trial hole before the visit. In this way the engineer will not need to make another visit at extra cost.

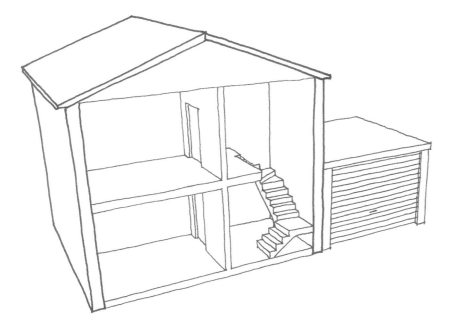

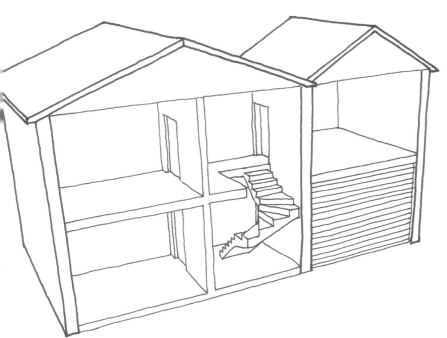

⌃ The stairs are the key. *These customers needed another bedroom and could not imagine how the space could be found. They had considered building over the garage, but could not figure out how to access it from the existing staircase (top). The solution that unlocked the whole design was to change the staircase so that it arrived in a different position at the first floor (above) allowing access to a new extension over the garage.*

Think carefully about the layout and access to rooms in extended upper floors. If the circulation is not efficient you can waste much of the space you are creating.

Extending over an adjoining garage can transform a house, making the combined building significantly more impressive.

If ground works are to be undertaken, consider installing a ground source heat pump to claim heat from the ground to supplement the heating in your house.

If other factors allow, building on two or more levels will reduce the cost per square metre, as one set of ground work will serve twice as much floor space.

Two common reasons for planning refusal of two-storey extensions are 'overlooking' (loss of privacy to neighbours) and 'overbearing' developments where the bulk of the proposed extension is deemed to be domineering to neighbours.

As this example shows, the answer to a design problem often comes in a way that is not expected. The phrase 'we'd never have thought of that' is one that is often heard by Architect Your Home.

⌃ Open kitchen. The modern styling of the rear part of this extension accommodates a huge sliding glass door, which allows the space to open up beautifully to the terrace and garden. Keeping the floor level and terrace level the same helps the continuity of the space.

⟨ Pebble-dash transformation. Other than one original window, which previously looked into a conservatory, the back of this house has entirely changed. The fussy scale and unattractive materials have given way to something both grander and calmer.

Project

Traditional front, modern back

In some cases it is better to demolish and build in the place of the existing garage rather than build over it. Here, for instance, the existing single-storey, adjoining garage of this semi-detached house has been replaced. The new part of the front elevation of the house has been designed to match the original, with the porch canopy being lengthened to stretch across the wider frontage.

At the rear of the house, however, the style is modern and contrasts sharply with the front and with its neighbours. The different external styles reflect the internal uses, particularly on the ground floor of the extension. At the front is a study, and at the rear a large modern kitchen is afforded maximum daylight and views to the garden. The modern style of the rear elevation incorporates a huge sliding glass door. The tiled kitchen floor extends out at a matching level to the terrace outside, which is paved to match. While more difficult to achieve, this detail enhances the connection between inside and outside beautifully.

On the first floor, two new bedrooms and a second bathroom have been provided. This extension has turned a modest three-bedroomed house with a tiny kitchen into a well-proportioned five-bedroomed house with a fabulous kitchen.

< **The original house.** *Before the work was done, this was a modest three-bedroomed house with a garage.*

∨ **Extended to match.** *The garage has been demolished and the house extended sideways in the existing style, with an elongated porch roof, corner bricks and even pebble dash to match the original.*

Two new bedrooms, a second bathroom, a study, a utility room, downstairs WC and a magnificent kitchen have replaced a single garage.

While the front of the house retains the original style, the rear is modern and incorporates an impressive sliding kitchen door.

The high-performance double-glazed windows will significantly reduce heat loss and energy consumption.

In an area where house prices are high, transforming this from a three- to a five-bedroomed house and the addition of an extra bathroom, will have increased the property value by at least double the cost of the works.

Retaining the original architectural style of the front of the house, while proposing a more daring style to the rear, where the impact will affect fewer people, meant that planning permission was not controversial.

Finding a selection of favourite images of contemporary homes from magazines and books is a great way to communicate to your architect the look and feel that you are hoping to achieve.

Return to original splendour

When a house has been allowed to fall into serious disrepair, and the refurbishment required is extensive, the cost of additional extension works can be partly consumed within the quantity of general works.

This 19th-century house had been the subject of a planning battle and, as a result, was left unoccupied for over ten years. Vandals had used the house as a place for parties, and the property, which was very large, was in need of significant works to restore it to habitable use.

To maximise what this house could offer, we proposed adding a combination of a two-storey side extension and a single-storey extension to the rear. It was hoped that the roof of the rear extension could form a huge balcony, serving the bedrooms at the rear of the first floor. However, it became clear that there would be problems getting planning approval for this as the balcony would probably overlook the neighbouring properties. The scheme that was deemed acceptable placed the balcony centrally at the rear so that the privacy of neighbours was protected.

The original building had an old render finish on its front external walls that was beyond repair. A new acrylic insulating render was applied, giving better thermal performance and a crisp flat finish.

▽ *Road-side elevation. The proportions of this magnificent family house have been strengthened with a large two-storey side extension that makes it even more prepossessing, but which is set back so as not to compete with the symmetry of the frontage.*

The single-storey ground floor extension of this project created a huge new kitchen family space opening out to the garden, replacing a maze of smaller, badly organised rooms.

∧ A softer face to the garden. *Extensions at ground floor level were added to the rear of the house. These are expressed in brick and are more broken up in their form compared to the frontage, creating a softer and more open face to the garden.*

The side extension was designed to be set back from the front of the house so that the original proportions of the front elevation could remain dominant.

∨ Computer visualisation. *Before committing to this design, the architect built a three-dimensional computer model of the building so that the customer could properly judge the proposals. This computer visualisation also helped the planning application process.*

Using an acrylic insulating render not only gave a very smart external finish, but also improved the thermal performance of the original external walls.

Using two skins of concrete block work for the walls of the extension kept construction costs down so that more budget was available for the internal fit out.

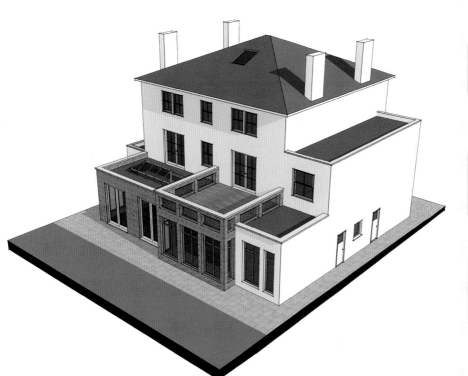

After initial planning refusal, careful design was necessary to ensure that the rear balcony would not cause a privacy issue, while still being an elegant feature of the house.

Computer modelling can be a great way to judge how a design will look. They take time to produce and are consequently expensive, but are great value if they help you make the right choice.

Going down

*Extending your home **underground** will neither overlook nor overshadow your neighbours **externally**. However, there are a **number** of factors that conspire to make this way of extending a home complex and **expensive**. It is particularly **important,** therefore, to make the space as lovely as possible.*

At the start of this chapter I suggested that the main options, in order of cost-effectiveness, for finding more space within a home were IN (making more space by rearranging the interior), UP (converting and/or extending loft space), OUT (extending by building out to the side or rear of a house) and DOWN (adding a basement). So why is the option to extend downwards the last on the list?

⋁ Sketch section. *This hand-drawn section cut through a house shows how room for living is found in the roof and below ground. A 'double-height' space at the front of the house allows daylight to flow down to basement level, and an excavated terrace garden to the rear alleviates the basement feeling in the kitchen.*

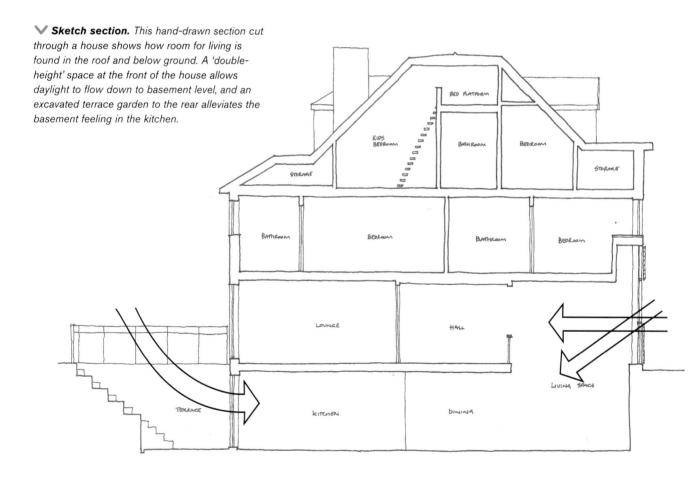

❮ *Let the daylight flood in.*
Removing part of the ground floor at the front of this interior, lets daylight flood down to the basement living space below.

Basements can be used for a whole variety of functions including additional bedrooms, cosy family kitchen/eating spaces or for a television den.

Excavating light wells beyond the walls of the house will reduce the claustrophobic feeling of being below ground.

Being set into the ground and the 'thermal mass' of the heavy construction make basements very well insulated and energy efficient.

A basement extension below an existing house is a very expensive undertaking and will generally only be feasible where property prices are very high.

A habitable basement must, generally, have a direct means of fire escape, or a route out of the house that does not pass through any other habitable rooms. This regulation would not apply to non-habitable uses such as a utility room or wine cellar.

Cross-section drawings like the one opposite are the best way to illustrate how much ceiling height each floor will have, and give a good sense of how the light will flow.

Basements

te simply, excavation is expensive work to undertake, and when it is eath an existing building that needs to remain standing throughout, it is n more expensive. Digging out, installing a temporary structural support, ving drains and services and waterproofing are all expensive tasks.

etheless, basement extensions are becoming more and more popular, despite costs, because in areas where property prices are high, people still want to find e space, especially when lofts or side extensions are not possible.

re is also a good environmental case for basements. The fact that they are w ground means that they are naturally insulated. The heavy construction ded to retain the earth provides excellent 'thermal mass' (where warmth is ed over an extended period). This can significantly reduce the energy sumption required for heating.

er than the expense, the main problem with developing a basement is that it be gloomy and claustrophobic. If the basement is to be used as a recording io or dark room, this can be a benefit, but, generally, people want to make the e as unlike a basement as possible, and this quite simply means windows daylight are needed.

ating windows and/or glazed doors at basement level requires that these look onto outdoor space and this means even more excavation. The larger the space ide, the more the feeling of being below ground is alleviated.

< **Below-ground suntrap.** *Seen from the outside at ground level, the stepped terrace garden forms a secluded suntrap in the heart of town (left). The kitchen space is flooded with daylight so it does not feel like a basement space (far left).*

If you are thinking of putting a kitchen or utility room in the basement, think carefully about the practicality of carrying washing or food up and down the stairs.

Good basement design is about making the space feel as 'un-basement-like' as possible.

The ground provides great natural sound insulation, so if you want a recording studio, the basement may well be the best option.

If you already have a cellar, enlarging it is less expensive than digging out from scratch. However, you may well need to 'underpin' the foundations, which is costly.

Part H of the building regulations relate to drainage **> see p.198**. In a basement you may be lower than the level of the public sewer and a sump arrangement may be needed for both rainwater and soil waste.

It is important to be open with your neighbours about what you propose to do. Do not ignore the need to deal with Party Wall legislation **> see pp.144–45** or you could face problems later.

The example illustrated here and on the previous page shows how a basement has been formed, providing a living room to the front and a kitchen/breakfast room to the rear of the basement level. The excavation has extended well beyond the back wall of the house to form a sunny terraced area with staggered planting steps to maximise the sense of space. The breakfast room looks out to a sunken terrace or light well, which is used as a lovely external private space.

Smaller light wells can also be effective to bring daylight down to basement windows. It is always worth going deep enough so that the windows can be placed at a standard window height. High-level windows do not give the same feeling of space and, if anything, emphasise the fact that the room is below ground.

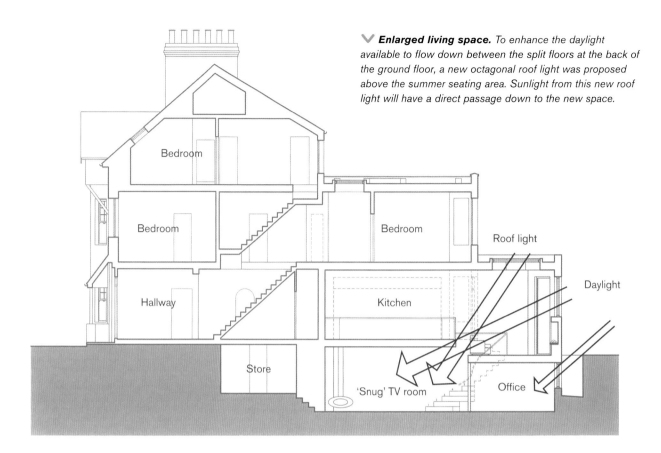

Enlarged living space. To enhance the daylight available to flow down between the split floors at the back of the ground floor, a new octagonal roof light was proposed above the summer seating area. Sunlight from this new roof light will have a direct passage down to the new space.

Bedroom

Bedroom

Bedroom

Roof light

Daylight

Hallway

Kitchen

Store

'Snug' TV room

Office

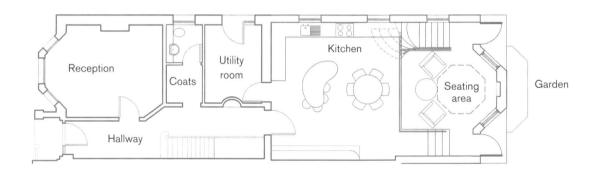

Reception

Coats

Utility room

Kitchen

Seating area

Garden

Hallway

∧ **Ground floor plan.**

⟩ **New basement level plan.**
The staircase down from the garden level to the 'snug' is designed to flow naturally into the new space. It is set off against a curved wall, which defines the study spaces.

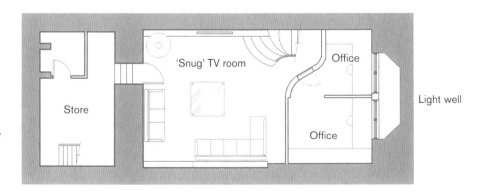

Store

'Snug' TV room

Office

Office

Light well

Adding a basement

One outcome of extending at loft level is that a house can, in some circumstances, become top-heavy. In this elegant semi-detached house in a prosperous area of West London, the loft had already been converted, creating a fourth and fifth bedroom.

The ground floor accommodation was not ungenerous for a three-bedroomed house, but now, as a five-bedroomed house, it was a little undersized. The owners wanted a separate 'snug'/TV room and to connect the dining area more effectively with the kitchen. In addition, they were hoping to find space for two small home office/study spaces.

With the loft space already taken, and little opportunity for a side or rear extension (due to garden size and proximity of neighbours), the remaining option was to investigate the feasibility of excavating a basement space.

There was a small existing cellar beneath the main staircase, with low headroom, but this did not have the potential to create the desired space.

One important factor to bear in mind was that the new 'snug' should not feel completely separate or cut off from the kitchen/dining area upstairs. The level of the garden was several steps below the existing ground floor level, and a better connection with the garden was also considered an important aim.

Accordingly, at the outline design stage it was decided to enlarge the kitchen at ground floor level, incorporating a kidney-shaped kitchen island, leaving plenty of space for a round dining table, and to have views out to the garden.

The area nearest the garden would be lower (and thereby closer to the garden level), creating space for an open seating area, with a 'summer' feeling and bathed in daylight. The different levels also served to break up the stairs down to the proposed new basement beneath the kitchen. This device allowed the stairs to seem less of a barrier, and also promoted good daylight penetration down to the new 'snug'.

Finally, the two new study spaces were situated below the lower seating level with an external light well to bring good daylight onto the desk spaces.

The owners of this house expressed a love of curves and this is reflected in the design with a couple of sinuous elements. I have already mentioned the curved (kidney-shaped) kitchen island, but in addition the staircase down from the garden level to the 'snug' was designed to flow into the new space almost like molten lava spilling into a new cavern, set off against an s-shaped wall, which defines the study spaces.

Finally, a retro-style globe open fire, suspended on its own chimney flue was designed to hover within the new 'snug', creating a cosy, yet funky, focus for the room. TV rooms are ideally suited for basements because the focus of attention will be the TV, rather than outside views, and reflection on the screen from bright outdoor light will not be a problem.

Basement spaces are ideal for inward-looking activities such as watching TV or for a home cinema. Very often, too much sunlight can cause distracting reflections on a screen, and the natural insulation provided by the earth helps contain sound.

Curves can add freedom to a piece of design, but use them judiciously. Too many curves in one space can confuse each other and end up looking a mess. Focus attention on one curved element by surrounding it with simple straight lines.

The earth is a wonderful natural insulator and, generally, basements are far more efficient in terms of heat loss than loft conversions or side extensions.

There is no getting away from the fact that excavating a basement is a complex (and, therefore, expensive) business. Even so, in this prosperous area, the high property prices suggest that the additional space will add value.

Where the basement space is open to the ground floor space, depending upon the distances involved, it can be within the regulations for the means of escape to go through the upper space. Check part B of the building regulations > see p.197.

When a basement excavation is proposed, it is important to ensure that your survey includes the variation in ground levels (topographical information), so that the excavations and party wall arrangements can be worked out.

Thinking ahead on building regulations

At the beginning of this chapter I laboured the importance of keeping the outline design stage fluid and not getting bogged down with detail. However, it is also important not to design something that will be impossible to achieve due to technical problems later in the process.

The whole idea of the outline design stage is to develop the broad-brush proposals that will form the backbone of the project. It is important to keep this phase loose and free, so that the principle of various ideas can be tried out in sketch form.

Momentum is vitally important to this process. It is very easy to get caught up with a specific query, such as will I get planning permission for this? Are the existing foundations strong enough? Or what sizes do roof windows come in? In general, I would advise people simply not to worry about such things at this stage and keep their eyes on the 'big picture'. In particular, steer clear of getting too involved in the building regulations, which involve a myriad of fiddly detail issues.

At the same time, it is important not to blindly go down a route that will simply turn out to be impossible or completely unfeasible once the later stages are reached. The art of keeping the outline process fluid while avoiding problems to come, really only comes with experience and represents a delicate balance for the designer. However, the technique of achieving this mainly falls into two categories.

Firstly, it is important to make general allowances for details that can be sorted out later. Knowing, for instance, that allowing 250 to 300mm (10 to 12in) for floor/ceiling thickness should be enough when working out approximate headrooms, avoids the time spent working out the precise make-up of the floor.

Another example of this could be seen when working out proposals for a loft conversion, various positions for the staircase will be sketched out to see what might work best. There is no point in sketching out something that is likely to be too steep, or not to have the necessary headroom, so an allowance will be made as the sketches develop. However, if each option had to be worked out precisely, then the whole process would get bogged down, and it would be impossible to keep sight of the overall project.

The second category is to know in advance those elements of detail that might have a fundamental effect upon the design, as opposed to those that can be ignored for the moment and left to be dealt with later.

For most projects, once the outline design has been established, the scheme design phase ➤ see also **Chapter 3: Scheme Design** pp.100–45 takes the proposal towards a planning application (or equivalent level of detail). We are still, at this point, quite a long way from the detailed work necessary to ensure that all aspects of the building regulations are catered for.

The vast majority of building regulation issues are eminently solvable at the later stage. For example, the exact slope of a drain, or the air capacity of an extractor fan, will not affect anything decided at this point. However, there are a few fundamental building regulation matters that need to be allowed for at the outline design stage, because they may trip the project up later.

In chapter 4, there is a comprehensive overview of the building regulations ➤ see also **The building regulations** pp.196–201, but here are the four areas of the building regulations that are worth some general consideration as part of the outline design process.

Structure

Most of the structural design and calculation necessary for a building regulations application will be done by a structural engineer later in the process, but it is important that the broad idea of how the project will stand up is understood and allowed for from the start.

For example, where a load-bearing wall is to be removed, consider if the supporting beam will be below or within the ceiling. What will the ends of the beam rest upon? Is there enough depth (or thickness) within the ceiling to house a beam? It would be premature to calculate the beam size in detail, but a rule of thumb says that the depth of the beam will be approximately 1/20th of the span.

Making intelligent allowances to accommodate future details will make the design process run more smoothly.

Fire escape

This is an important issue to understand as changing an escape route further down the design process may create fundamental changes to your layout and circulation. Again, without getting bogged down with the detail, try to ensure that all habitable rooms have a direct route out of the building, without passing through another room. Jumping out of a window can often constitute a direct means of escape if the room is on the ground or first floor, but basements and rooms on the second floor or higher need to have a direct way out.

Good design makes allowances for complications, so that the original concept can come to life. Poor design is an idea that gets changed out of shape on its route through the details.

Disabled access

Many people do not recognise that private dwellings are subject to regulations as regards disabled access. The most common examples are the need for level access, rather than steps at entrances, and often the requirement for a suitable WC on the ground floor (or entry level). If you are making changes to an existing house, not all of the regulations will be enforceable, but it is worth checking.

Many people see regulations as a nuisance, but they are all there for good reason. The energy efficiency requirements are in place to help meet the UK's targets set in the Kyoto Protocol.

Failing to get the principles of the design right at the early stages of the project can mean wasted work, major delays and additional expense.

Thermal efficiency

Part L of the building regulations ➤ see also **Approved Documents** p.199 deals with energy efficiency; the requirements were increased significantly in 2006 and are due to be tightened even further in 2010. New homes and extensions need to be able to demonstrate that they meet minimum standards, and many people are surprised by how difficult it is to meet the standard.

The calculations necessary to work out thermal efficiency are fiendishly complex, and it would be impossible to undertake a fluid outline design process effectively if you had to stop and calculate the rating for each option considered. However, it is important to bear in mind that the total area of glass (roof glazing, windows and glazed doors) may well be limited by the regulations, and a suitable allowance needs to be taken into account.

To avoid the need for wasteful changes further down the line, allow for building regulations, planning guidance and the rules of a residents' association or trust.

It is important to grasp only the broad principles at this stage, otherwise you may find that your design conversation becomes bogged down in pedantic detail, when you should be thinking big.

Case study

2. Outline design

Several aspects of this property were unusual for a house in a semi-urban setting. Firstly, despite being detached, it was built (rather lazily) to the design of a terraced house. The house was positioned awkwardly in the plot, just off centre, creating two garden spaces and two rather less useful outside areas.

The 1960s style of the house was very ordinary and the windows had been changed to uPVC frames that were very ugly. Two of the four external walls contained no windows at all.

Ideas and solutions

We wanted to provide additional accommodation for bedrooms and bathrooms on the upper floor, and more living space on the ground floor. It was feasible to develop the loft and second floor to gain extra bedroom space, so there would be no need to extend sideways above ground floor level.

We imagined two box dormers, back to back on both roof slopes. Effectively, this created a flat roof at the ridge level. The front and rear faces of the new level were set back from the elevations below to reduce volume and also to create the feeling that the top was lighter than the base ➤ see also **Adding a modern extension** pp.78–9.

The concept for the roof started to generate an aesthetic for the whole of the exterior. The brief required some visual weight and strength, and what began to emerge from the sketches was a very solid outer box with 'slices' cut from it. A more lightweight inner box could be revealed where the shell was cut away, and this extended up from the outer box to form the second floor level.

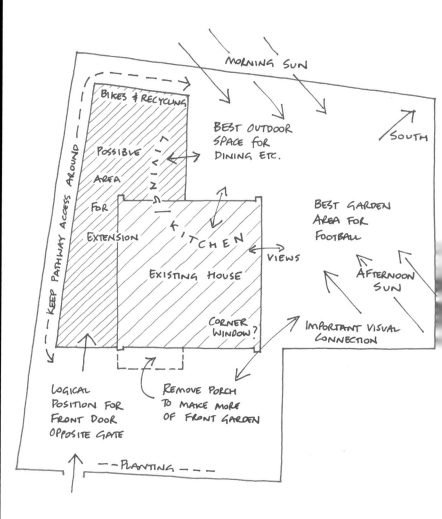

⋀ Sketch site plan. To gain the additional space required at ground floor level, we decided to extend into the external spaces that were too small to be effective as part of the garden. This would provide space in line with the entrance to the plot, which meant that the front door could be relocated.

❯ Ground floor plan. The three main functions of kitchen, dining and living areas form an open, but clearly zoned L-shaped space, connecting to the deck and garden. The study is slightly more separated and the utility space is contained behind an angled wall, designed to turn the view to the right as you come in.

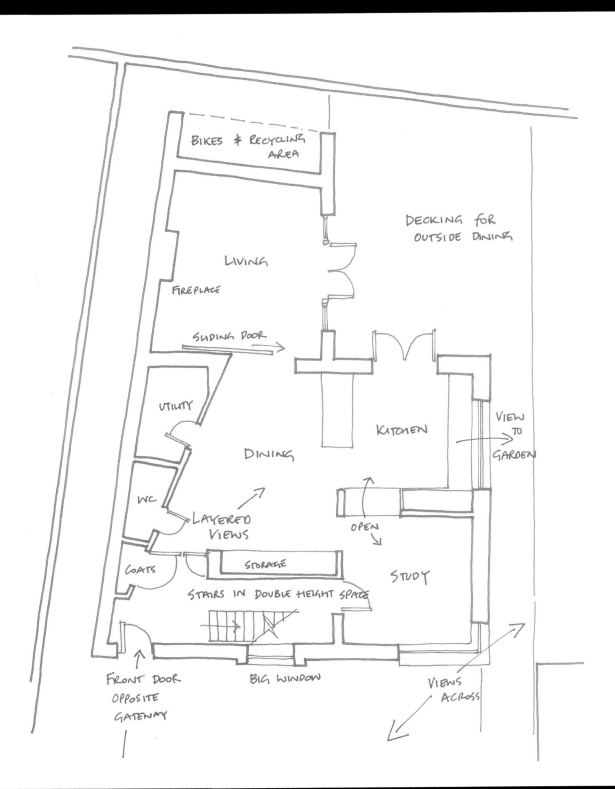

BIKES & RECYCLING
AREA

DECKING FOR
OUTSIDE DINING

LIVING

FIREPLACE

SLIDING DOOR

UTILITY

KITCHEN

VIEW
TO
GARDEN

DINING

WC

LAYERED
VIEWS

OPEN

COATS

STORAGE

STUDY

STAIRS IN DOUBLE HEIGHT SPACE

FRONT DOOR
OPPOSITE
GATEWAY

BIG WINDOW

VIEWS
ACROSS

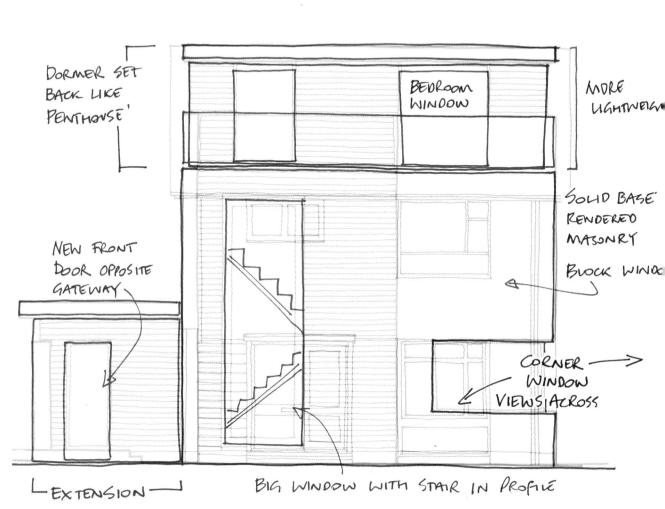

DORMER SET
BACK LIKE
'PENTHOUSE'

MORE
LIGHTWEIG

BEDROOM
WINDOW

SOLID BASE
RENDERED
MASONRY

BLOCK WINDO

NEW FRONT
DOOR OPPOSITE
GATEWAY

CORNER
WINDOW
VIEWS ACROSS

EXTENSION

BIG WINDOW WITH STAIR IN PROFILE

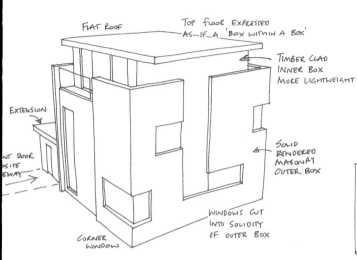

FLAT ROOF

TOP FLOOR EXPRESSED
AS—IF—A 'BOX WITHIN A BOX'

TIMBER CLAD
INNER BOX
MORE LIGHTWEIGHT

EXTENSION

NT DOOR
OS ITE
EWAY

SOLID
RENDERED
MASONRY
OUTER BOX

WINDOWS CUT
INTO SOLIDITY
OF OUTER BOX

CORNER
WINDOW

⌃ Box within a box. The desire to form something visually heavy and strong led to the idea of a heavy masonry box, which has been punctured with geometric openings to reveal a lighter-weight timber clad box within.

⌵ Sketching over. The original elevation (below) was traced over and over again to explore different forms and possibilities. Interchanging constantly from plan to elevation, the form evolved to become more striking and contemporary. The double-height window at the front was designed to frame a set-up view of the staircases in profile.

Feasibility appraisal

The purpose of outline design is to explore possible design solutions in enough detail to be able to appraise feasibility at a very basic level. So, with the outline proposals provisionally agreed, now is the time to take stock and undertake a feasibility appraisal.

The big questions that need to be addressed are, typically: Will I be allowed to build this? And if so, how much will it cost and how long will it take?

The bad news is that an initial feasibility appraisal will not be able to give definitive or accurate answers to these questions. There are still far too many variables that could send these predictions off course. The good news is that, unlike before, we now have an outline design against which informed and intelligent guesses can be made.

Do you need permission?

The most fundamental hurdle to cross is whether or not you will be allowed to build what is proposed. The first question to ask is what permissions need to be sought. Will the project need a planning application, or might it fit within permitted development? Now that you know roughly the size and shape of the project, it is possible to explore the guidelines ➤ see also **Permitted development** pp.106–9 to work this out.

If the project needs planning permission, you can seek advice as to how likely it is to be approved. You can simply ask the planning department of your local council by sending drawings in for a written response, or by visiting and seeing a duty planning officer. Many people find that the advice available from the planning department is frustratingly woolly and non-committal, so you might choose instead to seek the advice of an architect or planning consultant, who may be able to approach things from a more helpful perspective.

Of course, it is not just planning that might prevent your proposals from going forward. Fundamental building regulations ➤ see also **Thinking ahead on building regulations** pp.92–3 can trip you up, or there may be legal restrictive covenants preventing development or alteration written into your title deeds – these need to be checked out. If the building is listed ➤ see also **Listed Building Consent** pp.116–7, there may be particular preservation issues to confront.

Do not expect to be able to get any definite answers at this stage. The initial feasibility appraisal is about getting a good picture of what is likely to be the case.

In the same frustrating way, it is impossible to accurately predict at this stage how much building your proposal will cost, or how long the process will take. Clearly, however, people need to be able to set a budget, and with the outline design established, an approximate estimate of both time and money should be possible. But where should you go for such an estimate?

Getting quotes

Many people will now go to a builder and ask for a quote, but beware. Estimating is not a five-minute job, and most builders will not go to all of this trouble just to be helpful – understandably, they want your business. With only outline information to go on, there is plenty of scope for a builder to put forward a very keen price or timetable, knowing full well that he will be able to revise things once the detail becomes apparent.

I recently came across a project where the customer complained that the builder had originally told her that he would need 12 weeks to complete the work, when, in fact, it had taken nearly 30 weeks. His (predictable) defence was that when he quoted 12 weeks, he was not aware of all of the complexity added in later. In truth, he could have made an intelligent assumption, but this would have made him look expensive and slow, just when he wanted his customer to think the best of him.

To avoid this problem you need someone who is independent. The name for a professional consultant estimator is a quantity surveyor (or QS) and they come in many shapes and sizes. There are large firms and one-man bands. For smaller projects there are a growing number of online services that will provide budget estimates for a fixed fee. In the end, if you want someone with no hidden agenda, you need to pay them.

What about the neighbours?

Many people are tremendously concerned about what the neighbours might say. This sentiment breaks down into two camps. Firstly, those who worry that if the neighbours don't like what is proposed, they could prevent it happening by objecting to planning applications or refusing to agree party wall actions, and secondly, those who don't want any 'bad blood' with people who, after all, live just next door.

While the reality is that neighbours can rarely block proposals as easily as people think and neighbours who get upset usually get over it fairly quickly, in both cases life is easier and smoother if everything is done amicably. Now might be the time, with the bones of the design in place, but before anything is set in stone to approach the neighbours informally to discuss your outline proposals and try to bring people on-side. There is little to lose by this, and potentially much to gain.

The more developed your outline design, the more informed the estimate of cost and time can be. This is often a catch-22 situation, but you need to be able to balance speculative expenditure with unknown costs.

If it becomes clear that your design might well be refused permission, go back and rework the design from the start. Late modifications can warp the whole design.

Renewable energy systems such as solar or heat pumps are expensive up-front costs, but will save money over time on energy bills. Think how long-term savings might be allowed for in your cost predictions.

Getting an accurate cost at this stage should be a priority. Paying a professional cost consultant to give you an independent estimate, rather than a free quote from a builder, should be seriously considered.

More planning departments are charging for preapplication advice these days, so read the free design guidance on the planning department's website first.

It is important to clarify to any builders who may be prepared to price the project at this early stage, that there will be more detail to come and they will have to make several assumptions for now.

3 Scheme design

The scheme design stage takes the naked joy of the outline design, sobers it up, calms it down, measures it and clothes it, making sure that – in essence – it will work.

While resisting the temptation to jump headlong into every detail, the scheme design stage is about bringing reality to the proposals. Will these ideas fit into the space available in the way envisaged? Have you allowed enough height, thickness, depth or space for the details that will inevitably need to be incorporated in due course? Scheme level proposals are presentable, effectively for the first time, to the various bodies who may influence them, including planners, engineers, utility suppliers and builders.

practicality

aesthetic

environment

cost/value

regulations

communication

What is scheme design?

For the first time, your design, developed in **outline** *thus far, must begin to answer to* **reality**. *Scheme design develops your* **dreams** *into a state where they can begin to be measured, visualised, costed, judged,* **organised** *and serviced. Be open-minded because this* **evolution** *is necessary and fruitful.*

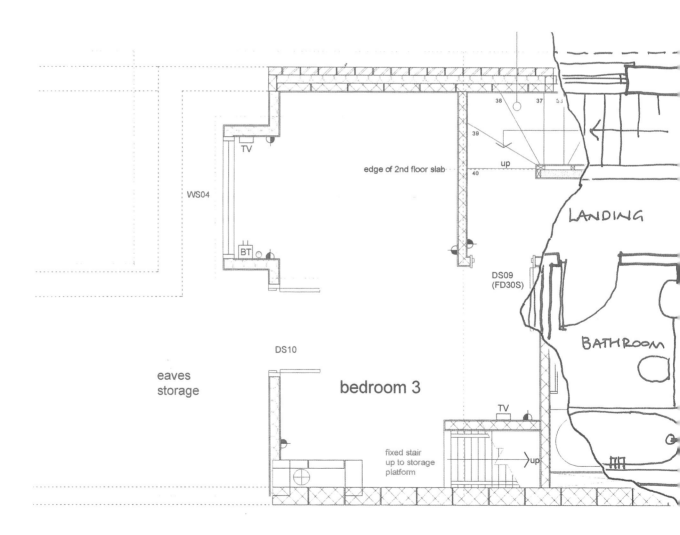

The tangible end result of the scheme design process is a set of drawings, commonly known in the industry as General Arrangement drawings (or GAs). However, it is important to understand that scheme design is a vital stage of the design process and involves much more than merely the production of drawings.

One of the most significant landmarks during the development of a design for building works (when it is applicable) is planning permission. Preparing for a planning application is a very important part of the scheme design, and much of this chapter looks at this stage.

Additionally, the scheme design phase considers the construction and structure of the proposals in depth for the first time. If suitable allowances for the construction are made at the outline design phase, the scheme design often runs smoothly. Similarly, the scheme design work needs to include assumptions and allowances for details that will evolve in later stages.

∨ **Hand-drawn outline design/scheme-level computer drawing.** *The hand-drawn, free nature of the drawings developed at the outline design stage gives way to the rigour of the CAD (computer-aided drawings) and their accompanying precision.*

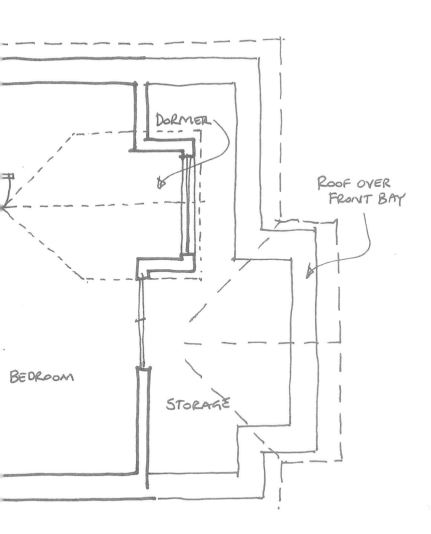

It may seem expedient to skip over the scheme design stage and jump straight into detailed design ➤ **see Chapter 4**. However, this can be a false economy in terms of both time and money.

Scheme level drawings enable you to accurately see how your proposals will look next to the rest of your home and neighbouring properties for the first time.

To assess and calculate the energy efficiency of a building or extension, accurate drawings are necessary to show the size of rooms, walls, windows and doors and their thicknesses.

Scheme design represents approximately 20 per cent of the fee that would be charged for a 'full service'. The Architect Your Home menu system allows you to choose only the services you want.

Scheme level drawings will form the backbone of what is needed for a planning application ➤ **see pp.112–3** and a 'full plans' building regulations application ➤ **see pp.200–1**.

Beware of too much precision. Sending a CAD drawing to a planner or neighbour implies that the dimensions are set in stone. A rough drawing implies flexibility, which can be more disarming.

Planning permissions

The most important factor in achieving successful planning is an understanding of the rules and criteria by which planning decisions are made. However, there are a great many popular misconceptions about planning permission, what is covered, when it applies, confusion with the building regulations, when it is necessary to make an application and the influence of neighbours, to name but a few.

The Town & Country Planning Act requires that planning permission is needed for all development. This does not necessarily mean that a planning application is always needed, so you need to know, what exactly is development?

Without going into the case law that has helped to define development, a good example is work in a garden. Clearly, general gardening, planting and digging is not development and needs no planning permission, but if the works are large scale enough to need a mechanical digger, and/or if structural calculations are needed for retaining walls, this could be deemed significant enough to constitute development.

Planning permission is entirely different and separate from building regulations. Most building works are required to pass through both separately, but many people get them confused.

Planning deals with what buildings are used for and how they affect their surroundings. This is not just about how buildings look or whether they affect someone else's privacy or view, but also many more practical issues, such as what effect the occupancy of a building will have on local parking and traffic.

In contrast, the building regulations set and control minimum standards of construction quality. Described in more detail in Chapter 4, ➤ see also **The building regulations** pp.196–201 the regulations cover a wide range of issues, from structural integrity and fire escapes to proper drains, disabled access and energy efficiency.

How an application is processed

Planning applications are administered by local government planning departments. Applications are received and appraised by planning officers who either attach a recommendation for approval or a refusal. The application is then put before the planning committee, which is made up of local councillors. Most committee decisions agree with the recommendation of the planning officers, but not all.

In order to control the number of decisions that the committee has to make, the planning department is given 'delegated powers' to approve or refuse clear-cut applications where there is no local controversy. For example, if an officer deems an application to be within the published guidelines of what is acceptable, and no objections have been received, the application may be approved under these delegated powers. However, if in the same case, a number of letters of objection have been received, the decision would be referred to the committee, with a recommendation for approval.

Over the years, the amount of information and level of detail required about the proposals has gradually increased. Planning officers frequently reject applications on the basis that there is insufficient information about such things as trees in close proximity to the proposed development, or the effects on the local bat population. It is well worth doing your homework on what information will be required before putting your application together.

One common misconception about planning permission is that it is all very subjective, and if the neighbours agree there should be no problem. In fact, planning law, despite being complex, is mostly very clear, and if a proposal does not meet the published criteria of what will be allowed, no matter how much neighbourly support you have, it will be refused. Conversely, if your proposals are clearly within the planning guidance, the objection of neighbours alone cannot be a reason to refuse permission.

Preparing a planning application

Planning applications can be prepared and submitted by anyone. In fact, there is nothing to stop you applying for planning permission to build on someone else's land (as long as you notify the owner of the land in question). However, having planning approval does not mean that the owner of the land will allow you to build there!

There are, of course, costs associated with making a planning application. Statutory application fees have to be paid when the application is lodged and these will vary depending on the size of the proposed project. If you use an architect to prepare and submit your application for you, they will need to be paid to do so, and you may also need to pay specialist consultants to prepare any reports or surveys that you may need in order to make your case. Tree surveys and traffic reports are common examples of work that may be needed and the cost of doing these can significantly outweigh the basic planning application fee.

While it may be tempting to try to be sparing with such expense, you may find that without the necessary supporting information, well-presented drawings and well-reasoned arguments, your application could be rejected, causing frustrating delays and even more cost than if you had done it properly the first time. Here, it is not just a question of what is 'needed' for your application, but more a question of what will give you the best chance of an approval.

The ever-increasing complexity of information required for a planning application means that it is often advisable to get someone with experience of the system to prepare and submit an application on your behalf. Architect Your Home make hundreds of applications on behalf of customers, and there is provision to do this within the services menu > see also **Gaining statutory consents** p.272. The money spent on using an architect at this point can save you time and money later on.

Planning applications usually take at least eight weeks to be processed. It is usual only to find out just before the eight weeks are up whether sufficient information has been included. To avoid delay, try to provide all the information up front.

Most planning departments publish fairly extensive 'design guidance', which is often available online. This shows examples of the style and scale of work in different situations that may be acceptable.

Planning policy is increasingly focused on environmental issues, and a proposal that clearly has environmental benefits will have this in its favour when decisions are made.

Central government sets the rates for planning application fees, so they are standard across England and Wales. The rates vary depending upon the scale of work proposed. An application for an extension is cheaper than for ten new houses.

Planning departments not only administer planning applications, but also cover Listed Building Consents and confirm permitted development.

Communicating your intentions to the planning department in a way that allows your scheme to be seen honestly, but in its best light, can make all the difference to your chances of gaining approval.

Permitted development

Permitted development is automatic planning permission for a list of situations for which you don't have to make a planning application. Unless they have been specifically removed, every house has permitted development rights as defined in the General Permitted Development Order (GPDO) of the Town and Country Planning Act.

The GPDO is broken down into different classes, many of which deal with agricultural or industrial situations, which do not affect home owners, but the first few on the list can be particularly useful to understand.

Class A sets out what changes can be made to a house without the need to make a planning application. Class B looks at roofs and defines the extent to which certain roofs can be extended under permitted development (this is examined overleaf). There are separate classes for porches, outbuildings, garden fences and more.

Whilst it may seem unfair, flats have no permitted development rights. Listed buildings may have them, but while this may sidestep the need for a planning application, it does not avoid the need for Listed Building Consent ➤ see also **Listed Building Consent** pp.116–17. Houses in conservation areas do have permitted development rights, but the criteria for what you can do are more restricted.

The criteria are complicated and it is sometimes quite easy to misunderstand their meaning, but if you are feeling brave they are all spelt out and can be viewed online at www.planningportal.com

Certificate of Lawfulness

You do not need to make an application for your permitted development; these are rights that you have as a home owner and you can simply start building (keeping in mind building regulations) ➤ see also **The building regulations** pp.196–9. It is advisable, however, to seek a Certificate of Lawfulness, issued by the planning department, stating that what you are doing is indeed within the necessary criteria. You are not required to have such a certificate, but it does give you the certainty of knowing that you are acting properly. Also, when it comes to selling your property, the conveyancing will be made smoother if this certificate is available.

Applying for a Certificate of Lawfulness is similar to applying for planning permission, but slightly less involved. Nonetheless, you usually need to prepare and submit drawings to demonstrate clearly that your proposals meet the criteria.

What you are allowed to do

The criteria for permitted development changed quite dramatically in October 2008. In some ways the rules made life easier for home owners, while in other ways new restrictions were introduced. For example, previously, the amount that a house could be extended under permitted development was restricted by a total additional volume limit. This meant that, in many instances, people had to choose where to use their allowance, to have a loft or ground floor extension. Now, there is only a volume limit on roofs and the restrictions on ground floor extensions are different.

Many people are amazed to find just how much they can actually do without having to submit a planning application. Changing windows and doors, or building an extension or outbuilding, such as a garage or home office, are possible, as long as you stick within the criteria.

The criteria change depending upon the type of house and whether or not it is in a specially designated zone, such as a conservation area. For example, a house that is not in a conservation area can build a 3m (10ft) deep two-storey extension to the rear, whereas a similar house in a conservation area can have a single storey under permitted development, but would need planning permission for two storeys.

The building must not extend towards a road and the heights of extensions are restricted within certain distances from boundaries.

The regulations make great play of the 'original', in particular, with reference to 'original' side and rear walls of a house. This clearly is open to debate in some buildings and most local areas consider anything built before 1947 to count as part of the original. I have seen plenty of examples where evidence of old maps have been used to show that a particular part of a building is old enough to be considered 'original'.

For the main part, the wording of the legislation is clear enough to avoid subjectivity and the need for interpretation. However, certain clauses, such as the requirement for exterior materials to have a similar appearance to those of the existing house are too subjective, and these will, unfortunately, require case law to establish clear definitions.

Staying within permitted development will usually avoid the delays commonly associated with planning applications.

As long as you stay within the limitations, the planning department can have no say in the appearance of what you build under permitted development.

Reducing bureaucracy encourages people to improve their homes rather than move into new housing. This is much better for the environment than allowing existing homes to fall into disrepair.

Using permitted development avoids the application fees associated with planning permission, although there is a small fee to get a Certificate of Lawfulness.

Although your project may not need planning permission, it may still need building regulations approval.

Don't think that just because you don't need a planning application, you will not need clear, well-presented drawings. You may need to prove you are within the criteria.

⋀ Permitted development at the front. *At the front of our 'typical' house the rules restrict alterations to a modest level. Here a porch, solar panels and a roof window have been added, all without the need for a planning application. Note that (other than the porch) none of the outbuildings and extensions are nearer the road than the main house.*

⟩ Rear extensions and alterations.
This diagram illustrates some of the various extensions and alterations that can, typically, be made to a house under permitted development. This example shows French windows, a box dormer to the roof, a glazed rear extension, a single storey side extension, a separate garage and a shed.

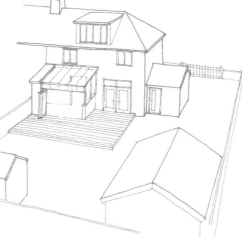

Permitted development: roofs

Class B of the General Permitted Development Order deals with extensions to roofs, and this is particularly important to anyone thinking about a loft conversion.

There are exceptions. Flats have no permitted development rights and listed buildings will need Listed Building Consent, but with roof extensions the restrictions include conservation areas where class B does not apply. Houses that are not in conservation areas can build roof extensions under permitted development within certain limits.

If you are simply converting a roof space for habitable use, and fitting roof windows, there are no issues regarding planning permission (although be careful of new restrictions on side windows). However, if you want to add a dormer or box dormer **>** see also **Loft dormers** pp.67–9, this counts as extending the roof.

Roof restrictions

The first fiercely enforced restriction, in my experience, is that no part of the roof extension can be higher than the highest point of the original roof. This usually means the ridge of the main roof of a house. Chimneys and parapet walls are not considered part of the roof. If you need your roof extension to be higher than this, then you would need planning permission, but it is extremely rare for planning approval to be forthcoming.

One recent project included a flat roof at the ridge level of the original roof. This would normally have been within the criteria, but it was proposed to fit two roof windows in the flat part of the roof, and their construction raised them approximately 75mm (3in) above the line of the flat roof. As a result, the project was deemed not to be within permitted development.

The second restriction is that extensions are allowed only to roof planes that do not face a highway. This is intended to allow dormer extensions at the rear of houses, where they are less likely to be seen by many people, but at the front, where a street-front elevation is more apparent, dormers are disallowed.

Again, the changes to the rules introduced in 2008 have added a subtle new aspect here. Whereas previously you could not (within permitted development) extend 'beyond the plane of an existing roof slope that fronts a highway', the restriction now says, 'beyond the plane of an existing roof slope that forms the principle elevation of a dwelling house and fronts a highway'. This subtle change is to the benefit of people who live on corner plots in particular.

One interesting point is that you are allowed within these criteria to extend a front roof plane along its length, but not outwards. This is important if you have a 'hipped' roof (like half a pyramid, see opposite). By extending the front roof plane along the length, a much larger box dormer can be formed, and this is allowable under permitted development because the roof has not been extended outwards.

The third restriction is externally measured volume. While the volume limits for other extensions have been dropped, roof extensions are only allowed up to a maximum of 40m³ (130ft³) on terraced houses and 50m³ (165ft³) on others. Remember, that this is the additional volume (not including the volume that the roof and loft take up already), and for most houses the limits are more than enough. However, to prove that you are within the limit, the maths required to calculate the volume of dormer extensions can get quite complicated!

Another restriction brought in when the rules were changed was that all dormers must be set back at least 200mm (8in) from the eaves of the original roof. The diagram below shows this, but the project illustrated on pages 68–9 would not fit with these new restrictions if it were to be built today.

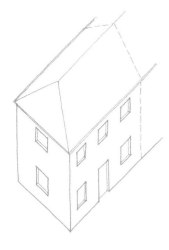

◁ *Original hipped roof.*
Many semi-detached houses have hipped roofs, where the slope to front and back is continued at the side, forming half a pyramid. This severely restricts the internal space that is usable when converting the loft.

◁ *Hip to gable extension.*
By building up the end wall into a triangle, and elongating the two main roof planes, the hipped roof can be transformed into a gabled roof, which has much more internal volume. This avoids creating any unsightly extensions at the front.

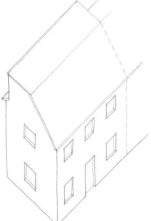

◁ *Box dormer to maximise space.*
With the gabled roof, a box dormer can be built to extend the full width of the property and create the maximum internal space allowable. A box dormer built onto the unaltered hipped roof would have to be much smaller.

The government considered taking roof extensions out of permitted development, which would force many thousands of extra projects through the planning application system. This was deemed to be impractical.

Given that planning departments have little say in the appearance of most loft extensions, people have been free to build as they like. It is true that many are very ugly, but some are fantastic.

There is a common idea that lofts get very hot in the summer, but if the building regulations are followed properly and suitable insulation and ventilation is installed, this should not be the case.

Adding a large loft bedroom is typically one of the most cost-effective ways to increase the value of a house.

Permitted development extensions must be within the 'curtilage' of the house. A few local authorities deem this to mean only your half of the thickness of a party wall. Check the situation in your local area.

When applying for a Certificate of Lawfulness **>see p.106** you may need to prove that you are within the volume limits by showing your workings out – just as your maths teacher always insisted!

Planning permission: your strategy

If your proposals do require a planning application, then it is important not to jump in with both feet, but to work out a planning strategy. This may seem time-consuming, but a properly worked through strategy may well save you a great deal of time and money in the end.

In simple terms, any planning strategy should be based upon the following questions:

- What do I want to achieve?
- Could I be refused?
- How can I avoid refusal?
- How should I present my case?

1. What do I want to achieve?

While this may seem facile, I meet many people who want a planning application to tell them what they can or can't have before they start designing. This is understandable because they want to avoid wasting money on designs that may not be acceptable. However, the planning system is based upon the idea that proposals are made, and are either approved or refused. All planning departments have various guidelines, which are very useful in setting the scene, but it is advisable to work with an architect to figure out what it is you want, who will illustrate the plans with proper scaled drawings.

2. Could I be refused?

Once you have your outline scheme, you can assess whether it is likely to sail through, or meet problems. This can be done in a number of ways. Firstly, your planning department will have a great deal of published information. Their 'Local Development Framework' (previously known as the UDP) sets out the policies for each area within the region.

For instance, if you want to open a restaurant in a part of the town that is clearly shown to be for residential use only, you are probably heading for trouble. This policy document usually has a host of information and design guidance to cross-reference. A local architect can often help you with this. If your local situation is really complex you may choose to bring in a planning consultant.

It is useful to find any recent precedent that can support your case; perhaps a neighbour has recently done something similar. You can view all recent planning applications and approvals at your local planning office, and these are increasingly available online.

3. How can I avoid refusal?

Once you have identified what the possible problems ahead might be, you now need to figure out what to do about them. The most important thing is not just to hope that the planning department won't notice – they will! It may well be that the design can be modified to sidestep the problems, or you may have extenuating circumstances that you feel will win the case. Very often you will need to have a study undertaken, such as a tree survey or traffic analysis, so that you can demonstrate the extent of the potential problem in question. If you don't do this research now, you may end up with a refusal and/or a long delay while you get them done later.

4. How should I present my case?

Whatever you do, take the trouble to present your case as fully and professionally as you can. Make absolutely sure that you have not missed anything out (such as a 'design and access statement' where necessary). If you think that an aspect of the proposal might be controversial, tackle the problem head-on and make your case. Your architect can provide you with all of the drawings and information that you need, either directly or in conjunction with any number of specialists or consultants (from bat specialists to traffic consultants).

Neighbours

One common misconception that I come across all the time is the role of the neighbour. People often think that if a neighbour objects, the sky will fall in, but the truth is that a neighbour can only flag up issues that planning are probably considering anyway. Whether a neighbour does or does not like something should not materially affect whether it is acceptable or not, within the criteria that the planners have (by law) to apply. The law is set to change with regards to household planning applications, and the role of the neighbour may become more significant, but for the moment it is not as important as many think.

Precedent

It may seem perfectly reasonable to want to do something that is already evident on similar houses in the neighbourhood. For example, people often think that because their neighbours have a roof terrace on their house or a dormer window at the front, that they will automatically get permission to do likewise. This is not necessarily the case.

For a start, many such alterations will have been done at a time when planning regulations were different, or even before they existed. Even structures built only a year or two ago might have gained permission prior to more recent changes in the local planning policy.

Similarly, these works might have been built without permission. If they have remained in place for a given time, they are considered 'established' even if they would not have gained permission in the first place.

If you need to change your design in order to have a better chance of getting planning permission, check whether the changes will affect your reason for doing the project.

Start with what you want and cross-reference any design guidance that your planning department provides. You may find that they are compatible!

Increasingly, the benefits of an environmentally responsible proposal will bear some sway if other aspects of the proposal are in the balance. Make sure you make your case.

If you push too hard on planning you might get refused, and that could cost significantly in time delays and the cost of preparing a resubmission.

Many people think that they will be able to get one thing approved and build something else. This is a very risky course of action. The planning departments have strong enforcement powers.

Many people start by asking their local planning department what they will be allowed to do. In an ideal world maybe, but in most cases, planners need a scheme in front of them to approve or refuse.

Putting your planning application together

Planning departments are so busy that they often only identify basic problems with an application just before the statutory eight-week deadline. This is a common cause of frustration for many customers.

Planning departments are rewarded on the proportion of planning applications that are processed within the eight-week deadline. On the face of it this would seem like a good idea, but very often officers will avoid consultation with applicants, so that they can simply refuse an application within the time frame. This counts as one towards their target. It would be preferable to allow applicants some consultation, so that they can make an amendment or provide additional information, if necessary. Even if this took ten weeks, it would be better than instigating another entire eight-week process.

Given this background, it is important to give yourself the best chance of an approval first time around, and this means being really thorough with your application. In short, you need to try to head off any, and every, possible reason that your planning department might have to refuse you because, in my experience, if they possibly can, they will.

Following such a route is considerably more involved and thorough than the minimum level of information necessary for an application, and will certainly cost you more to have prepared. However, this should be balanced against the wasted time and cost of having your proposals refused, in some cases, several times, or worse still, not being able to get permission at all.

Beware of fixed fees

Many designers, draftsmen and even some architects will offer a low-cost, fixed fee service to draw up and submit your planning application. It is important to ask yourself whether they are going to take the trouble to prepare nicely rendered drawings that show the proposals in the best possible light, write a thorough and well argued design statement and fully consider the best planning strategy for your scheme. In truth, for a low-cost, fixed fee, probably not.

An easy way

Rather than making paper applications, the government has introduced a much better system through a website (www.planningportal.gov.uk). This not only saves loads of paper (submitting a PDF file rather than six print copies of each drawing), but it also helps with the preparation of the application as it takes you through a sequential process.

Planning application checklist

When gathering together everything you need for your planning application, you should make sure of the following:

- All the necessary documentation is filled out correctly

- You have submitted the necessary location plan at the requisite scale

- You have calculated correctly the application fee

- You have submitted drawings that are well presented, professional, and accurate, and which present your proposals in as good a light as possible

- If you are concerned that your application may be refused for a particular reason, tackle this head-on in a written statement.

Drawings and written statements

It really is worth taking the extra trouble to get drawings that indicate attractive external materials. In some cases, you should also have a perspective view drawn up to give a genuine visualisation of how the proposals will look from key viewpoints.

Prepare a suitable written statement to submit with your application, and include any accompanying information that may be necessary. The best basis for this is to identify which planning policies and guidelines your application is relevant to. If your proposals fit within certain guidelines or policies, point this out, quoting the particular guideline.

For example, if you think protected trees may be affected, include a report from a tree specialist showing that your proposals are reasonable. If the application raises issues about traffic increase or parking, include a traffic study to head off any possible objections.

It may be that your proposals do not follow the published policies or guidelines. If this is the case, do not imagine that the planning officers might not notice this – they will. Tackle the matter head-on in your written statement. Quote the policy that you are going against, and make a convincing case to show that your proposals are perfectly reasonable – and perhaps also beneficial.

The online planning application process is easy to use and sequential. None the less, you should still study your local authority's published guidelines to give your application the best chance.

Submit one printed set of drawings at the same time as your online PDF drawings, to ensure that the planning department has at least one good-quality copy.

The planning portal system has meant that the old days of submitting paper applications, with six or more copies of each drawing, are coming to a close, saving huge amounts of paper.

Be careful to calculate the correct fee to go with your planning application. Your planning department website sets out the costs, but they are quite confusing. An application with the wrong fee may come back rejected after several wasted weeks.

Getting planning approval does not mean that you will necessarily be able to pass through building regulations. If you need to change your design to meet the regulations, you may need to go back through planning.

Communication with your planning officer can often be difficult and frustrating, but increasingly the use of e-mail is an effective way to ask questions. It is very important to keep things specific.

Planning permission case study

In this example, we applied for permission to build a large new house in a quiet residential conservation area. Our customer owned a house on the corner of a quiet road, and was looking to develop part of her large garden.

The key issues

In such a sensitive location, we knew that it would be difficult to keep everyone happy, but we were successful in getting planning approval at the first attempt. One of the main reasons for this was that we prepared a very thorough application, and just about every potential reason for refusal was addressed.

From the outset it was clear that the two most likely areas of concern would be the proximity of some protected trees, and the scale of the proposed new house.

The solutions

One of the first things we did as part of the outline design process was to commission a study by a tree expert. This study identified the important trees, and indicated the minimum distances from the trees that had to be kept free of excavation and building work. This study guided our design. As the site plan shows (opposite), the house was designed to allow the correct space around the trees. The expert's report and our adherence to it was all included as part of the design statement that went with the application.

To address any possible concerns about the scale and style of the proposal, we conducted an appraisal of the neighbouring buildings. This showed the general scale of the houses on the road, which were a mixture of styles, mostly built in the 1920s and 1930s.

In response to this, we designed a house inspired by the American architect Frank Lloyd Wright, who was building houses in Chicago at this time. His designs have a very strong horizontal emphasis that manages to be both contemporary and classic at the same time. We described the influences upon the design in our statement, and illustrated our proposals with drawings that attempted to show the colours of the elevations and the setting amongst the trees.

Finally, we made absolutely sure that every aspect of the application that we could think of was complete before submission. Even though we were lucky enough to have an unusually conscientious and communicative planning officer, we needed to undertake some last-minute negotiations to get it through.

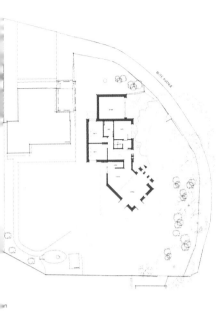

ground floor plan
1:100

▲ **Site plan.** *The important trees on this site can be seen on this site plan and the circles marked on the drawing indicate root areas where there should not be any building. The plan form of the house was, to a large extent, shaped by the available space avoiding these areas.*

▼ **Elevation.** *Only basic elevations need to be prepared in order to meet the minimum application requirements. However, rendering the elevations in colour, showing the scale of trees in the background and adding shadows to the drawings present the proposals in the best possible light.*

Understanding the likely reasons for a refusal is a good starting point when preparing an application. Address each one in turn, making your case, and quoting the policies in question.

Particular care was taken to illustrate the elevations of these proposals to show the colours of the materials used, and to try to communicate the setting amongst the trees.

Protection of important trees is often a very important factor in the success of a planning application. Demonstrating that arrangements will be made to protect these trees both during and after the works can help gain approval.

Simply achieving planning approval will very often transform the value of a house or piece of land.

Make sure all information in your application is correct. If it is shown at a later date that a drawing was inaccurate or that other information was not correct, your approval can be invalidated.

When writing a design statement, try to use language that the planning officers will relate to. In particular, make reference to specific paragraphs of the local policy document or planning guidance notes.

Listed Building Consent

Some buildings are listed in order to preserve special historic or architectural interest. Whether or not planning permission is needed for a proposed change, if your property is listed, you will need Listed Building Consent (LBC).

The regulatory system dealing with listed buildings is separate, but runs parallel, to planning permission procedure. They differ in several ways. While planning permission comes under common law, the protection of listed buildings is covered by criminal law, so unauthorised demolition or alteration to a listed building is, in fact, a criminal offence. Planning is also wider reaching, dealing with traffic and parking, for example, whereas the listed status of a building relates only to its historic or architectural interest.

In England and Wales there are three grades of listed buildings:

Grade 1 for buildings of 'exceptional interest and outstanding national significance'

Grade 2* for particularly important buildings of 'more than special interest'

Grade 2 for buildings of 'special interest'.

This system is administered by English Heritage and in Wales by CADW. In Scotland there is a parallel system with different gradings administered by Historic Scotland.

Common misconceptions

I have come across three common misconceptions in relation to listed buildings.

1. Only part is listed. The idea that only part of a building may be listed is quite wrong. If a building is listed, all of it, including unoriginal alterations or extensions, is subject to that listing. Changes to any part of it will require Listed Building Consent (LBC).

2. Grants. The second misconception is that you are likely to get a grant to help with the cost of work to a listed building. The fact is that while grants do exist, they are extremely rare and are almost never available to Grade 2 buildings.

3. No chance of consent. Many people think that there is little or no chance of getting consent to extend or alter a listed building. This is most certainly not the case, and we have been successful with many applications for LBC. In some cases, quite radical proposals are deemed acceptable. Planning Policy Guidance note 15 (PPG15) sets out the principles of when consent will and will not be granted.

Cost burden

The responsibility of owning a listed building can bring with it a significant cost burden. Firstly, there is a duty to maintain the building in a good state of repair – with many old buildings this can be a huge task on its own. Furthermore, there is the requirement to apply for LBC for any alterations that you propose to make to the building, which can be time consuming as well as costly. Finally, there are the costs associated with undertaking the works in the way that the conservation office insists on. At one grade 2* building, a small ramp was proposed to replace two steps, giving wheelchair access to a raised area of garden. The conservation officer involved agreed to the proposal, but insisted that it was built in a very specific type of stone to match the building. Consequently, this small ramp ended up costing over £11,000.

Making an application

Applying for LBC is much like making a planning application in the sense that you need to fill in forms and include drawings and statements about what you propose. In most cases, if you are looking to build an extension, you will need to apply for both planning permission and LBC. It is normal to submit both applications together to your local planning department.

Local conservation officers will deal with most applications, and English Heritage (or their Scottish or Welsh equivalent) will only be brought in when deemed necessary. Given that every aspect of a listed building, inside and out, is subject to the listing, your proposals may come under a very high degree of scrutiny. This can include your choice of interior door handles, and even (as in one project we were involved with) the colour and style of the screw heads used for interior door hinges.

Drawings submitted for LBC will need to illustrate a much greater level of interior detail than for a planning application, where the interior is generally only of peripheral interest. You will need to start with a measured survey, which will need to be done in much greater detail, showing internal elevations, and any detail such as wall panelling.

In exactly the same way as with a planning application, I would advise that it is worth preparing a really full submission. Include professional drawings that properly illustrate both the existing building and the proposals, as well as a written statement that deals with any areas of potential concern upfront.

There is a great deal of helpful information available on the Internet. In particular, the English Heritage website (www.english-heritage.org.uk) is excellent.

Check before you start

Given the sensitivity of the subject, it is always advisable, no matter how minor the works, to check with your local authority whether or not Listed Building Consent will be needed. Like-for-like repairs, undertaken in the correct way might not need consent, but repointing or painting very often will.

Owning a listed building can be a tremendous responsibility, and can be the cause of real frustration when even modest alterations are proposed.

Even quite radical changes can gain consent. In some cases, a contemporary alteration or extension is deemed preferable to one that pretends to be part of the original.

'Conservation' and 'preservation' are closely linked, but are not quite parallel. There is much debate about whether listed buildings should be allowed to become more energy efficient, for example. Sometimes two worthy aims conflict with each other.

While owning a listed building can be a tremendous cost burden, works that have gained LBC are zero-rated for VAT.

Unlike planning law, which is common law, listed buildings are subject to criminal law. Unauthorised demolition or alteration of part of a listed building is a criminal offence.

People can get very frustrated by the pedantic nature of many conservation officers. Remember that it is their job to be pedantic; be patient and try to establish effective communications.

Planning appeals

If your planning application receives a refusal that you think is unreasonable, or if you have received an approval, with conditions attached to it that you wish to challenge, you have the right to appeal against the decision.

The good thing about an appeal is that it is taken out of the hands of your local authority. Local authority planning officers act on behalf of councillors who, in the end, are answerable to voters. You may feel that your case has been refused unreasonably due to local pressure, and that an inspector with no community ties will have a more balanced view.

The bad thing about the appeals process is that it can take anything from six months to a year for a decision to be reached. This is a strong disincentive for many people who simply want to get on with their project.

There are three types of appeal:

1. Written representation

The applicant prepares a written statement arguing why the decision should be overturned, and the local authority prepares a similar statement arguing why their decision should stand. Each has a chance to answer the other, and then the inspector comes to a decision. There is no opportunity to speak to the inspector directly.

2. Informal hearing

This is a step-up from the written representation system. The inspector will convene a meeting with both the applicant and planner present. Anyone can attend, including objectors. Often a site visit with all present will follow. The decision report is made available several weeks afterwards.

3. Public enquiry

This is not usually appropriate for most home owner situations. The hearings are similar to a court process, often involving barristers and cross-examination, which can be very intimidating for the uninitiated.

Whilst a written representation is by far the simplest route to follow, there is certainly a case to suggest that an informal hearing gives an applicant the best chance of making a persuasive argument.

The rules governing appeals system were changed in 2009 and at time of going to press it is too early to see what effect this will have. The idea is to try to speed up the process significantly but the appellant's freedom to choose which of the three types of appeal to follow will be restricted.

▲ *Modern design in the countryside.*
This computer visualisation was used to help communicate the proposal for a radically modern house design in a rural riverside setting. After an appeal defined the exact nature of contravention that had caused initial refusal, this revised scheme gained permission without difficulty.

Approval after appeal refused

In this case a customer had bought a run-down bungalow in a flood plain. The site was idyllic with the river at the bottom of the garden, but neighbours were dead against a new, larger house.

The first design proposed to demolish the bungalow and replace it with a detached four-bedroomed house on two floors. Owing to the flood plain location, great care was taken to consult properly with the Environment Agency, and the house was designed on stilts so that it would be above the level of the worst flood recorded in the area.

The style was radically contemporary, with mono-pitched roofs arranged around a central stone 'drum', allowing lovely views to the river from a terrace at first floor level. However, at the first attempt, planning permission was refused. The reasons given to justify the decision included an out-of-keeping style, overlooking to neighbours, occupancy in the flood plain, even concern for the nesting of bats.

At appeal, the inspector upheld the local council's decision solely on the question of overlooking. While another refusal was a setback, the detail of the report allowed us to change the design specifically to accommodate the overlooking problem, and the local council approved the revised application without a murmur.

An appeal can take between six months and a year to be heard. Consider if there is a more expedient route to follow first.

In many cases contemporary design is supported in planning policy, even if the officer does not like it. It is not uncommon for planning officers to overstep their authority when it comes to aesthetics, and appeals are a good way to fight back.

The Environment Agency will comment upon any property within a flood plain, or that may be affected by flooding.

Should you appeal?

If you have been refused on a clear point of local planning policy, it is probably not worth wasting your time going to appeal. The inspector must make a decision based upon planning law. While there is clearly a huge amount of subjectivity involved (which can be worth appealing against), the inspector is not there to overturn local policy.

Similarly, the time delay caused by an appeal means that it is often not worth doing, particularly if a new application with minor modifications, will achieve planning approval. Many people become obsessed with fighting their cause with planning officers. Sometimes it is best to take a step back and determine whether it is really worth the stress.

One common frustration of the planning process is that often a refusal is given without a really thorough explanation of the reasons for the decision. Couple this with a general lack of consultation from many planning officers, and applicants are often left guessing what they might be allowed to do. The great thing about an appeal is that whatever the decision, you will get a report that explains the situation.

No statutory fee is involved in appealing. However, you are likely to need the assistance of an architect, or planning consultant (or both), in preparing your appeal and they will need to be paid.

Be aware that planning policy changes all the time and may have changed since a neighbour's work was approved.

At appeal you need to explain your proposals all over again, because you are dealing with the planning inspectorate, a central government body, and not with the local planning officer.

Structure and construction

*While you will generally need a **structural engineer** to work out the eventual mathematics of your design, it is important at the **scheme design** stage to have an **understanding** of the broad principles. Without a handle on how structures work, your **ability** to design with confidence and **fluidity** will be severely hampered.*

Structural changes

The majority of structural changes in domestic projects are usually more straightforward, and less costly, than people imagine.

The 'structure' of a building is quite simply the way in which the weight of the building (load) is carried down into the ground. For example, most houses in the UK have a pitched roof. Timber frames, called trusses, typically support the weight of a pitched roof; these transfer the load to the external walls. The external walls carry the load down onto the foundations, which ensure that the weight is spread and supported in the ground. Internal walls also carry the load down to the ground, either to provide a mid-point of support for the roof, or to help carry the weight of floors.

⌄ ***The ratio of span to depth.*** *The work a beam has to do is much more about the width of the span rather than the weight above. The further a beam has to span, the deeper (or higher) it needs to be. A useful rule of thumb is that the depth should be ¹⁄₂₀th of the span. These diagrams show how a wider span needs a larger depth.*

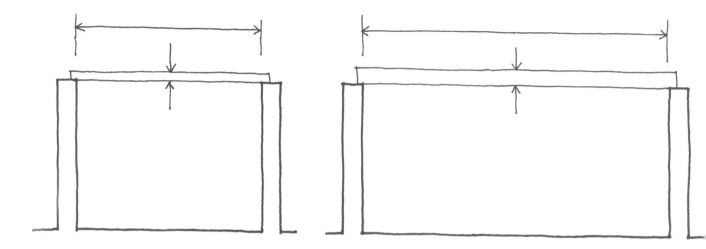

While the 'trussed roof and load-bearing wall' system is the most common type of structure in UK homes, there are many others, including timber-framed houses, but sometimes the structure of a building may not be immediately apparent. For example, in Georgian times the fashion for masonry buildings led many people to clad their homes with special tiles to make them look like brick. Similarly, many estate houses built in the last decade are timber-framed for speed of construction, and clad with a non-load-bearing brick outer skin.

Structural openings

Load-bearing walls typically have plenty of structural 'openings', such as doors and windows. When building a masonry load-bearing wall, openings are formed by building a bridge across the top. This is known as a lintel or beam. This lintel carries the weight of the wall above the opening across to either side of the opening.

When making an opening in an existing load-bearing wall, the weight above needs to be supported temporarily so that the opening can be made, and a lintel installed, before the temporary support is removed. This is as true of a new doorway as it is of knocking through between two rooms.

Span and support

A narrow opening in a load-bearing wall presents much less of a structural challenge than a very wide opening. This is because, for the wide opening, the distance that the load above needs to be carried by the lintel or beam is much greater. The width is called the 'span', and the greater the span, the stronger the beam needs to be.

Generally speaking, the strength of a beam is determined by its 'depth' (how high it is). A lintel that spans over a doorway is typically around 50mm (2in) high, whereas a beam that has to span across the width of a room might be 300mm (12in) high. A very useful rule of thumb says that the depth of a beam should be roughly ¹⁄₂₀th of the span.

Working with a structural engineer

It is advisable, for all but the simplest of structural tasks, to engage a structural engineer to work out the structure of your development. An architect can come up with the general idea for the structural design, but the engineer will work out what depth the beams should be, and how they need to be connected to the building. Often, the architect and engineer will work together, discussing the problem until the best solution is found.

When it comes to the application for building regulations, the engineer's calculations will usually be needed to prove that the design is structurally sound
> see also **The building regulations** p.196–201.

A good engineer is one who considers various options in order to find the most efficient structural solution that enables the vision of the design to be achieved. Some engineers will play safe with their calculations, oversizing beams, which can lead to a heavy appearance and unnecessary extra costs on site.

Understanding how the load of a building is carried from the roof down to the ground helps avoid having to make design changes later.

Good structural engineers will go the extra mile to seek a structural solution that does not compromise the vision of the design.

Over-cautious engineering calculations may suggest over-sized structural members. Huge energy is needed to manufacture steel beams, and keeping to the most efficient size reduces energy wastage.

Most people imagine that anything structural will be very costly. Very often the structural works required are straightforward and inexpensive, and it is the making good and finishes that add cost.

Proving that structural proposals will be suitable is an important part of a building regulations application. Calculations are generally needed from an engineer to meet this requirement.

If you communicate your proposals clearly to your engineer, he/she will be able to do the calculations efficiently. Fuzzy instructions can lead to wasted time and lots of extra expense.

Opening up

The majority of structural changes involve making openings in load-bearing walls. Making a new doorway or window, knocking through between a front and back reception room, or making a large opening in the rear wall of a house for an extension, are all types of structural opening.

The main structural elements used to make these openings possible are beams, lintels, columns and goalposts. These might be made from timber, steel or concrete.

Beams

A beam is a horizontal structure that carries the load of a wall (or whatever else is placed upon it) along its length to the points of support, typically at each end. Beams in houses are usually made from:

- **Concrete** These have steel reinforcement rods cast inside. They are either poured *in situ* or bought precast. Concrete is a low-cost material, but is very heavy, and is not dimensionally precise.

- **Timber** Beams range from a simple floor joist through to huge oak beams. A more recent advance has been glue laminated timber beams (see example illustrated), which are made from smaller strips of timber glued together to produce a large beam.

- **Mild steel** Phenomenally strong for their size, mild steel beams are available in different forms, including 'I' beams (or commonly an RSJ or Rolled Steel Joist), 'C' (channel section) or 'T' ('T' section).

A beam is only as good as the points of support that it sits upon, and very often it needs a 'padstone' of concrete, or special hard bricks, to rest upon and spread the load.

⋀ *Glue laminated timber beam. In this dramatic interior, a bridge has been built above a kitchen to allow access between bedrooms, while retaining the drama of the double-height space. The structure of this bridge is a timber beam made up of separate pieces glued together. Steel brackets are bolted to the beam to support the bridge deck and balustrade.*

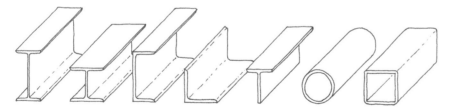

◁ *Standard steel sections. Lengths of mild steel can be bought in a variety of standard, cross-section shapes and each one is useful for different situations. Some common examples are: 'I' beam, universal column, channel, angle, 'T' section, circular hollow section and rectangular hollow section.*

Lintels

A lintel is a beam that forms an opening for a window or door. Precast concrete lintels are very common as they are cheap and easy to install in a brick wall, but they are not very attractive to look at, and are generally not acceptable visually unless covered with plaster or render.

Using a pressed steel lintel is a very clever way to span a window or door opening within an external cavity wall, and provide a flashing to guide water out of the building. You can cover steel lintels with brickwork.

Natural and cast, reconstituted stone is often used effectively, and can look very attractive, but it can be an expensive option.

Columns

A column is a vertical structure that carries a load downwards into one concentrated point. The span (and, therefore, the necessary depth) of a beam can be reduced with the inclusion of a column. Columns can also be used where two walls forming a corner are removed.

Concrete columns are often used in large-scale commercial buildings, but in residential projects, steel is by far the most common material. Steel can be slender in size, and is relatively easy to install.

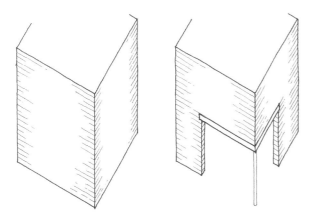

▲ **Corners.** *Beams are great in straight lines, but if you want to take the corner out of a building, the simplest way structurally would be to have one beam for each straight line, and a column where they meet at the corner.*

Goalposts

It is common, where a spine wall is being removed (typically, when knocking through from front to back reception rooms) to need a 'goalpost' arrangement. As the name suggests, this is a beam with a column at each end. The joints between the two are detailed carefully to ensure that the structure cannot skew out of shape. A goalpost also prevents the load being placed directly into a wall that may not be strong enough to carry it.

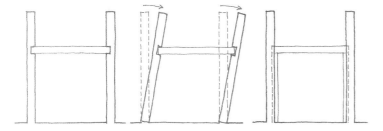

▲ **The danger of skewing.** *Walls often do more than just support the load from above; in some instances, they brace other walls and prevent 'skew'. When opening up and replacing such a wall, the simple span of a beam will not resist such skew and a rigid 'goalpost' arrangement might be required to provide the necessary stability.*

No one material is the most practical for all situations. Concrete can be great where weight and size are not important, steel is fantastic for strength, and timber is easy to work with and looks attractive.

The structure of a building has to look and feel right to the occupant. Even people without an understanding of structures will be made to feel uneasy with a large unsupported overhang or a floor edge that is too thin.

Glue laminated timber beams use a sustainable material (usually spruce softwood) in a highly efficient manner. This minimises waste during manufacture and is more energy efficient than steel.

Concrete is a low-cost material and can offer good savings. However, casting concrete on site can be time-consuming, and the labour cost might offset any saving over steel or timber.

Mild steel must be fire-protected. There are special paints that can achieve this, or you can encase it in plasterboard boxing.

Your architect and engineer will need to work together to find the best way of realising the design in a way that will be stable, safe and efficient.

Floor structure and construction

Where walls and beams give a *line* of support, floors create an *area* of support. Floors can do this by spreading their load directly onto the ground, or by throwing the load sideways to beams or walls. There are many different construction methods for floors, and here are some of the more common.

Ground-floor slabs

A common construction for a ground floor is to lay a concrete ground-floor 'slab'. Here, the load of the floor is spread directly and evenly onto the ground beneath, and is usually tied in to the wall foundations at the perimeter. For a ground-floor slab to be suitable, the ground beneath must be able to carry the load (your structural engineer will be able to say if it is not), and it will need to consist of several layers to ensure that it is stable, warm and waterproof. See below for how a ground-floor slab is constructed ➤ see also **Ground-floor slab** p.174.

Timber joists

When a floor is not supported continuously – for example, on a first floor – the most common way to carry the load of the floor is with floor joists. Joists are small timber beams that are set parallel to each other, close enough for floorboards to span between them. The Victorians used to build the ends of their joists into the walls that supported them, which was good structurally, but over time, the joist ends

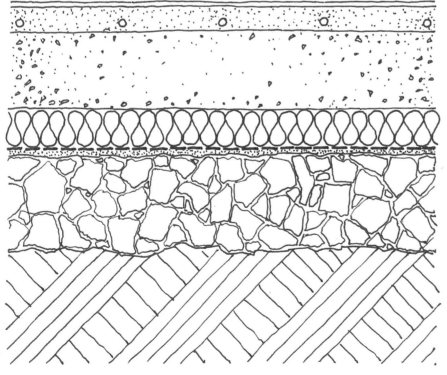

⟨ **Concrete ground-floor slab.**
A typical ground-floor slab is made up of many layers to provide stability, insulation and damp protection. Underfloor heating can be cast into the floor just beneath the surface, and this uses the 'thermal mass' of the concrete to great effect.

⟩ **Level threshold.** *In this extension, the timber floor inside has been designed to be at the same level as the decking outside, to maximise the continuity of the space. To achieve this, careful detailing is needed at the threshold, and floor construction should be considered from the outset.*

were prone to rot, if the wall was not entirely dry. These days, we tend to use steel joist hangers that have a shoe at the end to support the joist. Ceilings are nailed or screwed to the underside of the floor joists.

Suspended ground floors

Instead of solid ground-floor slabs, most Victorian houses were built with timber-joisted floors, not only at the upper levels, but also at the ground floor level. Since they did not have very effective waterproofing membranes, they felt that the most effective way to prevent damp from coming up through the ground was to raise the floor, leaving a ventilated space between the ground and the floor.

Generally, you can tell a suspended floor in two ways. Firstly, it will feel slightly hollow from above and the floor will have a slight flex. Secondly, there should be small grilles in the outside wall below the floor level. These are known as airbricks, and they allow the space beneath the floor to be ventilated. These are very important, because without this ventilation, condensation and damp can build up and cause all manner of problems.

Beam and block concrete plank floors

An alternative to timber is to use precast concrete joists. These come either as 'planks' cast in a factory, which can be delivered by truck and craned into position next to each other, or as a 'beam and block' system. Here, concrete beams, shaped like an upside-down capital 'T', take the place of joists, and simple concrete blocks fill the space between them. In both cases, if the project is of a sufficient scale, the speed of construction can be improved significantly, and often the floor thickness can be reduced. Also, methods such as these tend to give a more solid feel to the floors.

Sometimes either a suspended or solid construction for a ground floor will be perfectly acceptable, and the best way to choose is to see which your builder is more comfortable using.

Concrete floors can usually achieve the necessary strength with less thickness than timber construction. Particularly where height is important, or overhangs are emphasised as part of the design, this may be a preferable construction method.

There is a significant move to use timber in buildings as it is more sustainable, and requires less energy use, than concrete. Generally, this applies to softwoods such as spruce, which grows quickly in great quantity and can be managed responsibly.

Old floors are rarely level. When extending, you may find that matching the levels of floors can cause considerable extra work and cost.

Level disabled access can mean that designing the ventilation for the space beneath a suspended floor becomes trickier. 'Periscope' vents can be used to deal with the change in level.

On scheme level elevations it is a good idea to indicate the levels and thickness of the floors within a house with dotted lines. This will help people understand how the inside relates to the outside.

External walls

If you are planning alterations or an extension to an existing property, it is important to understand the essential structure of your building, so that it connects effectively with the new construction.

Old timber-framed houses tend to display their structure as an external feature (see opposite), with the framework filled in with panels to form walls. The panels are very often made of wattle and daub (woven strips of wood plastered with a clay mixture), but sometimes the panels are filled in with brick.

Modern timber-framed houses are often a little more tricky to identify, as they tend to conceal their timbers, and clad the whole frame with an outer skin, which may be brick, timber cladding or a rendered panel.

Many pre-war houses have load-bearing external walls with solid brickwork, either 225 or 330mm (9 or 13in) thick. Some have a render or pebble-dashed external surface, but these were either done at the time of building so that cheaper brickwork could be used, or at some point later as an attempt to waterproof the walls.

It is easy to imagine that in years gone by there was a 'golden age' of craftsmanship. However, when the quality (or lack of it) of concealed Victorian brickwork is exposed, it becomes clear that shoddy building work is not just a modern phenomenon.

ᵛ *Brick cavity walls.* In this mews-style house, reclaimed London stock bricks are used for the outer skin of the cavity wall, with concrete blocks for the inner skin.

ᵛ *Mixed masonry.* The elevations of this large house are broken up by mixing a plain painted render finish (over blockwork) with natural rustic stone walling for the chimney.

▲ Timber frame expressed externally. *In old timber-framed buildings, like this 14th-century bookshop in Sussex, the timber framing of the walls is visible on the outside. More recent buildings often copy this effect by sticking timbers onto the outside, but authentically this was a strictly functional arrangement.*

Cavity walls

Later in the 20th century, cavity walls became a popular construction method, and this remains the case today. As the name suggests, the wall has two skins with a space (or cavity) in-between. People often think that cavity walls are all about better thermal insulation, but while this is certainly the case, it is not why they were introduced. Quite simply, masonry is porous, and sustained wet weather on a solid wall will eventually allow damp inside. The idea of a cavity wall is that the outer skin can get wet, but the water cannot pass through the cavity to the inner skin, which always stays dry.

The air cavity has the added bonus of improved thermal performance, and if additional insulation is added, the thermal qualities are significantly increased. Very often the outer skin is built of attractive facing brickwork, while the inner skin can be built with lightweight, aerated concrete blocks that are low cost, quick to lay and improve the thermal performance even more. The internal walls can be plastered.

When building a cavity-walled extension onto a house that has solid brick walls, think carefully about the connection between the two. It is very important that the inner skin of the cavity wall does not make a direct connection with part of a wall that might act as a bridge for damp.

An alternative to a brick outer skin is to build both skins with concrete block-work. A standard layer (or 'course') of blocks is the same height as three courses of bricks. It is, therefore, at least three times quicker to build a block wall than a brick wall. Blocks are also (typically) much cheaper than bricks, and the saving of labour and material costs combined is considerable.

There are many innovative construction methods that look great on paper, but using the method that your builder feels most comfortable with is probably the most efficient and cost-effective.

If you want to know what a particular brick type will look like, ask to see a completed building rather than a small sample. If you want to match bricks for an extension, you will usually have to specify reclaimed bricks.

Concrete is a controversial material. The extraction process and manufacture uses huge amounts of energy, yet concrete can be a good insulator.

Concrete blocks are low cost and quick to lay. Two skins of block-work with a cavity and an acrylic render to the outside is a very cost-effective way of building an energy efficient external wall.

The two skins of a cavity wall usually need to be tied together for stability. Your building inspector may want to check these have been installed correctly so that they will not form a bridge for damp.

The choice of external finish materials will significantly influence the feeling that a building communicates in its environment. Do you want your house to say open and jolly or strong and sombre?

< **Mixing both construction and finish.**
This house has had a matching masonry extension on the ground floor and a timber-framed loft conversion. The combination of render and timber cladding is expressive.

Care must be taken to avoid 'differential movement', if an extension is built using a different construction method to the original.

The word 'facade' means 'face' and the elevations of houses are often read like faces, expressing different emotions and attitudes. Think very carefully about the proportioning of windows and choice of finishes.

Adding internal wall insulation to old buildings can be difficult. In some instances, an external insulative cladding can be added to improve energy efficiency.

Reclaimed bricks from an old demolished building can give an instantly attractive appearance, but are often at least double the cost of newly made equivalents.

Concrete blocks rarely show an acceptable external appearance, and the most common solution is to apply an outer layer of render. Traditionally, this would have been a sand and cement mix, effectively like external plastering, although there are now much more sophisticated acrylic-based renders that are more flexible, frost-proof and also very waterproof.

Another increasingly popular external wall finish is timber cladding, which can be nailed to softwood battens fixed to the wall behind. The most popular timber for this is Western Red Cedar, which can be treated or left to turn a weathered silvery colour.

The building regulations require that external walls facing a boundary have a limited area made from 'combustible' materials. This dates back to the Great Fire of London when fire spread too easily from building to building.

Your planning drawings should indicate exactly what type of brick is to be used, and very often samples will need to be provided and approved by the planning officer.

< Timber framed and timber clad. *This very eco-conscious extension to a masonry house has been built with a timber frame on a brick base. The timber cladding has been set vertically to emphasise the height and dynamic of the modern design.*

Internal walls

If you want to take down an internal wall, or plan to add new walls inside your property, you need to think about the construction of your existing walls, and the options available to you.

In residential buildings, internal walls tend to be constructed from masonry or from studwork (a framework with a covering such as plasterboard).

In old houses, you may find internal walls made from bricks, usually 'half-a-brick' (the width of a brick, approximately 100mm/4in) or 'one-brick' (the length of a brick, approximately 225mm/9in) thick, plus the thickness of plaster. Studwork is made from timbers, usually 100 x 50mm (4 x 2in), with thin strips of timber (laths) nailed across them to form a surface.

In more recent houses, blockwork is a likely choice for solid internal walls as it is cheaper and quicker to build. Metal studwork is quickly replacing timber as the base for a plasterboard covering. When planning out your project, allow 100 or 125mm (4 or 5in) of thickness for an internal wall.

∧ **Translucent glass panel walls.**
Two floor-to-ceiling glass panels with a translucent finish have been used here to great effect, creating privacy, while retaining a feeling of lightness and openness.

Load bearing or not?

One common misconception is that solid walls are structural and studwork walls are not. This can be a very dangerous assumption because there are plenty of examples of load-bearing studwork walls, and likewise, solid walls that are not load bearing.

The easiest way to determine whether an internal wall is carrying any load is to see if any floor joists or purlin props ➤ see also **Roof structure** pp.134–5 in the roof space are bearing onto the wall. In addition, floorboards are typically set at 90 degrees to the supporting joists, so if the floorboards in the room above are parallel to a wall, it is likely that the joists beneath are bearing into that wall.

An internal wall may also perform a structural function, even if it is not carrying any direct load from above. As described on page 123, a wall may be performing a bracing task to prevent a building from 'skewing' out of shape.

Connecting walls

With an older building, problems often occur when trying to cut into or connect to existing plaster finishes. Old plaster was often mixed with horsehair to strengthen it, but over time, it can start to crumble. One way to deal with this is simply to strip off all of the old plasterwork (with the laths if it is a studwork wall), and apply new plasterboard. While extremely messy and quite involved, this is certainly an effective solution. However, plasterboard is very flat and featureless, and in some old buildings the charm of the surface of a lath and plaster wall is important.

Curved walls

Often a great internal feature, curved walls can be formed in a number of ways. Blockwork can be built to a slight curve, with the flat surfaces taken out in the plastering, but tight curves are difficult. The most common way to form a curved wall is with studwork. Plasterboard can be bent around a gentle curve, and if one face of the board is soaked, it can be bent even more. For tighter curves, 'skin' plywood can be formed around timber studs in layers to give a very stable surface.

Glass blocks

Glass blocks are another popular component that can be built as a straight wall, or with a curve for beautiful effect. These blocks are typically 200mm (8in) square and 100mm (4in) thick and are laid like bricks with a mortar joint. The laying process is very tricky, as the blocks need reinforcement rods within the joints, and the pointing of the mortar needs to be immaculate, otherwise the wall can look terrible.

Glass blocks are surprisingly expensive, and the care and skill needed to lay them means that they can be a costly choice. The key to their effective use is to get light behind them, this will allow them to sparkle, otherwise they can look very 'dead'.

Glass walls

Glass is very popular, but its combination of fragility, cost and weight make it tricky to use. Fixings need to be carefully considered and designed, and allowance for possible movement of the building must be built in to avoid cracking. Glass is particularly popular in bathrooms as it divides space almost invisibly, is waterproof and can be cleaned down easily.

Routes for cables or pipes will need to be channelled out of a block wall. Stud walls have ready-made voids for services.

The purpose of a skirting board is to cover the inevitable cracking between floor and wall. If you are trying to create a very clean, modern look by not using skirting boards, you will need to address this.

It is worth putting insulation into internal walls. If you have a guest room that is rarely used, this will save heating energy when it is not in use.

On a building site, speed is often the most pressing factor that affects cost. Metal studwork can be built much quicker than timber studwork, and it has ready-made openings for services.

Where an internal wall is separating an escape route (for example, a hallway) from a habitable room, it will need to achieve a half-hour fire rating. Blockwork, or a stud and plasterboard wall with two layers of plasterboard, are both suitable.

It is very important that all parties involved in the building process are clear as to the proposed construction of internal walls. Engineers may assume heavy masonry, if drawings do not clearly show otherwise.

Moving walls

Fitting out a new apartment in a converted factory provided several challenges. The brief was to create a layout that could function as a luxurious one-bedroomed flat, but could be changed easily to be a two-bedroomed flat. The innovative use of internal walls proved to be the key to the design solution.

The key issues

With only one glazed external wall, the basic layout for the apartment was reasonably straightforward. The main problem was how to introduce a wall that would divide the large living space to create a second bedroom when needed.

The solution

The design of a curved wall in the centre of the apartment creates a visual focus for the space, and helps to introduce a door position that still feels right when only one bedroom is needed.

The wall that forms the second bedroom is hidden in a slot behind the kitchen units when not in use. This wall is constructed as a timber stud wall, with plywood panels rather than plasterboard. Ply was used as it is strong and will not crack as readily as plasterboard, which is vital given the inevitable movement and vibration involved in sliding the wall in and out of position.

When the two-bedroomed mode is needed, a piece of the timber flooring is lifted to reveal a sliding track. The wall can be rolled out and into position. Slip bolts keep the wall in place, and a small panel closes the space.

▽ **Changing rooms.** *The plan on the left shows the floor layout in one-bedroomed mode, with a large open living area. Sliding the wall out along the dotted line from behind the kitchen units subdivides the central space at the top of the plan on the right, so as to form a useful second bedroom when needed. The whole operation takes about a minute and a half.*

⟨ *Changing into two-bed mode.*
The floor of the main bedroom was raised to allow space beneath for a concealed bed that could be slid out like a giant drawer. The first step of the transformation is to pull out the bed. The slot in the ceiling indicates where the dividing wall slides out.

Converting this apartment takes only a few minutes, and can be done by one person. Choosing a high-quality sliding track was important, so that the heavy wall slides easily.

The curved wall is finished with panels of brushed aluminium laminate, with a black frame.

Condensing boilers are energy efficient and can be situated up to 6m (19½ft) from an external wall. Here, this means that the only external glazed wall is kept completely clear.

Other than the sliding tracks, the sliding wall design did not incur many additional material costs, but the complex installation added significant labour cost.

We had to allow for a direct means of escape from both bedrooms, to the main entrance even though the second bedroom could form part of the open-plan space.

The tricky and unusual nature of this project meant that it was particularly important that the builders fully understood the idea proposed, before they took on the project.

⋀ *Instant wall.* The sliding white wall is brought out from its hiding place and glides into position. The hinged section can then be closed like a giant door and the transformation into a two-bedroomed flat is complete.

Roof structure

The roof is the most complex piece of structure in most homes. You may take one look at the 'forest' of angled timbers in your loft space and be mystified as to how they are working to hold up the roof, so here is an overview of the main types of roof structure.

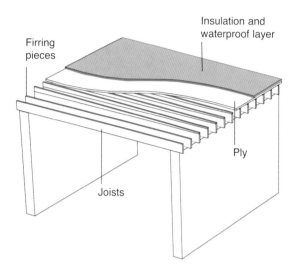

Flat joisted roof with firrings. *On top of the joists, additional pieces of timber cut to form a slope (called 'firring pieces'), are fixed. The ply deck is laid on top of these, and, typically, the insulation and waterproof layer on top of that.*

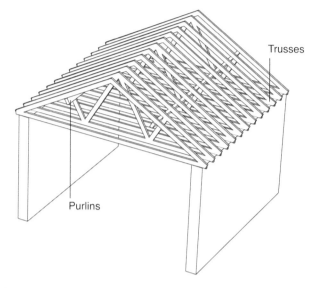

Traditional trussed roof. *This diagram shows three trusses (see the W shape) spanning from wall to wall. Purlins span from truss to truss, and rafters are supported by the purlins.*

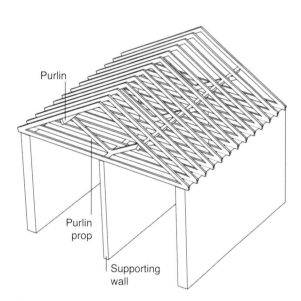

Propped purlins. *In this diagram, the purlins are propped by timbers that carry their load down to an internal supporting wall. Such walls in old houses are often constructed from timber studwork, so don't assume that if it is not brick, it is not supporting.*

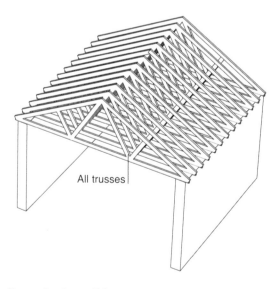

Trussed rafters. *This method is very speedy as every rafter is part of a separate truss, made in a factory and then craned into position from the back of a lorry. Lots more timber is used than is absolutely necessary, and the loft space is substantially reduced.*

Flat roofs

A flat roof can be a useful design solution, but I want to put right two common misconceptions about flat roofs: first, that they are inherently unreliable, and second, that they are flat.

All flat roofs are given a slight slope. This is usually 1 in 40 so that any rain collecting will drain away to the desired points. I have often heard people say that they would never contemplate a flat roof on the basis that it would always be prone to leaking. This may have been true in the 1950s, but roof membrane technology has moved on to such an extent that it is simply no longer the case. After all, think of the many office and commercial buildings with flat roofs that have no problems.

In construction terms, a flat roof works in exactly the same way as a floor, although each is affected by different problems. Most commonly, a flat roof will be constructed from dead level timber joists in the same way as a floor. The slope is then created on top of the joists by using tapered strips of timber called 'firring' pieces.

Structurally, there are 'live' loads (people and objects that move about) and 'dead' loads (the weight of the building). A flat roof is usually not designed to carry the normal loads of daily life that a floor would carry. However, it will be expected to support the live load of occasional maintenance, the load of a heavy fall of snow and the pressures that wind may put upon it.

Clearly, the other thing that a flat roof needs to do is to keep the weather out. Essentially, a weatherproof layer is laid over insulation on a slight slope so that any water drains across to a drainage point. Roofs can slope from one side to another guiding the rain to a gutter, or can slope to a single drainage point. For more on weatherproofing > see also **Flat roofs** pp.156–7.

Pitched roofs

The majority of houses in the UK have sloping (or pitched) roofs, usually covered in tiles or slates. Like floors and flat roofs, the structure of a pitched roof is essentially there to carry the weight of the covering across to the points of support. Since the external walls provide the main structural support for most houses, most pitched roofs are based upon 'trusses' that carry the load of the roof across to the walls. Often there will also be one 'spine' internal wall that will help carry the weight and this may mean that the truss simply becomes a prop (see diagrams opposite).

The load (or weight) of the tiles is passed down the line as follows: the tiles are carried by tile battens, which are supported by rafters (sloping joists), which, in turn, are supported along their length by purlins. Purlins are members that transfer load across the slope of a roof to props or trusses that, in turn, transfer the load to the supporting walls.

A more recent construction method is to use 'trussed rafters', where each and every rafter is a truss. This allows for very speedy construction, but creates a forest of timbers within the loft space.

There are many different types of tiles, from traditional clay to the more common (and cheaper) concrete. Traditional slates are natural pieces of slate, but modern, machine-made alternatives are available. Be careful to check that the pitch you need can be achieved with the tiles that you want to use. Many tiles are not effective on a slope of less than 35 degrees.

Flat roofs are relatively quick and cheap to construct, and also provide a useful platform for a roof terrace, storage tanks, air-conditioning machinery or solar panels.

When undertaking a flat-roofed extension to an old pitched roof building, it is often more attractive for the roof to be concealed behind a parapet of the wall > **see pp.156–7** than have the roof overhang the wall.

Since heat rises, insulation in the roof will retain heat in winter. Conversely, in summer, ventilation that allows hot air to escape out from the roof can keep a building cool.

A large, new, pitched roof can be quickly and cheaply constructed using trussed rafters. These can be craned off the back of a truck, and put directly into position in a matter of hours.

Other coverings for pitched roofs, each with different criteria under the building regulations, include thatch, corrugated sheet materials, rolled sheet metals and timber tiles (called 'shingles').

Samples of the external materials should be submitted for approval by the planning department. Major delays and extra costs could be incurred if you have to change something once it has been installed.

Using roof space

Since loft conversions and extensions are such a popular way to add space to a home, the structural adaptation of a roof to accommodate living space is a very common requirement.

When the project is simply the conversion of a loft space, without any extension, there are generally two main things to achieve structurally. First, the timbers that form the trusses, and/or purlin props, need to be removed to open the space up for accommodation. Second, the floor of the loft needs to be made strong enough to carry the live loads of a habitable room.

While this may seem very detailed at the scheme design stage, the reason that roof space should be considered now is that it may radically affect floor to ceiling heights. This may be the deciding factor as to the viability of the project as a whole.

Creating a floor

A loft floor is usually formed by the ceiling joists of the rooms below. Ceiling joists do not have to support as much weight as floor joists, and so are not usually designed to be strong enough to carry any additional load. When converting a loft space, it is important that new floor joists are set in place to form the new floor. Of course, this can be done in place of the original ceiling joists, but that would mean taking down all of the ceilings below.

It is possible to set the new joists above the existing ceiling joists. This has the great advantage of separating the floor from the ceiling below, thus reducing the amount of noise that might be transferred between the rooms. However, setting the new floor above the existing ceiling takes up a great deal of additional height, and very often, height in a loft space is at a premium.

A good solution is to stagger the new floor joists between the existing ceiling joists, keeping the acoustic separation and losing only a small amount of height.

Removing supports

Looking at the diagrams on page 134, you can see that both trusses and purlin props do essentially the same thing – that is, provide support for the purlins, which, in turn, support the rafters mid-span.

If we take the example of a typical terraced house, the purlins will be supported at each end by the party walls. However, most commonly, the purlins will not be strong enough to span the full width of the roof, so they are given support at points along their length by purlin props or trusses.

∨ **A new loft floor.** On the left side of the diagram, the ceiling joists simply support a ceiling. To the right, new (deeper) floor joists are set between, but not touching, the ceiling joists. Acoustic insulation is added and the floor deck is fixed to the new floor joists. The new structure boasts acoustic separation and minimal loss of headroom.

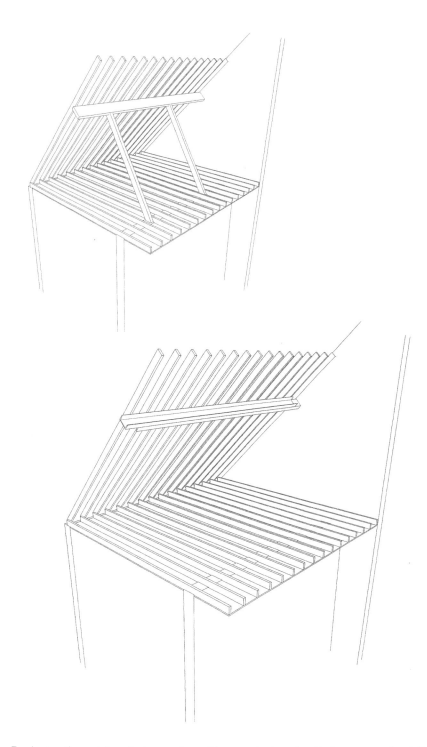

◀ *Remove supports to open space.*
*The purlin props (top) are needed
because the purlin can only span so far.
Replacing the purlins with a stronger
steel beam (bottom) will negate the need
for the props so that they can be
removed and the space opened up.*

Consider the likely headroom of a possible loft conversion. Height will be lost due to the new floor structure, and when you ventilate and insulate the roof slopes.

Roof spaces can be restricted in size, so keep the design as simple as possible. Leaving roof structure exposed might sound appealing, but may look fussy.

Glue laminated timber beams are a much better environmental option than steel when replacing purlins, but generally they are larger.

Despite the structural alterations necessary, converting a loft space is usually the most cost-effective way of creating significant additional space within a home.

While there is no minimum headroom for a loft space within the building regulations, you must have a minimum headroom of 2m (6½ft) above a staircase.

Trying to visualise and communicate how large or small a loft space will feel is difficult because of the sloping ceiling surfaces. I often build a simple cardboard scale model to give an idea of the space.

Replacing the existing timber purlins with new steel purlins that can span the full width does away with the need for the intermediate support so, once in place, the original props or trusses can be removed.

One common problem is how to fit a steel beam into both party walls of a terraced house, without having to poke into the neighbour's property. This is best achieved by using two channel sections, back to back. As long as they have a long enough overlap, they can slide into position and be bolted together to form a capital 'I'.

> **Garden elevation.** *South-west facing, this side of the house expresses the most detail, with all of the doors opening out to the deck and football area, and the corner windows emphasising the solidity of the block from which they appear to be cut.*

side elevation

> **Face front.** The front of the house was a composition of drama (with the tall window), function (with the front door repositioned), strength (with the clean heavy planes of masonry) and lightness (balcony and timber cladding).

existing ridge height - maximum height of proposed roof

2nd fl

1st fl

G fl

front elevation

3. Scheme design

The scheme design process takes the childish abandon of the outline design and insists that it grows up.

With this project the *joie-de-vivre* that can be seen in the hand drawings on pp.94–7 has given way to the much more serious business of fitting the design to the site in a way that will gain the necessary permissions, will comply with regulations, be buildable and stay on budget.

On the floor plans the room sizes have been carefully considered and routes planned for services. Structural allowances have also been made so that the structural engineer can take the drawings and carry out his detailed calculations, coming back with beam sizes and connection details.

The main purpose of these drawings is to explain the scheme as a whole.

All the floor plans are shown and all four elevations have been drawn so that the next stage – detail design – can be undertaken within the framework that these scheme level drawings provide.

As an additional aid to the design and communication process, a computer 3-D model was made so that we could appreciate the form as it would appear from different angles.

Such 3-D drawings can be very useful in fully understanding how the proposals will appear, but these are not standard issue alongside scheme level drawings, as they take a lot of time to prepare, and, therefore, will add to the architect's fees.

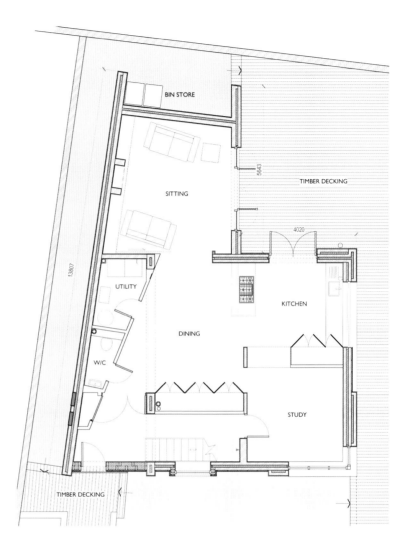

ground floor plan

⌃ **Entrance level.** *The square plan of the original house can be detected, with the extensions to the top and left of this drawing. The side extension has enabled the front door to face the gateway, and the kitchen and sitting rooms both have French doors opening onto the exterior decking area.*

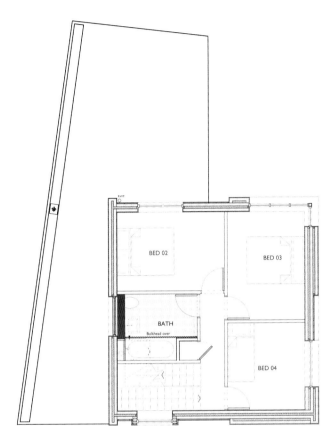

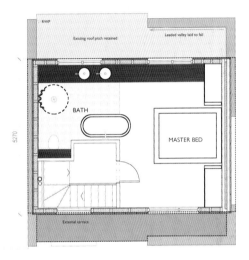

first floor plan

second floor plan

⌃ **Bedroom levels.** *The original first floor had three bedrooms and a bathroom, as does the proposed new arrangement. However, this layout allows for a much more dramatic building and, unlike its predecessor, rises to a penthouse-style, top floor master bedroom/bathroom suite, with outlook to the front and the back of the house.*

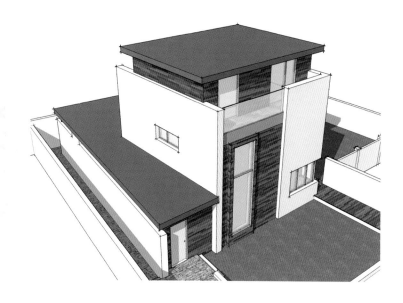

‹ Solidity to the north-east. *A single bathroom window punctures the strong north-east facing wall. It is as if the house has turned its face toward the sun, with only this bathroom and a utility room served by the functional light on this facade.*

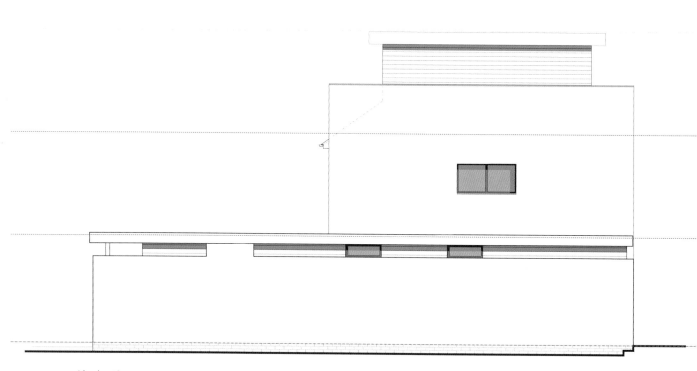

side elevation

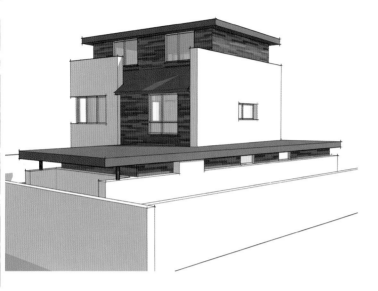

Bedroom windows. *Set well away from any neighbouring houses, the windows on the rear elevation of the house serve three of the four bedrooms, and give different character to each. Like the front, the solidity of the masonry box gives way to the lightness of the timber cladding.*

rear elevation

Party wall legislation

In a terraced or semi-detached house, the wall that separates the two properties is known as the 'party' wall. Party wall legislation is there to protect this wall (and more) from damage due to building works by either side.

It is important to take on board that the Party Wall Act is not a way for people to try to prevent their neighbours from undertaking building works, and party wall consent cannot be withheld unreasonably. However, it is quite possible for disputes to arise and delays ensue, so it is important to sort out any party wall issues well in advance of work starting.

What is covered by party wall?

The Party Wall Act covers more than party walls alone, and people often get caught out. In brief, the legislation protects property from any structural damage that may arise as a result of a neighbour's building works. For example, if you are working near to the boundary of your property, particularly if you are digging foundations, you may need to get party wall consent, depending upon the depth of digging and the distance from your neighbour's property.

There is a very useful booklet that can be downloaded from www.communities.gov.uk about party wall legislation, and this sets out all of the instances where a party wall agreement is required.

If, for example, you want to form a new basement beneath your property, even if your house is detached, you will almost certainly need party wall consent, unless your neighbour's house is a considerable distance away. If you are planning a loft conversion and need to upgrade purlins ➤ see also **Using roof space** pp.136–7, the loads on the supporting wall will increase, and this has the potential to cause cracks in the party wall of a terraced or semi-detached house.

Meeting the requirements

There are essentially two ways to meet the requirements of the Party Wall Act. The easiest way, which is by far the most common, is by a simple exchange of letters between the neighbours. For this to be effective the letters must cover the salient points. It is possible to download a model form of the letter from www.communities.gov.uk.

This letter informs your neighbour of your intention to do the works and explains the nature of the works. It assures that any damage caused by the works will be put right at the expense of those doing the work. The letter then points out the rights of the neighbour to insist upon the appointment of a party wall surveyor (described below), if so desired. Finally, the letter asks the neighbour to sign a waiver so that works can proceed without the need for a special surveyor. If everything is amicable, most neighbours will sign the waiver.

Party wall agreements

When a neighbour is not prepared to sign the waiver, a party wall surveyor will need to be appointed at the expense of those doing the work. Unlike with lawyers, it is not necessary for each side to have their own surveyor, since technically, in party wall matters, the surveyor is representing the interests of the wall!

The surveyor will inspect and record the existing condition of the appropriate parts of the properties, and will then study the proposals in detail. He may request that additional details are drawn or structural calculations are presented, before he is satisfied. Once he is sure that the works should not cause any damage to the neighbouring property, he will advise both parties and broker on a suitable written agreement.

It is very important that party wall matters are not left until the last minute. Neighbours are perfectly within their rights to insist upon a two-month delay, once they have been notified of works proposed and, if they want to be awkward, they can insist that all sorts of hurdles are cleared before they are prepared to sign an agreement.

A schedule of condition

Whether or not you are working with a professional party wall surveyor, a really good way of protecting the interests of both sides is to have a 'schedule of condition'. This sounds very technical, but in essence is simply a detailed record of the state and condition of the party wall on both sides before any work starts. This can be undertaken by an independent professional or by the home owners, but it is important that both parties sign off on it before building work starts. Any existing cracks are noted, measured and photographed and the information is bound together in a small report. The great thing about this is that if any damage is caused, it is clear whether or not it was pre-existing or caused by the works, leaving little room for argument.

Do not think that just because you are not doing any work directly to a party wall, you will not need party wall consent. Check the requirements of the party wall legislation to see if it applies to your project.

Last-minute changes to proposals can wreck a design. Make sure that party wall agreements are in place as soon as possible to avoid later compromises.

In tight urban locations, a proposal might require many party wall agreements. One project, where two new houses were squeezed into a yard, required 27 separate party wall consents!

Dealing with your neighbours in an amicable fashion at an early stage can garner support for your scheme during planning, and can avoid costly delays.

The Party Wall Act is the law and is an entirely separate piece of legislation to planning or building regulations. There is no reason why a party wall agreement should be refused, if your proposals are properly designed and calculated in detail.

Like everything else, good communication is about finding the right balance. Involve neighbours too soon and they might try to dictate, leave it too late and you risk getting their backs up.

4 Detail design

Whether you work out the details carefully with your architect in advance, or you leave them to your builder to make up as he goes along – someone, somewhere will be doing the detail design on your project.

Shoddy details can spoil your project in myriad ways. Technically, the details need to meet regulations and keep weather out; economically, they need to fit within the budget, and aesthetically, they need to extend and underpin the effect that you are aiming for overall.

Most of all, good detailing involves an investment of time and concentration, in order to get exactly what you want.

practicality

aesthetic

environment

cost/value

regulations

communication

What is detail design?

People often **imagine** *that there is a 'standard' level of* **detail** *that* **builders** *will need to work from, but there is not. Quite simply, the more effort spent locking down detail in drawings and* **documentation** *in advance, the more* **control** *you will have over what the builder is doing.*

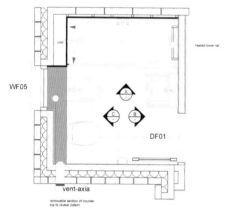

WF05

DF01

vent-axia

bedroom 1 ensuite bathroom plan

removable section of counter
top to reveal cistern

Vent-Axia Solo Selv 12T extractor fan with airflow shutter and washable filter.
Mains transformer with 12V SELV output with presettable overrun timer (5-25mins.)
Units to be semi-recessed and wall mounted at high level or ceiling mounted as indicated
on drawings. Ductwork to be vented as shown. (T: 01293 - 441 605)

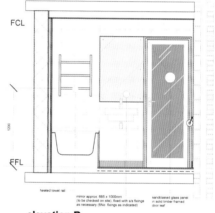

FCL

heated towel rail

FFL

heated towel rail

mirror approx. 685 x 1000mm
(to be checked on site), fixed with s/s fixings
as necessary (6No. fixings as indicated)

sandblasted glass panel
in solid timber framed
door leaf

elevation B

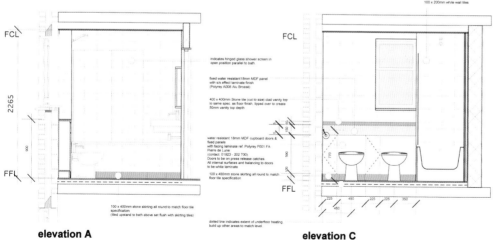

FCL

2265

900

FFL

100 x 400mm stone skirting all round to match floor tile
specification.
(tiled upstand to bath above set flush with skirting tiles)

elevation A

100 x 200mm white wall tiles

FCL

indicates hinged glass shower screen in
open position parallel to bath

fixed water resistant18mm MDF panel
with s/s effect laminate finish
(Polyrey A008 Alu Brosse)

400 x 400mm Stone tile (cut to size) clad vanity top
to same spec. as floor finish, lipped over to create
50mm vanity top depth

water resistant 18mm MDF cupboard doors &
fixed panels
with facing laminate ref. Polyrey P001 FA
Pierre de Lune
(contact: 01923 - 202 700).
Doors to be on press release catches.
All internal surfaces and balancing to doors
to be white laminate
100 x 400mm stone skirting all round to match
floor tile specification

dotted line indicates extent of underfloor heating
build up other areas to match level.

770

FFL

225   450   225   225   350
450

elevation C

Bathroom details. An example of a detailed and dimensioned plan (top right) together with three of the internal elevations for an en-suite bathroom. The jump in scale and information is clear when compared to the scheme level plan (opposite).

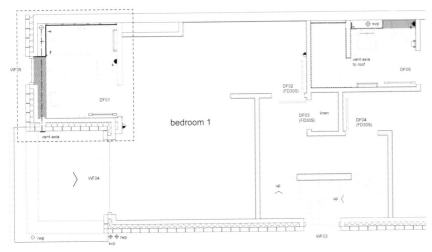

1st floor plan

⌃ **Scheme level floor plan.** *The dotted box indicates the* en-suite *bathroom, shown here at scheme level as part of a whole floor layout, and shown in detailed form (opposite) with just some of the detailed design drawings prepared for this room.*

Many builders are happy to work from little more than an outline (the proverbial 'back-of-a-fag-packet' sketch). What this means is that they will be free to make up the details as they see fit. The extent to which they consult you on this will differ from builder to builder. Clearly, this saves money on having drawings done, but the downside is that you have very little control over what is built, and it is impossible to pin down a cost against anything so vague.

Scheme-level drawings ➤ see also **Chapter 3: Scheme design** pp.100–45 are a vital starting point, but these do not describe the detail of what is proposed. Detail design starts to tackle this specific information. Whether you engage an architect to do this work for you, leave it to your builder, or work it out for yourself, one way or another it needs to be done.

If using an architect, the tangible end-result of the process will be detail level drawings, which you may choose to have done for the whole of your project, or just for select details that you want clarified.

Since the majority of building regulation issues are detail matters, it is during the detail design stage of a project when they are most pertinent. A few of the broader regulation issues have been dealt with ➤ see also **Thinking ahead on building regulations** pp.92–3, but this chapter looks at building regulations in more detail ➤ see also **The building regulations** pp.196–9.

The more specific your requirements, the more developed your detail design needs to be. In short, to get exactly what you want, it needs to be designed and drawn in detail.

God is in the detail. There are countless examples of great concepts that have ended up looking awkward, clunky, or that simply don't work, as a result of leaving the detail to the builder.

Include exact information regarding insulation, draught-proofing, and so on, in detail-level drawings, so that your builder knows exactly what is required.

One way of keeping costs down is to identify those areas where the control of the detail is especially important, and to focus the design budget on these.

The details that the building inspector will want to clarify can be sorted out on site with the builder, under the 'building notice' method ➤**see pp.200–1**. However, the more details that are not considered in advance, the more unpredictable the project will become.

It is important to be clear with all parties who is responsible for the various details. For example, ensure that your builder is fully aware of those details you expect him to handle, or you may have a problem once work begins.

Walls

*For each **type** of wall and its construction method, there is a range of **important** details to be considered, which will **depend** upon the circumstances and **function** of the wall. How much of this detail you choose to leave up to your builder will differ from **project** to project and builder to **builder**.*

External walls

The basic construction of the wall will have been decided at scheme level stage, but the detail of how that is executed needs to be considered now.

Typically, external walls need strength and stability to provide structural support, and should have an effective means of keeping bad weather out, the warmth in, and fire from spreading.

The most popular construction for external walls in domestic projects is a cavity wall: two masonry layers (or skins), with an insulated space between them. The main purpose of the cavity is to prevent water from getting to the inner skin, so it is important not to bridge the space in any way that might allow water to travel across. However, the whole wall needs to act as one to be stable, so wall ties are used. These are installed as the wall is being built, to connect the skins. Usually made from galvanised or stainless steel, they have a 'drip' detail, so that any water that tries to cross the cavity, drips off safely before getting to the inner skin.

Where a cavity wall comes out of the ground is a very important detail (see diagram). Generally, the wall sits on the concrete foundation below the ground level. Several courses of bricks are built up to a level of about 150mm (6in) above the ground. At this point a tough plastic layer, known as a Damp-Proof Course (DPC) is laid into the mortar joint. The DPC on the inner skin laps over the Damp-Proof Membrane (DPM) that is laid beneath the floor slab. The assumption is that the brickwork below the DPC is wet. The DPC in the external skin prevents damp creeping up the wall, and the DPC, lapped with the DPM, separates the inner skin and floor from the damp below.

An alternative to a plastic DPC on the external skin is to use engineering bricks for the courses below the DPC level. Engineering bricks are much harder and do not absorb moisture like normal bricks, so negate the need for the plastic DPC.

In addition, at this stage you need to consider other cavity wall details, such as where it meets a window opening, or the threshold of a doorway, where it supports a floor on the inside, or a roof at the top, and (in the case of a rear extension) where it joins an existing, older external wall. All these variants, and more, are

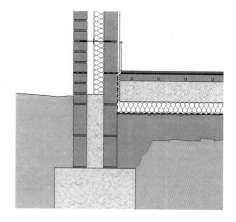

⋀ Floor to wall junction. *This detailed section through the base of a cavity wall shows blockwork below ground, an insulated cavity, with a brick outer skin. The Damp-Proof Membrane (DPM) laps up from beneath the floor insulation to the Damp-Proof Course (DPC) in the wall.*

Timber cladding combined with acrylic render. *In this example from the case study, the external walls are constructed from two-skin cavity blockwork, coated externally with an acrylic render in some areas and clad with horizontal timber in others.*

required for this one construction method, that of a cavity wall. A similar set of variants would apply for each and every alternative construction method, such as a timber-framed construction or hung external tiles.

The details described above are very typical, but relate only to one of many different circumstances. For example, when there is a suspended ground floor, instead of a solid ground-floor slab, there would be no DPM to lap with, and the DPC for the inner skin would act in a similar way to that of the outer skin. However, in this case, remember that the space below the floor needs to be ventilated. It would be different again if there was a basement.

Clearly, the scope of this book cannot illustrate all of these possibilities. The important thing to understand about detail design, however, is that it is best not to simply copy details from a book, but rather try to understand what the detail design needs to achieve. In the above case, the key issues are strength and stability, for support and keeping the water out and the warmth in.

If the building method is well understood and familiar to your builder, there is less need for detail drawings than for a more unfamiliar method.

Using engineering bricks at low level is an alternative to installing a plastic DPC. While they are more expensive, they can be very attractive, and often come in a dark purplish colour (known as 'blue' engineering bricks).

While people get very excited about solar panels and wind machines, the energy saved by good wall insulation is more significant per pound spent than any of the clever energy systems available.

It takes approximately three times as long to lay brickwork than to lay concrete blocks; therefore, the use of concrete blocks offers significant cost savings.

It is so important that wall ties do not form a bridge for damp to cross a cavity that a building inspector will often check with a torch to see that the ties have been laid level, and that lumps of mortar have not dropped onto them.

Wall details will often be drawn as small sections (like the example opposite) at a scale of 1:5 so that each element can be clearly identified and communicated.

Internal walls

While internal walls do not need to keep the weather out, they do need to separate rooms effectively, and may need to provide support for floors or a roof structure above.

Studwork (timber or metal) and masonry are the two main types of internal wall, but there is a great deal of detail beyond this simple choice, which needs to be taken into consideration.

Fire-separating walls

Many internal walls need to provide fire separation, which is rated under the building regulations in terms of the time it would take a fire to burn through a wall. For most homes a half-hour fire rating is the most that is required, but in some cases a one-hour rating is necessary. Masonry walls tend to meet these criteria easily, but when holes are made in these walls for services to be put through, it is sometimes necessary to incorporate special fire-stopping material. Two layers of plasterboard on a stud wall will usually achieve the half-hour rating.

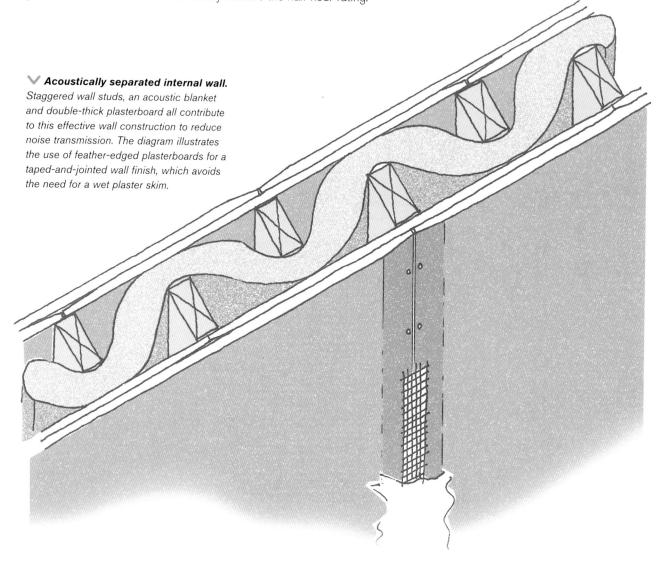

∨ *Acoustically separated internal wall.*
Staggered wall studs, an acoustic blanket and double-thick plasterboard all contribute to this effective wall construction to reduce noise transmission. The diagram illustrates the use of feather-edged plasterboards for a taped-and-jointed wall finish, which avoids the need for a wet plaster skim.

Acoustic separation

Providing suitable acoustic separation between rooms is becoming an increasingly important part of both the regulations and people's requirements. Sound usually needs to be dealt with in two ways: heavy material is used to block out high-frequency sound such as conversations, and a physical disconnection – for instance, an air gap – is provided to reduce thumps and other low-frequency noise. The weight of a masonry wall will, clearly, be good for the former, but often the air gap is more problematic. The diagram opposite shows how a stud wall can be created with staggered studwork, an acoustic blanket and double layers of plasterboard to give a very effective (though not fully soundproof) construction detail.

Fixing points

One detail that is often forgotten is to provide suitable places within a wall for fixings. Walls may need to have anything from radiators to washbasins, coat hooks, clocks or paintings fixed to them. Plasterboard is strong up to a point, but is not designed to carry any 'point-loads' and very often a wall that has been finished needs to be cut open to put suitable supports inside so that wall lights or other items can be fitted.

Plastering and wall linings

With masonry walls the common practice in the UK is to cover with a rough base layer of sand and cement mix (or sometimes a rough plaster called bonding) before the finer, skim coat of plaster. Stud walls are generally faced with plasterboard, which is flat enough to receive the skim coat without the base layers.

More common in commercial projects, and, generally, in continental Europe, is an alternative method that cuts out wet plastering. Known as tape-and-jointing, all the walls are covered with feather-edged plasterboard. Also known as tapered-edge, this has a slight narrowing at the edge of the boards which is formed in the factory. Again, the diagram opposite illustrates this slight narrowing.

When fixed to the wall, the two edges butted together are covered with a scrim tape, and then jointing compound (which is quite like filler) is smoothed over the slight recess to cover the joint and tape and give a smooth flat finish.

On masonry walls (in particular, the inner face of external walls), the tape and joint system can be used as an alternative to wet plastering, if the walls are clad with plasterboard. This can be screw-fixed to thin battens of timber or pressed steel, or can be glued to the walls with blobs of adhesive. This is known as 'dot-and-dab' and is a very speedy and effective method. Once lined, the same tape-and-joint finishing can be applied, as described above.

The advantage of the tape-and-joint system is that it avoids the mess and drying times of wet plastering, and also gives a very flat finish.

Lath and plaster

When working with old buildings, be aware of the difficulties in working with 'lath and plaster' walls and ceilings. Before the invention of plasterboard, it was common to nail hundreds of thin strips of wood (known as 'laths') to studs for a wall or joists for a ceiling. This lightweight surface was rough enough to receive plaster, which was often strengthened by mixing in horsehair. Trying to connect to or cut into such a surface without causing extensive cracking can be very tricky.

People often ask for rooms to be made soundproof. Full soundproofing is, usually, not practical in a home. However, it is always good to incorporate some level of acoustic insulation between rooms for general privacy.

Wet plastering can give a good finish only if the plasterer is very competent. In most cases, wet plastering leaves an imperfect finish, which is hard to detect until the walls are decorated and lighting is installed.

Timber wall panelling can create a beautifully warm interior, and although timber is expensive, it is quick and relatively clean to put up, as well as being a fully sustainable material.

The time saved with metal studwork – both the erection time and for the ease of running services makes this, generally, the most cost-effective construction for an internal partition wall.

Interior walls that separate two dwellings, such as those between two flats, must meet very high standards for acoustic insulation as well as fire separation. The requirements of the building regulations have increased significantly in recent years.

If you have heavy items, like clocks, wall lights or large artworks, that you want to hang or fix to a studwork wall, tell your architect at the detail design stage so that the builders can be instructed where suitable construction needs to be allowed.

Roofs

*An **effective** roof is the most basic **element** of human **shelter**, but there are various ways of approaching the design in terms of shape, **structure** and finish, which will be **suitable** and appropriate for a range of different **buildings**.*

Pitched roofs

Pitched (or sloping) roofs need to be given careful thought at the detail design stage. There are many alternatives, each suitable for different circumstances and with different cost implications.

Thatched roofs are perhaps the closest link to the original development of pitched roofs, but even these are very much based upon the same principle as any other covering, namely, that the materials overlap from the top of the roof so that water will run down the slope without getting in.

Clay tiles, in various forms, and slates cover most of the older roofs in the UK, while interlocking concrete tiles, and slates made from composite materials, are more cost-effective modern solutions. The other significant developments of the last half century are the inclusion of roofing felt (a waterproof layer beneath the slates or tiles) and insulation.

Different roof coverings overlap in different ways and, in many cases, only a small part of each unit is exposed. Traditional slates, for example, have such a large overlap that less than half of their surface is exposed. This is necessary because rain driven by the wind could be forced some way up the slope under a slate. The invention of interlocking tiles, with ridges to stop the invasion of water, means much less overlapping and, therefore, less covering is needed.

The most common pitched roof has roofing felt fixed to the rafters in such a way that it dips slightly between the rafters for water drainage. Over this are fixed timber strips or battens, which are usually nailed through the felt into the rafters. The tiles or slates are fixed to the battens. Flat slates are simply nailed to the battens, and tiles are hung onto the battens from the small ridge cast into the back of the tile.

Pitch angle

One matter to be very concerned about is that of the pitch angle. Slates and clay tiles are, generally, fine on steep roofs, but the lower the angle the more they struggle to be effective against driving rain and strong winds. Most tile manufacturers will specify a minimum pitch angle for their product, with many being no good for angles of less than 35 or 32 degrees.

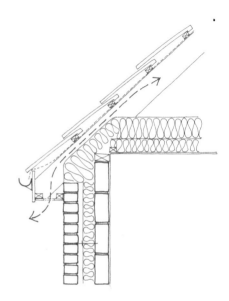

⋀ Typical eaves construction.
This diagram shows a detail section cut through the junction of a cavity wall and a pitched roof. The overlapping roof tiles hang on the battens, and the dotted line beneath indicates the roofing felt. The arrows indicate the necessary passage of ventilation that must not be blocked by the insulation.

❯ Wrap-around lean-to slate roof.
This modest ground floor extension has a pitched roof, with traditional slates. Note the hipped roof around the corner (on the right), the use of lead flashings to waterproof the joint where the slates meet the brick wall, and the rendered parapet walls adjoining the neighbour (on the left).

Roof insulation

If the loft space within the roof is to be occupied, then it will be necessary to insulate the slope of the roof (rather than the loft floor). Many people forget the importance of a ventilation gap between the insulation and the roof covering. This is vital to avoid condensation problems (that are more often than not mistaken for damp coming in). The ventilation gap is also pointless, unless there is suitable space for air to flow in and out. An array of special ventilation tiles and ridge tiles is available to accommodate this, and very often ventilation points can be incorporated easily into the detailed design of the eaves (see diagram opposite).

Water drains naturally off a pitched roof, which means that imperfections will usually not be catastrophic, particularly if they are high up on the roof. A flat roof has to be absolutely watertight.

If you are trying to match a new section of roof with an existing roof, you may need to seek reclaimed tiles or renew the whole roof. It is very difficult to get a good match, mainly because the effects of weathering are impossible to replicate effectively.

Less energy is used in the firing of clay tiles than in the production of concrete tiles. If you want to make a truly carbon-based choice, balance the energy profile against the distance the product has to travel.

While interlocking concrete tiles may not be the most attractive option, they are very efficient because they need less overlap, and can be quicker to lay than their traditional rivals. Overall they generally offer a significant cost saving.

For a listed building, anything other than like-for-like repairs to a roof, undertaken in the traditional manner, will probably need Listed Building Consent. The good news is that such work is zero-rated for VAT.

An experienced specialist tradesman in lead or copper roof work will know much more about the appropriate details than you or your architect, but without consultation this might not match what is wanted.

Flat roofs

Flat roofs are effectively floors made weatherproof. In some ways they are the simplest form of roofs to build, and in other ways the most complex.

Flat roofs tend to represent the most efficient use of space and materials, but without careful detailing, you can encounter endless maintenance problems.

Insulation

An important consideration of the detail design of a flat roof is the way that it is insulated. While a pitched roof can have insulation in the loft floor (if it is not occupied), there is no loft space with a flat roof. Insulation separates flat roof design into two categories: 'warm' roofs and 'cold' roofs.

This is all to do with preventing condensation. You may think that condensation probably does not add up to much, but in a roof it can cause real problems. Essentially, the warm air within a house carries with it moisture in the form of water vapour. If that warm air hits a cold surface (like the inside of a single-glazed window) condensation will form.

⌃ Extension with a flat roof.
This full-width extension has a flat roof concealed behind a brick parapet wall. In the centre of the flat roof a large lantern-style roof light allows daylight to pour into the room beneath.

With a 'cold' roof, the ventilation is between the weatherproof layer on the outside and the insulation. Most of the warm air stays within the insulated space, but it can get through to the inside of the cold roof surface, and can then condense. As long as this space is ventilated, the condensation will not build up and no problems will occur.

With a 'warm' roof, there is a layer called a 'vapour barrier' between the insulation and the warm air inside, so that no warm air can get through to touch any of the cold surfaces. Cold roofs are, generally, more reliable as they don't depend upon a continuous vapour barrier; however, warm roofs don't need to be as thick and are often preferred when maximising a ceiling height is important.

Weatherproofing

The reason why flat roofs are so much more reliable these days than they were 20 or 30 years ago is that the technology of the weatherproof layer has improved. Flat roofs used to be made with bitumen-based material called asphalt, which had to be melted in a big cauldron before being applied. There are many and various flat roof systems now available that are much more reliable and durable than asphalt, and are also easier to apply.

For example, a material called EDPM, which is essentially a tough rubber sheet, does not need any special skills to apply. It comes in one large sheet and is cut at the factory to fit the roof in question. Firstly, plywood is laid on fillets of timber to form a sloping deck and create the drainage fall. A thick layer of rigid insulation is then laid on top of the ply deck. The insulation has a ready-made vapour barrier applied to the underside. Lastly, the EDPM sheet is glued down on top of the insulation, and can be dressed into channels to form gutters, and tucked under the tops of parapet walls.

Edges

Another very important detail to consider for any flat roof is the edge. The roof can either create overhanging eaves, or the wall can go up past the level of the roof, creating a parapet. The two diagrams below show typical detailing for a flat roof eaves and a flat roof behind a parapet.

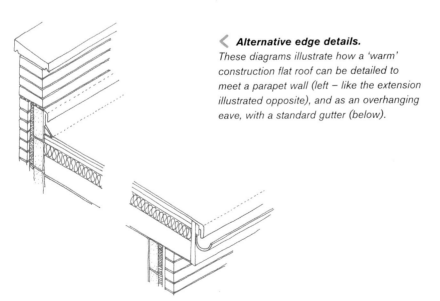

‹ Alternative edge details.
These diagrams illustrate how a 'warm' construction flat roof can be detailed to meet a parapet wall (left – like the extension illustrated opposite), and as an overhanging eave, with a standard gutter (below).

If a project is to be built in two phases, a flat roof at the end of phase one will become a floor during phase two. No significant construction is wasted in this situation.

Flat roofs can have a significant visual effect on a building. Overhanging eaves can look fantastically modern if detailed nicely, or a parapet can work well on an older building.

EDPM is manufactured from rubber, which is both a natural product and sustainable as it is harvested from living trees.

Under standard circumstances, a flat roof will be cheaper to build than a pitched roof as there are fewer materials and processes involved.

When flat-roofed extensions are granted planning approval a condition may be added to the permission stating that the roof cannot be used as a garden or terrace, in order to protect the privacy of neighbours.

If you propose to use one of the many new technologies available for your roof covering, ensure that you have clear installation instructions, so that your builder understands how it must be fitted.

Metal roofs and flashings

Sheet metal is a wonderful roofing material, which has a long tradition of use on old buildings, as well as being used for many innovative new products and systems.

As a roof covering, metal has traditionally been regarded as an expensive but long-lasting solution, and it can be seen on cathedrals and public buildings. Generally, the roofs of private homes were not covered in this way, but junctions and valley trays were, and still often are, formed in lead.

Lead roofs

Lead is a tremendously useful and versatile material as it is reliably waterproof and can be easily formed into shape on site to suit the circumstances of a particular roof. Lead also has a quiet beauty, with its soft edges, visual weight and dead-grey colour. Sheets of lead are supplied in rolls. The sheets can be joined by folding two adjoining edges up and rolling them over. This creates an upstanding seam and characterises the appearance of a lead roof. One of the joys of a lead roof is that the craftsmanship involved is very apparent in the finished result.

However, lead is a very heavy material, which can influence the necessary structure, and is also very expensive. The price of lead has soared recently – many churches have had problems with the lead from their roofs being stolen. As a result, lead work is usually still reserved for junctions and flashings, where it is invaluable.

Zinc roofs

Zinc is another sheet metal that has long been used for roofing. Lighter and thinner than lead, it is shiny when new, weathering down to a lead-like appearance over the years. It is possible to buy pre-weathered zinc that has the soft, aged look from the start.

While zinc can be formed on site, it is much stiffer than lead, and it cannot be shaped so readily in place to fit an unusual shape, as the folds need to be made with a pressing tool. As a result, zinc is more commonly used as a roof covering rather than just for junctions. In a similar way as with lead, sheets are joined with raised seams, and the effect can be very pleasing.

∨ *Zinc roof* *This 'butterfly' (or reverse pitch) roof to the extension featured on pages 78–9 (below right), uses 'semi-weathered' zinc panels to give a soft grey finish. While similar to lead, the folds in a zinc roof tend to be visually sharper and of course it weighs much less.*

∨ *Lead – old and new.* *This early Victorian dormer window (below middle) has both its arched roof and its cheeks clad with lead. The lead work on the cheeks even includes a decorative motif. The raised seams can be clearly seen on this wrap-around extension roof (below left), which illustrates how lead can be used to form the roof covering, gutter and fascia of this roof, giving a wonderfully complete and durable result.*

∧ **Octagonal copper-clad 'onion' domes.** *In the right setting, the vivid and unique green patina of a copper roof can be magnificent. These striking domes, built as part of the Richmond Theatre in West London, are a great example.*

Copper roofs

Like zinc, sheet copper has a long tradition of use as a roof covering. Copper is also relatively light and stiff in sheet form, and can be pressed and joined with seams. The most notable thing about a copper roof is its wonderful colour that changes from red-gold as a raw material to a vivid pale green due to oxidisation.

Designing with metal

In all these cases, the general construction detail involves constructing the roof deck in plywood to form a slope ➤ see also **Roof structure** p.134, with insulation beneath, and then forming the metalwork on top of the ply layer.

Whereas all of these traditional sheet metal roofs are formed on site, some systems on the market today tend to incorporate as much pre-forming as possible, in order to reduce the amount of skilled and lengthy work to be done on site.

Coated sheet steel, usually shaped to add strength and create interlocking seams, is now available as a 'sandwich' panel, with the steel face pre-bonded to an insulation and vapour barrier, and sometimes even to an internal finish. These can be bolted directly onto the structure with no need for a ply deck.

This sophisticated manufacturing process does not, of course, come cheap. These products are used on large commercial projects, such as warehouses and factories, where the scale and tight organisation of the operation means that the time saved more than offsets the cost of the system. In domestic projects, this is more questionable.

When you have a roof with awkward shapes, lead is an unbeatable, versatile material for forming weatherproof junctions around dormer windows, in valley gutters, and connecting to brickwork.

A lead roof, made by a skilled roofer, can be a very beautiful thing as the craftsmanship is so evident in the end result. The nature of lead gives both visual weight and softness, because all of the edges are slightly rounded.

The manufacture of metals requires a great deal of energy, but the use of any thin sheet material has an inherent efficiency. Metal roofs also have a very long lifespan and are eminently recyclable.

Sheet metal roofs are an expensive option for home owners, but their reliability and durability offer great value in the long term.

In many historic listed buildings, lead is also used for gutters and down pipes. Removing or replacing them with plastic gutters would not generally be permitted.

There are several different ways to form a 'seam' between two sheets of metal and each can give a different visual effect. It is worth a little research to ensure you get the one you want.

Windows and doors

*Windows and doors not only provide **light**, access and **ventilation** to our homes, but also, like the **eyes**, nose and mouth of a **face**, they play an important role in defining the **character** expressed by the **facade** of the building, and as such must be chosen carefully.*

Windows

Window frames are made from all manner of different materials, and windows come in all shapes and sizes, but by far the most often used are fixed windows, casement windows and sliding sash windows.

Fixed windows

Quite simply, fixed windows are frames set into a wall with glass fixed directly into them. Since there is no openable frame in this type of window, the visual thickness of the frame is kept to a minimum. Traditionally, the frame, most commonly made from timber, was rebated and the glass held into the rebate by a small strip of timber called a glazing bead.

Casement windows

Of the two openable categories, casement windows have a frame set into the wall, and then inner rebated frames (rather confusingly called sashes) carry the glass. The sash is then hinged like a door within the frame, although there are also pivoting versions. The hinges can be set to the side (like a door), or at the top or bottom, depending how you want the window to open.

Casement windows are made from either timber, steel, aluminium, uPVC, or in combinations of these. Each have their place alongside their advantages and disadvantages, and your choice of window type and material should be considered carefully. You can also find products that allow secure partial opening for safe ventilation when the property is unoccupied.

Sliding sash windows

Sliding sash windows are very common in the UK, particularly in properties dating from Georgian through to Edwardian times. These windows are much less common abroad and in France I have heard them referred to as 'English-style' windows.

High-performance sliding windows. *Half of each of these windows is fixed in place and the other half slides sideways. The frames are very well sealed and, combined with triple-glazing, they are very efficient at keeping the warmth in. The slatted 'Juliet' balconies, nicely detailed with steel frames and timber slats, add depth to the elevation.*

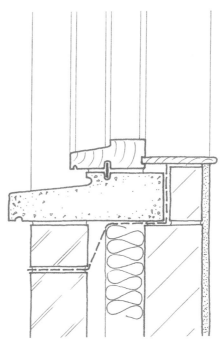

Windowcills. *The cill is the base of the window frame, which is, generally, hit by the hardest weathering, so the cill is important for keeping the weather out of the wall. Consequently, the detailed design of the windowcill is vital. Cills are formed in many different ways. It is common to have a 'sub-cill' of stone or masonry below a windowcill, which is generally a projecting element of the window frame itself.*

Timber window frames will need periodic maintenance, as will painted metal frames. For this reason many people gravitate towards uPVC. While they are not entirely maintenance free, uPVC frames certainly need less work in the medium term.

A feature of most beautiful buildings is elegant windows, and the slenderness of the framing is a very important factor in stylish windows. It is often difficult to keep the framing in a suitable proportion when using double glazing.

While uPVC window frames do not significantly degrade in use, they are not biodegradable and are not easily recycled.

Windows made to a standard size and purchased 'off the shelf' are significantly less expensive than ones that have to be made to a specific size. Unfortunately, it is rare to find that your window opening perfectly suits a catalogue size.

To increase the area of glazing that your extension may be permitted under part L of the building regulations **>see p.199**, you may need to use triple glazing to improve thermal performance.

A comprehensive set of drawings will often include a window schedule containing a list of all the windows in the project, and indicating which details apply to particular windows.

Box-sliding sash windows. *While their mechanisms are quite complex, traditional box-sliding sash windows are, generally, elegant and functional, largely because the mechanism means that the glazing bars can be very slender.*

The complexity of a sliding sash window is inherent, because as the sash slides vertically, gravity pulls the weight of the upper sash downwards. To prevent this, and to make the lower sash slide upwards more easily, the sashes are fixed to ropes at either side (known as sash cords), which rise to the topside of the frame, over a pulley and down to a lead counterweight. These counterweights are concealed within a tall box that looks like a wide frame.

In most examples, the box frames are partially built into the wall so that they look reasonably slender from the outside. However, when two separate sash windows need to be placed next to each other, the space needed for the two counterweight boxes will mean that a thick piece of solid construction is visible between the two windows.

While this all seems very complex, sliding sash windows can be very beautiful, give a large area of open air when fully opened, and both sides can be cleaned from the inside.

Sometimes, replacement sash windows are produced using a friction system, which is not nearly as satisfactory as the traditional counterweight method. Sash windows are also manufactured in other materials such as uPVC. The nature of uPVC framing is that it is, generally, much less elegant than wood, because the framing of the sashes needs to be thicker.

⌃ Folding/sliding doors. *Using these wonderfully tall glazed folding/sliding doors gave this generous kitchen extension a wonderful sense of space and a great connection to the garden. The doors (shown here half-folded across) can be folded completely across to the left to open up the room to garden in summer, or closed across, with only the panel on the extreme right acting like a standard door on its own.*

◀ **Giant sliding glass door.**
This kitchen/breakfast room can be opened right up to the terrace and garden beyond by sliding back the huge glazed panel. A good-quality mechanism is vital for such a door, otherwise it would be too heavy to slide easily.

When selecting folding/sliding doors, try to choose an odd number of panels. This will mean that the last (odd) panel can be used as a door on its own without moving any other panels.

While creating an almost entirely glass wall across the rear of a house can look wonderful inside, be careful not to make the opening look incongruous from the outside.

Large areas of glazing can be a weak point for heat loss in a house, but can also create benefit by gaining heat as a result of 'solar gain'. The energy benefits can be calculated as part of a SAP calculation **>see pp.199**.

A set of folding/sliding doors will be significantly more expensive than a series of French windows. A set of seven panels across an opening of 5.5m (18ft) costs approximately £8,000.

There have been many accidents where people have run into glass doors. Building regulations require toughened glass in certain areas and 'manifestation', which involves some surface treatment – often small stickers – at eye level.

Some folding/sliding glass doors are made so well that they can achieve a remarkably good thermal performance. Always check the 'U-value' rating of the system that you are considering. A rating of 1 or less is excellent.

Glazed doors

Opening up the house to the garden to generate an 'inside-outside' feeling is a very popular option. People want to open the doors during the summer, so that the space can simply flow outside, and to have lots of light pouring in.

The solution to this can be as simple as French windows, usually a pair of doors that are almost entirely glazed within a frame. These are essentially large casement windows that are designed to the floor and are able to cope with the flow of people across the cill.

Sets of French windows can be fitted side by side (when doing this think carefully about where the doors will open) and this can be very effective if you wish to open up a room to the outside.

One important thing to understand is the need for an adequate frame around the glass. People often want the maximum glass area, but if the frame of the opening door is not strong enough to carry the weight of the glass, it will eventually fail or twist and cause problems.

The downside of French windows is that they only swing open, not right out of the way. Many people want to open up the whole wall in good weather, and a very popular solution is to use a folding/sliding system that allows a series of glass panels to concertina to one side leaving a completely open space. These can be very effective, but it is well worth choosing a good-quality system, as the cheaper ones tend to get jammed, which over time can be very irritating.

In the project illustrated above, one huge sliding glass panel can be pushed aside to leave a wide opening from the kitchen out to the terrace and garden. Careful detailed design to ensure that the level of the floor matched the terrace level outside, with a matching tiled finish, enhanced the continuous feeling from inside to outside. An in-line drain was included to prevent rain penetrating across the level threshold.

External doors

Whether it is to the street or to a communal hallway, just about every dwelling has a front door. Front doors can be imposing and grand, or welcoming and warm. They can be high security and exclusive, or be punctured with postboxes and cat flaps. Generally, they need to resist the weather, should be large enough to allow furniture in and out, and in most cases will take quite a lot of wear and tear.

Most residential front doors are made from timber. Victorian and Edwardian houses had panelled timber doors, usually painted, often with glazed panels and ornate door furniture. Contemporary houses generally have timber front doors and, in many ways, these tend to be a development of the traditional form, although often less reliant on symmetry.

Steel doors are available, but are very heavy and usually need a steel frame too. I am glad to say that other than where security is a particular threat, these are rare for residential properties. There are also uPVC doors, which I cannot recommend in any way as they are ugly, environmentally dreadful and unpleasant to touch.

In the main, residential front doors in the UK open inwards, which is more welcoming for visitors, but is not as secure as ones that open outwards (which are more common in continental Europe and the USA). Kicking down a door from the outside that opens outwards is nigh on impossible, whereas kicking down an inward opening door only requires the lock to break away. A solution to this is to have several locking points (which can be operated by a single key turn), so that the top, middle and bottom of the door locks into the frame.

▽ **Three panels.** *This doorway is given much more importance externally by having three panels. The panel on the left is solid, with boards arranged horizontally. The central panel is the actual door, which has a vertical grain, a series of portholes and a tall thin handle. And on the right a translucent panel of glass admits light but protects privacy.*

▽ **Level threshold.** *Part 'M' of the building regulations ➤ see p.199 often requires 'level access' at entrances so that wheelchairs do not have to negotiate steps. This makes it more difficult to keep out the weather, but there are a number of satisfactory detail solutions that can be used, such as the recessed rubber weather strip below.*

◄ **Converted chapel.** *This former Salvation Army Hall has been converted into apartments. The chevron arrangement of timber on the front door was designed to fit with the Victorian Gothic style of the building.*

Front doors need to be weatherproof, secure and wide enough to bring furniture in and out. Think about which way the door will swing and whether glazing is a good idea. This provides more light, but less security.

The choice of front door design can set the tone and mood for a whole house. This is well worth taking trouble over as it can have a strong impression. Think also about daylight in the hallway.

Many doors, frames and thresholds are made from tropical hardwoods: steer clear – this is the rainforest! Remember that effective draught-proofing is important for energy efficiency.

Money spent on a good quality front door is rarely wasted as there is generally only one! However, some of the sophisticated steel-reinforced security doors and bespoke panel doors can cost a great deal.

In the photograph on page 2, a contemporary oak front door in a Victorian terraced house can be compared to its neighbour that still has the original front door. The glass fanlight above the door has been sacrificed and a much taller door, with more elegant proportions, installed. This shows a lovely use of oak, and because it opens outward, it is very secure. Its neighbour retains a 'cottagey' feel, which many people would find more comfortable.

One very important detail of any external door is the threshold. Traditional doors often have a step, sometimes clad in brass, which resists the wear of foot traffic, and also forms a weather seal. Modern building regulations increasingly require level access ➤ see **Building Regulations part M** p.199, which makes the weather seal much more tricky. The example to the left shows one way of creating a threshold detail with level access.

It is common in the UK for external doors to swing into a building. However, there is no regulation preventing external doors from opening outwards as long as the door will not swing into someone's path.

Think what you want your door to say to the world about you. Do you want it to be impressive or protective, to uphold privacy, or be welcoming? Look at other homes and see what feeling their front doors give.

Internal doors

While internal doors are not susceptible to the weather and rarely have security issues, they need to provide a certain amount of soundproofing, and many also need to be effective as fire doors.

The important thing to understand about fire doors is that they are rated by the time they would hold a fire back, so you get a half-hour fire door or one-hour fire door and so on.

Aside from their functional requirements as a means of access, internal doors play a very important aesthetic role. In houses with classic features, dado and picture rails, the proportions of the door, both the overall dimension and how it is divided into panels, is very much part of the visual balance of the whole room. This explains why salvaged panelled doors from other houses can often look completely incongruous when installed into a house with different proportions.

▽ *Timber-veneered doors. These flush double doors have a lovely tall proportion, and are finished in a dramatic dark timber veneer, with 'parliament' hinges that allow them to open right back onto the wall at either side.*

Fire doors. These half-hour rated fire doors have been cut from 3m (10ft) long door 'blanks'. Roller catches in the top of the frame hold them shut when closed.

Think about whether an internal door will swing – into a room or out, and on which side it should be hinged. Doors that open inconveniently are annoying, very impractical and sometimes dangerous.

Tall internal doors can create an elegant proportion, whereas a standard height doorway in a room with high ceilings can look squat and ill-considered.

Constantly heating rooms that are seldom used, such as guest bedrooms, can be a tremendous waste of energy. If you are going to turn off the heat in a certain room, ensure that the interconnecting doors fit well and are draught-proof.

Victorian pine doors that have had their paint stripped off are a favourite for many people. Some dealers in such doors are unscrupulous – check that doors are not twisted, are properly dried out, and be careful not to pay over the odds.

There are particular guidelines within the building regulations about how near doorways can be to the top or bottom of a stairway, when a landing is needed, and which way the doors can swing.

A half-hour rated (30 mins) fire door (FD) with a smoke seal (S) is often indicated on architect's drawings with the abbreviation FD30S. Accordingly, an FD60S would be rated for one hour.

New doors can be bought as proprietary 'blanks' and the standard height is 1.981m (6ft 3in). You can, however, get 3m (10ft) long door blanks and cut these to size. I particularly like doorways that are made full height to the ceiling (unless the ceilings are very high indeed) as this can give a very tall and elegant proportion.

The example illustrated above shows how a pair of very tall double doors have been installed to allow the maximum daylight to pass through to the stairway, which previously was very gloomy and dark. These doors are half-hour fire rated and the dark line that is visible in the thickness of the door is a smoke seal that would swell up in the event of a fire.

Internal doors can also be used very effectively as dividers between rooms that have been knocked through. In many cases, a pair of double doors, or even four (sometimes glazed) folding panels, can allow separation when desired and can be folded back for a more open-plan effect. Sliding door panels can also be used in such situations, but whatever the chosen configuration, it is worthwhile spending some time and attention getting a good-quality mechanism that will not squeak, jam or disengage itself.

Plumbing

A basic **strategy** *for the plumbing of a home should be considered from the start of the process,* **evolved** *during scheme design, and* **developed** *with particular focus at the detail design stage. It is important to think of* **routes** *for supply pipes, but* **waste drainage** *often requires the most attention.*

Plumbing strategy

The detailed design of a pipe-work system is usually done by a plumbing subcontractor, or (if you have an elaborate or very large scheme) by an independent services engineer. Unless you leave sufficient space in the areas where the pipes need to run, you will often find it necessary to incorporate nasty boxing to conceal pipes.

Plumbing in a home, generally, falls into two categories: supply plumbing and waste plumbing, and each presents its own issues.

Supply plumbing

This is the system of pipes that delivers water and gas to where it is needed. It includes cold water from the street into your property, hot water from the tank to the bath, or gas from the meter to the kitchen hob. I include in this category pipes

≪Cantilevered wash basins. *The two wash basins in this bathroom are mounted onto a boxing that is built off the wall. This not only gives a useful shelf, but also allows a concealed route for the necessary supply and waste pipes.*

< Feature boxings. *Using boxings to conceal pipework is made into a feature in this bathroom with a walnut-veneered finish. These boxings not only hide pipes, but also contain the flush cistern for the WC and provide some separation between the WC and the bath.*

that take water on a circuit, such as radiator pipes. Generally, the pipes used are small in diameter and are pressurised, so the routes taken can go up, down or in any direction.

Until recently most of these pipes would have been copper, but, increasingly, plastic pipes are used. This is because plastic pipes are easier to install, need fewer bends, as they are, essentially, flexible, and need fewer joints, as they come on a reel rather than in lengths. Certain services still need to be installed using copper pipes.

Since supply pipes are mainly small and can go pretty much in any direction, they are easy to incorporate within stud walls, and under floors between joists. Think carefully about any beams that might get in the way, and how the pipes might have to pass around or through these.

The other important thing to consider is water temperature. For example, a pipe containing very cold water, passing through a room, will need to be insulated (or 'lagged') to prevent condensation. Similarly, a pipe containing hot water will lose heat if the water has to travel far, so it is a good idea to have short runs of pipe. If a basin is a long way from the hot water tank, you will need to run the tap for a long time before hot water comes out. Then, once the tap is shut off, hot water is wasted, as it is sitting in the pipe.

Waste plumbing

This is usually more problematic to design into a scheme because it relies on gravity, so the pipes need to slope downwards. Waste plumbing also needs much larger diameter pipes. Where supply pipes are often 15mm (⅝in) in diameter, waste pipes taking water from washbasins and baths need 50mm (2in). Waste pipes from WCs need 100mm (4in). There are also limits as to how far sideways a waste pipe from a WC can travel before heading down to the drain below ground.

It is generally a good idea to set bathrooms, kitchens and utility rooms above one another, if possible, so that they can all be connected to one vertical waste pipe. However, if this does not fit in with your design, there are all sorts of ways to solve the problem. A new vertical pipe can be installed in a different position (although it must connect to the drain below ground, and this can be expensive), or a macerator can be used to pump waste to a point of drainage via small diameter pipes. These can be fitted almost anywhere, but like any mechanical item, may break down (which is no fun!), and they can be noisy.

Designing forwards

Designing 'forwards' is a concept that I am very keen to promote, and often the best way to explain this is to give an example of designing 'backwards'. I have come across many situations where people want to add a bathroom on an upper floor and seem to think they must locate it in a certain place. This is usually because a builder has told them that they 'have to have' the bathroom in a particular position because that is where the plumbing will 'have to go'.

What the builder is actually saying is that this is where the plumbing would be easiest for him to install. To me, this is entirely backwards. First work out where you want the bathroom, and then work out what plumbing is required. It is always achievable, but if the additional cost is prohibitive, you can always rethink the layout.

The most practical arrangement is to stack all of your plumbing requirements above one another. However, this may not give the best layout. Balance ease and economy against layout for best results.

Pipework is generally ugly so try to design concealed routes into the walls and floors of your home.

Aim to keep rainwater, grey water (from baths and basins) and soil waste (from WCs) separate. Rainwater can go to a soak-away and grey water can be recycled, reducing both the sewage burden and water consumption.

Macerator pumps are fairly expensive (a recent project included one that cost around £1,000), but they can sidestep plumbing gymnastics by allowing you to have a bathroom in the desired position.

The building regulations require that every home must have at least one gravity-drained WC, so that in the event of a power cut the home still has a functioning facility.

If you are going out to buy your own sanitary ware, make sure that you agree in advance with the plumbing contractors what diameter of waste pipe is needed, as some fittings are not compatible.

Heating

*There are lots of choices when it comes to heating, including different **fuel** sources, **boiler** types and **heating** methods. With **environmental** concerns and rising energy **prices**, your choices will have a long-term effect upon your home.*

Heating strategy

A fact that most people are surprised to discover is that about three-quarters of the total energy used in a home is used for heating and hot water. This is why basic insulation in walls and roofs, whatever the energy source, is such an important issue during the detail design stage. A well-insulated house requires a fraction of the energy needed to heat one that is not insulated, and the 'payback time' for good insulation is very small indeed when set against energy costs.

Energy options

Gas is the most popular choice for domestic fuel, because it has been relatively cheap for many years. However, prices have risen consistently in recent years, and they look set to continue in this vein.

< *Low-voltage underfloor heating.*
This remarkable technology uses a 'conductive plastic', which is only 2mm (¹⁄₂in) thick, can be cut with scissors, and can be laid under most types of flooring. The system is a little more expensive to install due to the need for transformers, but the running costs are remarkably low.

If you have a gas boiler, you can back this up with a solar-thermal system. This takes the form of panels or tubes on your roof in which water is heated by the sun – the hot water then flows into your tank (see overleaf). This reduces the workload required of your boiler. If the system is well designed and your hot water use is intelligent, the consumption of gas can be reduced dramatically.

Another popular way of supplementing your heating needs is with a heat pump. This technology enables heat to be taken from the ground (ground-source) or air (air-source) and put into your tank. Again, this can reduce reliance on gas, but the installation costs can be significant.

One often-overlooked energy source is electricity, particularly using an Economy 7 system. This uses cheap electricity during the night. A simple electric immersion heater in your hot water tank can be surprisingly economical, if used this way.

It is possible to supplement your use of electricity from the national grid by generating your own. Solar panels that generate electrical power are called photovoltaic cells, and, while these are currently much more expensive than solar thermal systems, they can service a wide spectrum of your energy needs in addition to providing power for your heating.

Distributing the heat

When it comes to choosing what system to use for distributing heat around your home, there are three main categories: radiators, underfloor heating and air conditioning.

▪ Radiators The most common form of heat distribution and, as a result, the cheapest to install are radiators. They are the usual option when adapting an existing radiator-based system – for example, when building an extension. The problem with radiators is that they require relatively high temperatures in isolated places, which necessitates high-energy input and creates an uneven temperature in the room.

▪ Underfloor heating This is rapidly becoming the most popular choice. Costs have reduced dramatically and when starting from scratch, costs are comparable with other systems. The most usual type of underfloor heating for a whole house is a warm-water system, using racks of pipes set out evenly beneath the floor in all rooms. This gives a lovely, even heat and, because the water needs only to reach a relatively low heat, does not require much peak energy.

Generally, electric underfloor systems are more expensive to run, while being easier and cheaper to install. They are used where underfloor heating is wanted in one area only, such as a bathroom or kitchen. New low-voltage systems are now available that have the benefits of ease of installation, combined with low running costs (see opposite).

▪ Air conditioning Heating can also be distributed via air-carried systems. These either heat (or cool) air in a room and blow it around, or bring heated (or cooled) air into rooms via ducts. Such systems are relatively rare in the UK (the requirement for artificial cooling (air-con) is so infrequently needed in this climate), and are often unpopular because of noise issues. The ductwork necessary is large and cumbersome.

Artificial cooling may seem like a good idea on a very hot summer's night, but in practical terms, how often does a home really need to be cooled? Such systems are expensive to install, and use large amounts of energy.

Because underfloor heating is entirely concealed, there are no radiators to clutter up the clean lines of your interior design. The radiator industry has hit back with various ranges of very simple, beautifully designed radiators.

Combining good insulation with renewable energy through solar or heat-pump technology can bring a home near to complete energy self-sufficiency. We should all aim to be as close to carbon-neutral as we can.

Many renewable energy systems are assessed in terms of 'pay-back time' (the time it takes for savings on energy bills to be greater than the installation cost). Also take into account the additional value that such a system might add to your property.

Replacing an inefficient boiler with a new, condensing one will make a huge difference to the SAP calculation of your home's energy efficiency. This can give significant flexibility of design within part L of the building regulations **>see p.199**.

Calculating the energy efficiency of your home, which takes into consideration the amount and effectiveness of the insulation you have, will also help in working out the amount of heating output needed.

Solar-thermal systems

In this example, a semi-detached house in West London has utilised solar-thermal technology on the roof to provide hot water to supplement the heating requirement. This significantly helps to reduce the carbon footprint produced by this property.

Before we started work on this house, we assessed the environmental performance of the property, by calculating the carbon emissions produced from every room. A key criterion was to achieve a minimum target of 60 per cent reduction on carbon emissions produced from the property. One of the main uses of energy in a property is the heating system, so we looked at this first.

Reducing carbon emissions is not just about the use of visible and fashionable systems, such as solar-thermal technology. In fact, much less 'sexy' initiatives – for example, a more efficient boiler and better insulation – can make a great difference to energy efficiency for very little effort. We chose to combine solar panels on the roof with a new condensing boiler, double-glazing and insulation. A great source of information regarding how carbon emissions can be reduced is available through the sustainable energy academy website: www.sustainable-energyacademy.org.uk

The conventional wisdom says that solar-thermal systems only really work when they are mounted on a roof that faces due south. This property has a west-facing roof, so we compensated by increasing the solar panel area by 25 per cent. This has proved that the system works well even when the roof does not face due south.

Solar-thermal panels. *Despite facing west, the solar-thermal panels on the roof, combined with good insulation, double glazing and a new boiler, have dramatically reduced the carbon emissions of this house.*

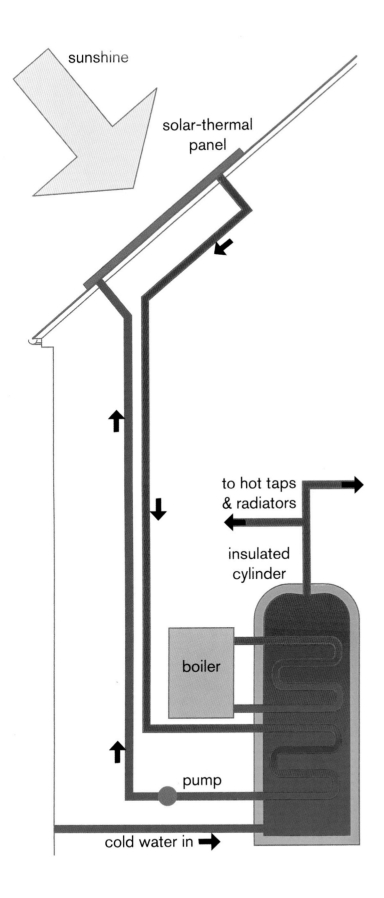

sunshine

solar-thermal
panel

to hot taps
& radiators

insulated
cylinder

boiler

pump

cold water in ➤

◁ *Solar-thermal theory.* Sunshine on
the panels heats up a pumped circuit of
water, which is transferred into the water
in the cylinder. The boiler, therefore, has
less work to do to heat the water in the
cylinder, from where it goes to feed hot
taps and radiators.

Do not be put off the idea of solar-
thermal technology just because your
roof does not face due south. This
project illustrates that it can still be
a very worthwhile exercise.

Solar panels look similar to roof windows,
and a positive mainstream attitude
towards green issues has turned them
into something of a 'badge of honour'.

In excess of 15 million homes in Britain
have the potential to reduce their carbon
emissions by 60 per cent by using a solar
thermal system. The reduction in emissions
across the board would be colossal.

None of the improvements involved in this
project were expensive. Improvements to
your heating system can also save you
money in the medium term.

Part L of the building regulations **>see
p.199** requires significant levels
of energy efficiency for new works,
extensions and conversions. This project
exceeded the minimum requirements.

Architects are increasingly aware of
green issues and renewable energy.
If you are keen to reduce your carbon
emissions, an architect will be able to
suggest various ways of doing this.

Floors

There are many types of **floor** *construction methods to choose from; some are very* **fast** *to construct, some are low* **cost**, *some are* **lightweight,** *and others are extra* **thin**. *Each project will have its own unique* **criteria,** *and the choice of floor should be made accordingly.*

Ground-floor slab

The most common way of building a ground-floor slab is illustrated in the diagram below. A layer of compacted hardcore (rubble), with sand on the top, forms a smooth base (called a 'blinding' layer). A plastic waterproof sheet, known as a DPM (Damp-Proof Membrane) is laid over, followed by a thick layer of rigid insulation, such as polystyrene. The rough concrete slab is laid on top of this, usually with some steel reinforcement mesh to strengthen it, and lastly, a top layer of sand and cement mix (a 'screed') is laid to form a smooth flat top layer. Underfloor heating pipes are commonly cast into this top screed layer.

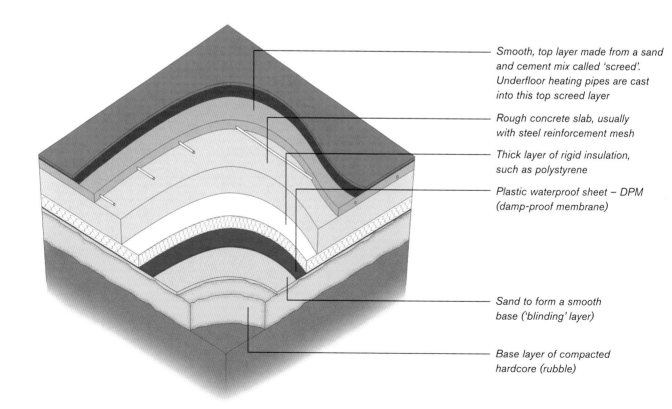

Smooth, top layer made from a sand and cement mix called 'screed'. Underfloor heating pipes are cast into this top screed layer

Rough concrete slab, usually with steel reinforcement mesh

Thick layer of rigid insulation, such as polystyrene

Plastic waterproof sheet – DPM (damp-proof membrane)

Sand to form a smooth base ('blinding' layer)

Base layer of compacted hardcore (rubble)

Timber-joisted floor

The depth (or height) of the timber joists will depend upon their span, but whatever the span, they must carry some form of deck. Traditionally, timber boards are used for the deck, but today interlocking chipboard sheets are common.

Where acoustic insulation is important, there is often a soft, or rubberised, strip laid on top of the joist, so as to avoid any direct transfer of sound to the joists. Services, such as heating pipes and wiring, are run between the joists. If small holes in the joists are drilled in the middle for wires and pipes to pass through, this usually makes no difference to the strength.

Ceilings are formed by screwing plasterboard to the underside of the joists. You can use two layers to further improve acoustic insulation between rooms. Ideally, joists should be set at specific spacings (or 'centres'), so that the joints of the plasterboard fall on the line of a joist.

Beam and block floor

Precast concrete beams shaped like an upside-down 'T' span across from wall to wall, in a similar way to timber joists, but instead of nailing floorboards to the top, concrete blocks are laid between the beams, sitting on the web of the upside-down 'T'.

Unless the spans are very modest, it is usually necessary for a crane to lift the beams into place, which adds considerably to the cost, but the time saved can be significant. As a result, a beam and block floor is a very popular choice for commercial projects, where the economies of scale can afford the crane.

The other advantages are that the concrete beams can span further than timber of the same depth, so it keeps the floor thickness down, and some systems do not even need a screed on top, hence there is no waiting around during the curing process.

Simple things, such as openings for pipes, can cause more headaches than a timber-joisted floor, but the acoustic and fire separation qualities are naturally better.

Poured concrete floor

In many parts of continental Europe, the most common form of floor construction is to use poured concrete.

To form such a floor above a space (as opposed to directly on the ground, as described opposite), a temporary deck of plywood is formed, supported by removable legs or 'props'. Steel reinforcing bars are laid out on the deck to the structural engineer's instructions, and wet concrete is poured over the top, encasing the steel bars. It is then allowed to cure.

Once the concrete is set, a sand and cement screed is usually laid on top to give a smooth finish, but a machine (called a 'power-float') can be used to give a smooth top finish to the floor slab itself, negating the need for a separate screed. Lastly, the temporary props and deck beneath are removed.

The ability of a poured concrete floor slab to span in all directions often provides the thinnest option for a floor. This can be important if you are struggling for maximum ceiling height.

When extending an existing house, it usually makes sense to continue with the original construction method. Changing from timber to concrete floor construction can cause movement between the two.

Concrete floors are often chosen because they are thinner and allow greater ceiling heights, but if voids need to be left for recessed lights, the advantage can be lost.

When the sustainability of timber is set against the high levels of energy needed to produce concrete, you can see a very compelling case for timber floor structures over concrete ones.

A screed layer needs time to dry out and cure, during which no other work can take place in that area. Factor this in, and plan for work to take place in other areas of the building.

Do not forget that work done to a ceiling will affect the floor above. Cutting holes for recessed lights may undermine the way in which the construction creates separate fire zones. Special fire-resistant 'hoods' can solve this problem.

Drawing your project in section (as if cut vertically from top to bottom) is the best way to communicate the arrangement of ceiling heights and floor thicknesses.

Bathroom details

*It is becoming increasingly **popular** to replace a **traditional bathroom** with a wet room. Rather than having a shower tray, there is a drain in the **floor**, but to do this, it is vital that the floor is reliably **waterproof**.*

ⱽ **Oak floor.** People often think that timber is an impractical floor for a bathroom, but as long as it is not going to be regularly soaked, many timbers can work well. The solid oak in this bathroom brings a natural warmth of colour to a clean white room.

ⱽ **Floor and wall tiling for a complete wet room.** This cool shower-room uses two tones of grey porcelain tiles in a large format to create a wet room. The grey tiles set off the white sanitary ware, which sparkles under the halogen lighting.

Simple and sculptural. *The hero of this bathroom is the beautiful freestanding bath. It is allowed to shine because of the simplicity of all the other elements. Note how the large rectangular floor and wall tiles give way to a mosaic version of the same tile in the shower area, and how the glass wall is designed to stand with no visible support.*

While a wet room can look fabulous, the work required to achieve it is far more complex and involved than adding a conventional shower tray.

If a bathroom is fairly small, do not cram too much into it. If there is not enough room for a separate shower and bath, put a shower over the bath. Resist the temptation to go for twin washbasins unless there is plenty of space.

Bathroom windows and orientation are often neglected, but it is worth considering where morning sun will come in. Sunlight on water can be beautiful and gives a naturally uplifting start to your day.

A luxurious shower requires good water pressure and lots of hot water. Be aware that simply purchasing a large showerhead may be the tip of a cost iceberg in creating high-pressure hot water for your bathroom.

Other than special shaver sockets, power points and light switches must not be sited in bathrooms. The best solution is to set the light switch just outside the bathroom door or use a pull-cord switch.

To keep a wet room floor level consistent, it needs to be allowed for at an early stage of the design process. The structural engineer should be made aware of this, as extra layers of construction will be needed.

Bathroom floors

Timber-joisted floors with a chipboard deck will move (or deflect) when weight is put upon them. Beneath a carpet this tends not to be a problem, but under a tiled floor this can lead to cracks in the grout, or tiles themselves.

The best way to stiffen the floor is to apply two layers of plywood, glued together, with any joints staggered and screwed down at close intervals. As with a flat roof, it is also necessary to design a slight slope to direct any water towards the drain. There must also be sufficient depth within the floor for the drainage trap and pipe to flow away to the main drain.

On top of the plywood deck, it is now common practice to lay a waterproof membrane to prevent any water that gets through the tiles from getting into the floor. This membrane is usually dressed up the wall by 150mm (6in), or so, to ensure that, even if the bathroom floods, no water can get through. The stone or tiled finish is then laid on top of the membrane, and the drain cover set in place.

Bathroom simplicity

One of the keys to designing a successful bathroom is to keep things as simple and clean as possible. It is always possible to add visual complexity with your fittings or decoration, but if you leave pipes and fittings exposed, it will invariably look like a mess.

In the bathroom shown opposite, two semi-recessed washbasins and a 'back-to-wall' type WC are mounted on a simple vanity unit that runs the length of the room. This provides good storage and hides the water cistern and all the pipework. The clean lines of the example above is a model of how good detailing can produce a beautifully simple bathroom. Trying for this sort of effect without investing and concentrating on the detail design will inevitably look clunky and disappointing.

Kitchen details

*Kitchens include a **unique** combination of functional, **ergonomic**, durable, stylistic and **technical** requirements, where the quality of the **details** will often be critical to the success and **longevity** of the project.*

Having established the layout of your kitchen at the outline and scheme design stages, now is the time to furnish these layouts with details. A kitchen is where the importance of detail design comes to the fore, as it is, for many people, the most complex combination of functional requirement and stylistic design in the home.

Ergonomics is defined as the science of obtaining a correct match between the human body, work-related tasks and tools. In a kitchen, the need for good ergonomic design is vital, as you can spend a long time standing at a cooker or work surface, and moving between the different parts of the kitchen.

Assuming that the positions of the main areas and elements – siting of the sink and fridge, preparation and cooking – have been established, it is now very important to consider where the necessary storage will best be situated. For example, allow adequate space next to the oven and hob for pans and cooking equipment.

Kitchen surfaces

Worktops, walls and floors are frequently wet. They require durable surfaces without little cracks or crevices where dirt and moisture can build up. The junctions between splashbacks and worktops are particularly important, and the areas around sinks and hobs can deteriorate quickly if the detail design is not appropriate. If you choose timber worktops, make sure that they are shaped to drain surface water away, as they can absorb water over time.

Consider the height of your worktops. The standard height is 900mm (35in) from floor level, but it may be more comfortable to set them at 1000mm (39in), if you are relatively tall. If you are designing a kitchen for yourself, try different heights by placing a board on some books on a table and adjusting until you have the most comfortable height. However, if you are developing a property for sale, you are probably safest sticking to 900mm.

◄ Classic detail. *This generous kitchen is very simply laid out and fabulously equipped. The conventional styling gives a beautifully warm and traditional feel, without compromising the function and ergonomics of the kitchen working space.*

The choice of floor finish in a kitchen is very important, as it will take a great deal of punishment, and need cleaning, more than any other floor in your home. Tiles are more durable and easy to care for than timber.

The beauty of a kitchen is often derived from how well it is designed in terms of function, and the success of the details. There is often a genuine pleasure in cleaning something that wipes down in exactly the way intended.

If the use of natural light to illuminate tasks is well thought through, the saving on artificial lighting could be significant, thus reducing energy requirements.

A well-detailed kitchen, with high-quality, durable fittings and cupboards, will be relatively expensive, but will last a great deal longer than a cheap, flimsy kitchen, which will need to be upgraded or replaced in two or three years.

Ventilation is very important in any kitchen to evacuate smells and steam. Extraction hoods over hobs are a very effective solution. Where possible, choose the type that ducts the extracted air outside, rather than the filter and recycle model.

It is vital to discuss how you like to cook, so that the kitchen can be designed accordingly. For example, extra extraction and high splashbacks are great for regular wok cooking.

⏫ Angled extractor. The design of extractor hoods has developed tremendously in recent years. This steeply angled unit does not crowd the cook's headroom.

⏶ Careful detailing for a tiny kitchen. In this studio apartment storage boxes and shelves are arranged into an elegant composition, the fridge is recessed into an old fireplace, and the hob has been especially made with three cooking rings.

❮ Hob lighting. This suspended extractor not only takes away smells, but also provides task lighting just where it's needed.

❯ Glass breakfast bar. This kitchen island has an elevated glass wraparound bar at a higher level than the worktop. The detailing of the glass included invisible UV bonding, so that the vertical glass supports could be fixed to the glass top, without the need for a frame or connecting bolts.

Kitchen lighting

Consider how daylight will fall over your work areas, and set windowcill heights accordingly. If natural light is coming in from above, make sure that you will not be working in your own shadow. If this is unavoidable, consider using reflective surfaces to bounce light onto the place you are working. Mirrors or glass splashbacks can do this very effectively.

Lights set under wall units can be very effective, but people often forget about lighting over a sink, which is often set beneath a window. After dark, you could be washing up in your own shadow, which is not to be recommended. Directional ceiling-mounted down-lights are often a good solution.

Kitchens also need good general lighting to avoid too much light and shade. Low-energy lighting from a fluorescent source is often the best lighting option.

A poorly lit kitchen is not only impractical, but can also be dangerous. Good lighting is necessary in areas for specific tasks, such as chopping and washing up, and general lighting is needed for cleaning.

Lighting control systems allow you to preset combinations of lights at different levels of brightness to suit particular moods or tasks being undertaken in a variety of circumstances.

Low-energy fluorescent lighting placed in a concealed location, such as behind a pelmet, or beneath wall units, is very effective and attractive for a kitchen.

Light fittings vary tremendously in cost and quality. If you need to keep a tight hold on your budget, place lights in a concealed location, where they do not need to look attractive. This can save a great deal of money.

For safety reasons, there are set minimum distances between kitchen sinks and where power points and light switches may be located.

Keep a record of the exact type and colour code of your lamps (bulbs), so that when one needs to be replaced you can ensure it matches the others in the room.

Lighting design

A whole subject in itself, **lighting** *involves a huge array of different* **options**. *In essence, however, you need to identify the tasks, items or* **spaces** *that need to be* **illuminated**, *and work out what lighting might do the job.*

Too many people are seduced by the design of a light fitting in itself, rather than focusing on the light that it emits. There are so many beautiful light fittings available on the market that this is quite understandable, but the key to good lighting design is to estimate the required luminance and work back from there.

An important thing to remember when designing a lighting scheme is that we mainly experience lighting in the way it bounces off surfaces. It will bounce brightly off shiny and light surfaces, and will be absorbed by soft and dark surfaces. Pointing large numbers of down-lights onto a dark carpet will create very little luminance, whereas shining lights across a pale wall surface will spread light throughout a room. The most common types of light source used in homes are listed below.

Incandescent lighting

Light bulbs (40w or 60w) provide the most usual type of incandescent light source. They run off mains power, are cheap to produce, and give a strong, warm light. The lamps themselves (the technical name for a light bulb is a 'lamp', whereas the technical name for what most people would call a lamp is a 'light fitting') are quite large, so while these are well suited to pendant fittings, they look very bulky when recessed into a ceiling.

Low-voltage halogen. *These recessed, halogen down-lights are very popular, because they are small in size, but produce a beautiful lighting effect. In this kitchen their light reflects off the wall surface to illuminate the work surface.*

Incandescent globes. *This cluster of acrylic globes hanging from a single ceiling rose are funky and fun. Each globe has one incandescent lamp (bulb) inside, which can be changed for a compact fluorescent to be more energy efficient.*

Low-voltage halogen

These low-voltage lights are much smaller than incandescent lamps, and are used in recessed ceiling down-lights. They have a lovely twinkle, and give a beautiful warm light. Typically, they run off a 12v power supply, so need a transformer to convert the 240v given by the mains. However, do not be confused by the idea that low-voltage lighting is low energy – this is by no means the case, as these lights create a lot of wasted heat and use a great deal of power.

Fluorescent tubes

These tubes were given a very bad name by flickering overhead strip lighting (often experienced in schools), but there is no doubt that technology has moved on. Fluorescent tubes can be used very effectively, especially when concealed (behind a pelmet, for example, or beneath a kitchen wall cabinet), and give a very even, almost bland light. Tubes are available in different shades of white, from a very warm yellow to a cold white light. Fluorescent tubes are much more energy efficient than halogen or incandescent alternatives.

Compact fluorescent

Often referred to as low-energy lights, the compact fluorescent light not only produces much more light per unit of power, it also has a much longer lifespan than halogen or incandescent lamps, which further enhances its environmental credentials. Again, these lights tend to give a rather bland character of luminance, but can work well when blended with a halogen source. There are some light fittings that combine compact fluorescent and halogen lamps in one fitting.

LED (Light-emitting diodes)

We seem to have been told for the last decade that LED technology is the future, but still we wait for this very promising theory to replace halogen lighting effectively. LEDs are cold to the touch, long lasting and use tiny amounts of power. The problem is that they are still very expensive, and you need lots and lots of them to produce any satisfactory amounts of luminance. Hopefully, by the time this book is published, a wonderful new type of LED will have hit the market and revolutionised lighting design.

When designing the position of light fittings (above staircases, for example), always consider how easy (and safe) it will be for someone to get to that position to change the lamp when necessary.

Sometimes the most beautiful effects can be achieved by blending the light from different sources. For example, combining fluorescent for general luminance and halogen for highlights.

While it is important to try to reduce energy usage by choosing low-energy lighting, the most effective way to control energy use is to ensure that lights are turned off when rooms are not in use. There are automatic systems that can assist in this.

Low-energy lighting is generally still more expensive to buy than incandescent or halogen, but this cost should be balanced against the lower running costs and frequency that lamps need to be replaced.

Building regulations require that one-third of all the light fittings in any new project are low-energy. However, some people are getting around the rule by simply adding low-energy lighting that they have no intention of turning on.

Industry terminology can be confusing, and can lead to misunderstandings, if not explained. 'Lamps' are what most people call 'light bulbs', and 'light fittings' are what most people call 'lamps'.

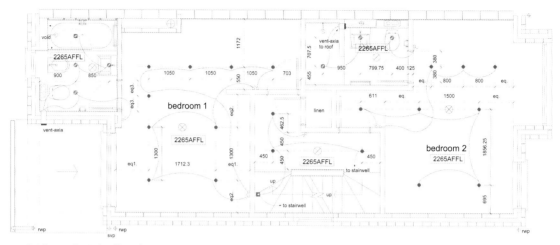

1st floor reflected ceiling plan

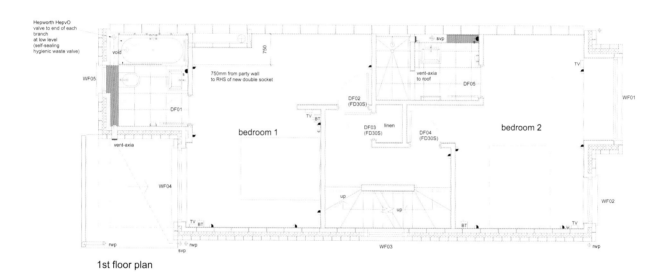

1st floor plan

Lighting layouts

Once you have decided upon your lighting design, it will need to be communicated to the builders and electricians who are going to install it. The most effective way to do this is with a lighting layout plan.

Since most lighting is mounted in the ceiling, it is usual to prepare a 'reflected ceiling plan' (RCP) for each level of the building. This is shown as a normal 'floor' plan, but as if the ceiling and everything contained in it is reflected down onto the floor. The example illustrated here shows the first floor plan of a house, with a RCP of the same first floor above it. Light fittings are shown in position, and there are curved lines that indicate which lights are activated by each switch. This can be done with codes if the lines make the drawing too complicated to read clearly.

⋀ Floor plan and reflected ceiling plan.
These plans correspond – the lower is a floor plan that shows layout and the upper is the reflected ceiling plan (RCP) that shows the positions and switching of lighting and other equipment. The key (opposite) identifies the symbols used on the drawing.

KEY:

MK Ceiling Mounted lamp holder (1174 WHI)
with standard 60W bayonet light bulb
with pull switch

Pendant light from ceiling rose t.b.c.

DeltaLight 'Compac 226 SBL A' ref. 202 45 06 SBL A
2 x TC-D 26W

DeltaLight 'Kubic HP ALU' ref. 271 41 80 ALU
1 x QT14 75W lamp **with triangular plate to top & bottom**

DeltaLight 'Luxor S1' ref. 202 11 14
1 x QR-CBC51 50W lamp
with Tube RB 202 02 08 B Baffle (all dimmable)

DeltaLight 'Artuur 180 A' ref. 202 25 10 A
1 x QR-CBC51 50W lamp

DeltaLight 'Artuur 180 A' ref. 202 25 10 A
1 x QR-CBC51 50W lamp
with IP54 Clear Glass cover over baths / showers

DeltaLight 'Genie 90 S SBL ANO' ref. 213 12 05 ANO
1 x QR-CBC51 20W lamp
IP65 rated

DeltaLight 'Dox 2 Down-Up T A' ref. 219 51 51 A
2 x QR-CBC51 (50W lamps to rear courtyards
35W lamps to front entrance porches)
IP65 rated

900mm Fluorescent batten

Vent-Axia Solo Selv 12T extractor fan with airflow shutter and washable filter.
Mains transformer with 12V SELV output with presettable overrun timer (5-25mins.)
Units to be semi-recessed and wall mounted at high level as indicated
(T: 01293 - 441 605)

double dimmer switch

single dimmer switch

electrical single socket
shaver socket to bathrooms

electrical single socket outlet

electrical double socket outlet

BT   double telecom socket

Smoke detector
(7.5m radius of detection).

Gas supply to fireplace
to current regulations

DS02   Denotes half hour fire doors
(FD30S)   with intumescent smoke seals
          and integral Perkomatic self-closers

TV   TV aerial socket

RJ45 Double Data Socket.
Cat 5 cables to all data points
to be terminated in position t.b.c.

Speaker socket for future
home cinema system
to ground floor lounge only

NOTE: Positioning of all switches and sockets to comply
        with Part M of the current Building Regulations
- All sockets (TV;BT; plug sockets etc.) mounted 450mm AFFL to underside
- All switches (light; doorbells; entry phone etc.) mounted 1200mm AFFL to top
- All lights switches to be dimmable
- All switches & socket fittings in s/s

If your lighting and power schemes
are complex and the drawing gets too
complicated, separate the two issues and
produce one RCP to show lighting and a
separate plan to show power points.

If you want recessed lights to be arranged
in lines, perhaps down the centre of a
corridor, check the positions of joists first,
as they may restrict your choices.

Movement sensors, developed for security
alarm systems, can be used to activate
and deactivate lights, so that unoccupied
rooms do not waste energy. Remember to
combine this with a timer.

It is easy to increase costs by adding more
lights and power points. The cost of each
is much more than just the cost of the
equipment; remember the labour costs.

Smoke detectors and fire alarm
equipment may be required to meet the
building regulations. Include these on the
electrical layout plan.

Using symbols on your drawings with a
clear key to explain what those symbols
represent is a very important way of
communicating what you want where.

Where to put everything

Power, telephone and TV points, and lots of other items, can also be indicated on a
RCP. The symbol key is absolutely vital, so that there is no confusion. As you can
see, the drawing identifies and positions each item. Take time to think about where
you want to place electrical equipment, so the sockets are put in the correct places.

With the advance of in-house automation and new technologies coming into play, these
plans become more and more complex. Do not bury your head in the sand. Sorting
out the complexities at this stage will ensure that all the right services are included
within floors and walls, rather than having to run ugly cables on the surface later.

Stairs

In design terms, **stairs** *are a wonderful* **opportunity**. *Staircases need to meet some* **obvious** *and essential* **functional** *requirements, and yet there are many types to help you achieve this, both in* **form and style**.

Stairs need to meet a range of detailed regulations, but they can still be sculptural and beautiful items. By definition, stairs span up from one floor to another, and this means finding space that is twice as high as the room in which to site them. Visually and aesthetically, double-height space is an exciting design opportunity.

Basic staircase

In their most basic form, staircases are very simple structures. A straight staircase can simply be made from two parallel beams (called stringers) that span diagonally from the lower floor to the upper floor. The treads (the part you stand on) and the risers (the vertical part between one tread and another) are fixed between the two stringers. Straight staircases are usually made from softwood and can be bought cheaply from builders' merchants. A staircase is often set against a wall, with one stringer supported directly on the wall.

⌃ Staircase with glass guarding. This staircase shows a lovely combination of materials, with an oak open string, natural carpet on the treads and risers and glass protection to the open side with a stainless steel handrail. The protection to the open side is technically known as a 'guarding' (as it guards against you falling off), although many people refer to this as a 'balustrade'. In fact, a true 'balustrade' is made up of separate banisters.

‹ Staircase arrangements. Here are some of the many possible arrangements for a staircase that needs 15 risers. As they demonstrate, by using combinations of straight treads, winding treads and half-landings, a staircase can be arranged in numerous ways to fit into whatever space is available and to depart and arrive in different positions on each floor.

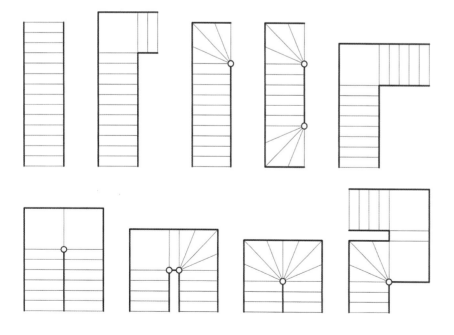

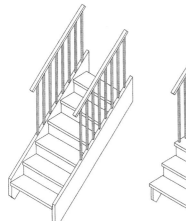  

Closed string, closed-tread.   **Open string, closed-tread.**   **Open string, open-tread.**

Staircases can also be made from materials other than timber (or combinations of materials); common choices include concrete, steel and glass (the design of which can get very complex).

Spiral staircase

A staircase made up entirely of winders is known as a spiral staircase (although some people like to point out, rather pedantically, that they are in fact helical rather than spiral). People often think of spiral staircases as being a space-saving solution. In fact, they take up a similar amount of space, because what they gain in length, they lose in width. Spiral treads are usually supported by a central column, and either span to a helical stringer around the outside, or cantilever out radially from the central column. They are often beautiful and sculptural in their own right.

Open-tread staircase

One way to make a staircase look and feel lighter is to omit the risers to make an open-tread staircase. To meet building regulations, stairs should not include any open space of 100mm (4in) or more through which a small child could fall. This means that the truly open-tread staircases that were so popular in the 1960s are not allowed now. There are various ways to close the gap with the addition of an intermediate bar or frame (as the diagram above right shows); this gives the sense of an open-tread staircase, and yet meets the regulations.

Part K of the building regulations ➤ see also **The building regulations** p.198 sets out the necessary standards for many details, including the pitch angle (steepness) of a staircase, and the maximum and minimum depth and height of treads and risers. The government's approved document for part K is very clear and sets out what is, and is not acceptable under the building regulations.

Handrails and guardings

While handrails and guardings (see note opposite) are very important factors in the look of a staircase, they are primarily there for safety, and there are specific building regulations outlining what is required. Any design that you choose has to be strong enough to cope with falls and accidents.

In most houses guardings are made of banisters, but you can use a host of alternative materials, including glass, wires, mesh or extended wall planes.

Regulations preclude very steep staircases, but even the allowed maximum angles can be challenging for an elderly person, or someone with reduced mobility. Part M of the regulations sets out standards for 'ambulant disabled' access staircases.

There are so many components to a staircase that it is generally a good idea to keep the design of the details as simple as possible.

In many cases it is possible to reuse and modify an existing staircase. Timber staircases can be turned around, cut in half, extended or modified in all sorts of ways.

An 'off-the-peg' staircase from a builders' merchant can be a very cheap solution, but if you have a space that requires a specific pitch angle, you may need one to be custom-made.

No part of a guarding should be 'climbable'. This precludes the modernist favourite: 'ocean-liner' style guardings, which had horizontal bars beneath and parallel to a handrail.

It is vital that the height of all the risers on a flight of stairs is the same. Unless you are absolutely sure of the floor-to-floor dimension, simply indicate on your drawing that the risers must be equal.

Staircase design

Staircases come in many and various forms, and are made from a host of different materials, using different structural compositions. Here are three contrasting examples of staircases designed by Architect Your Home architects.

1. Staircase suspended with multiple steel wires

This staircase replaced a very steep staircase that went in the opposite direction. By forming a solid half-landing three steps up, the rest of the stair had a more acceptable pitch angle. Another image of this staircase can be found on page 38.

The idea was to allow as much light as possible to pass sideways from the well-lit, south-facing front room to the gloomy dining room. To do this we chose not to use stringers, and used 74 stainless steel tension wires to support the treads. These were fixed, with regular spacing, into a steel beam above the ceiling and connected to the treads below. The wires provide support for the weight of the stair, but also form a guarding to each side. A steel framework was designed to hold the treads together, so that they would not move independently or swing sideways. The openings are just less than the 100mm (4in) maximum. A series of tiny fixings under each tread allowed fine-tuning of the tension of each wire.

∧ *1. Suspended on steel wires. A solid half-landing allows stairs to be less steep and the steps up are almost invisibly held.*

∨ *2. Part straight, part spiral. This dramatic, twisting staircase is an essay in oak and mild steel.*

∧ 3. Bottom half of timber staircase... *As it emerges around the corner of the white wall, this staircase changes from a closed to an open stringer, exposing the zigzag profile of the treads and risers. The glass guarding extends down from above, with the handrail simply supported on the wall side.*

∧ ...and top with glass. *Above the level of the upper floor the glass, held with fixings that are almost entirely concealed within the thickness of the floor, cantilevers upwards.*

The design of the oak and steel staircase was planned around where the ideal place to leave the lower floor would be, and where the ideal place to arrive at the upper floor would be.

The design of the wire-suspended staircase was developed to appear as lightweight as possible. It allows the maximum amount of daylight to pass through the space.

Oak is strong, with a beautiful grain structure and a lovely golden tone. It is a very sustainable material as it is grown in huge, well-managed forests in North America and Europe.

2. Part straight, part spiral stair in oak and steel

This staircase was designed to sit within a double-height space, connecting two living areas. One of the key design criteria for the project was to bring lots of drama and daylight to the lower level, so the staircase needed to look right in the space, and not block the daylight.

The part spiral, part straight arrangement of treads was set out so that the top and bottom of the stair arrived in just the right place for each level. Getting the angles and curves exactly right, so that all the regulations were met, took a great deal of time and had to be drawn in precise detail. The structure of the stair, including a twisting stringer and balustrade, was formed in mild steel. This is strong, relatively easy to fabricate and inexpensive, but can look very hard and cold. Combining mild steel with the oak treads and handrails softened and warmed the appearance.

Home owners need to understand that cantilevered glass guardings look simple, but the complexity required to achieve this visual simplicity is often considerable, and this can mean expense.

3. Timber staircase with cantilevered glass

Built against a sidewall, this staircase is quite complicated, because from the top it descends between two solid planes, then opens out to expose the zigzag of the treads, and turns at the bottom. At the top, the stairs are held on both sides by closed stringers. These are concealed behind the wall finish. We used an open-stringer for the lower section, which terminated before the turn at the bottom.

The glass guardings are cantilevered around the opening at the upper level. They continue down as one plane to provide the side guarding at the lower level. While the effect is very simple, the amount of detailed design needed to get all of the necessary support into the walls and the floor edge was considerable.

Many magazines publish images of staircases in properties from countries where regulations are different. Just because you have seen a picture in a magazine, don't assume that you will be allowed to do the same.

Cantilevered glass guardings look simple, but because they are held only at the bottom, they need a lot of very precise, and expensive, design and engineering to retain that clean, simple look.

Joinery

Timber *is used extensively inside our homes. Where it is part of the main construction it is called* **carpentry**, *but finished works such as* **doorframes** *and skirting boards are classified as* **joinery.**

Architraves and skirtings

Today, many people want to avoid the use of architraves, skirtings and other details as far as possible, to maintain a clean, simple look. In the past, these devices were used to conceal difficult building junctions and to hide imperfections. There are now more modern solutions.

When deciding whether to include architraves and other finishes, consider where they appear in other rooms. Do you need to create a continuous look, or does the room stand alone from the rest of the property? Also be very mindful of the risk of not including architraves and skirting: as plaster settles, will it reveal unsightly cracks?

It is important to recognise that in a tall, elegant room, the thicknesses and heights of these features were calculated following classical proportioning systems. This becomes most apparent when a room that does not have elegant proportions has inappropriate or disproportionate mouldings (such as skirtings, cornices and dado rails) applied – the effect is difficult to pin down; it just feels wrong.

Architraves

Internal doors and door linings are almost always made from timber. While timber is flexible and can swell or shrink depending upon humidity, plaster is inert, inflexible and will crack if subjected to movement. Where the two materials meet – a timber doorframe and a plastered wall – the differential movement between the two will inevitably cause cracking. Architraves are simply cover strips used to conceal the joint and any cracks. They can be very decorative; in classical houses in particular, the architrave should always be in proportion to the doorway, and the doorway to the room itself.

One way to get a clean architrave detail is to use an extra wide doorlining that projects 20mm (¾in) or so wider than the wall (see right). The plasterboard can be trimmed accurately and butted into the side of the lining, so that the potential place for cracking is an internal corner, which a flexible jointing filler can cope with.

Skirtings

Devised to cover the difficult junction between plastered walls and floors, skirting boards also developed as part of a well-proportioned wall elevation. Builders often like using skirting boards, because then the plastering work does not have to be neatly finished right down to the bottom of the wall.

⋀ *Traditional decorative architrave.*
This architrave is simply a piece of moulded softwood, which is used to cover the joint between plaster wall and timber doorlining.

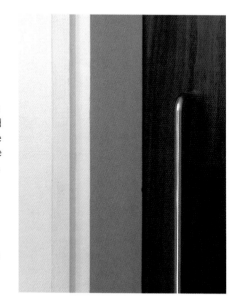

⋀ *Extra-wide doorlining.* *Here, the doorlining has been made wider than the thickness of the wall, and the plasterboard cut neatly to butt into it. Flexible jointing filler can cope with the internal corner.*

⋀ Moulded softwood skirting. *Skirting boards protect the base of a wall, and neatly hide the joint of wall and floor finish.*

⋀ Flush skirting with shadow gap. *For clean lines and a protective band, a flush skirting is a neat solution.*

Contemporary-style houses often look good without any skirting boards, but in any home where there is likely to be normal wear-and-tear, you do need to consider how to protect the wall from marks and damage. Skirting boards protect the base of a wall from the knocks of furniture legs and vacuum cleaners. Traditionally, skirting boards were formed in plaster or timber, although MDF is also common these days.

One design for a contemporary detail is to create skirting boards that are completely flush with the surface of the wall. Use two sheets of plasterboard, with the outer one stopping short of the floor, and finished with a corner bead. The skirting is then fixed on, flush with the wall surface, leaving a small shadow gap. Such a detail would be tricky where an existing wall finish is to be retained. Overboarding with new plasterboard would give the best result, but would be costly and make the room slightly smaller.

Picture and dado rails

Traditionally, both rails performed a useful function and contributed to the internal proportions of a classical room. Picture rails, as their name suggests, are shaped to be able to carry hooks from which pictures may be hung. They are set high on a wall and form a horizontal band, interrupted only by windows that may cut across their line. Dado rails are, essentially, crash protection for walls. Set at approximately table height, they will take the impact if furniture is bumped against the wall.

Cornices

Often mistakenly referred to as 'coving', cornices are possibly the grandest of the traditional, classical bands that would run around a room. Designed to cover the junction between ceiling and wall, cornices developed into very complex decorative elements in classical rooms.

Most commonly, cornices would have been cast in plaster, fixed up in lengths, and the joints filled with plaster. Many beautiful plaster cornices have been painted so many times that the detail becomes obscured. Stripping cornices back with a professional steam-stripping process can restore their grandeur. If sections are damaged and need replacing, it is quite possible (although expensive) to have a cast of your cornice made on site, and new plaster sections made to match.

If you choose not to include protective features such as skirting boards, factor in that you may need to redecorate more frequently.

Do not try to add picture and dado rails to walls in a room that does not have a high ceiling. This will only emphasise the lack of height.

Cornices and ceiling roses formed in polystyrene can be bought very cheaply, but these should be avoided. They damage easily, and will not biodegrade once discarded.

There is a misconception that simple, modern-style interiors are cheaper to build than ornate, classical styles. In fact, most ornamental details were designed as practical devices to save time.

In listed buildings, the arrangement of skirting boards, architraves and cornices is often highly prized by conservation officers. Make sure that you seek Listed Building Consent for any alterations.

When having specific decorative mouldings made to match those in an old house, it is often necessary to draw the exact shape in section at full scale, so that a special cutting tool can be made.

Carpentry and joinery

On a building project, working with timber falls into three categories: carpentry, joinery and cabinet-making.

Carpentry involves what is often known as 'first fix'. This includes building the structural framework, joists, rafters, timber studwork, forming openings for doorways, and laying battens for fixing wall linings or flooring.

Joinery produces the built-in timberwork that you will touch and see, including what is known as the 'second fix' items. This includes timber windows, doors, staircases and steps, banisters, handrails, built-in wardrobes, skirting boards and windowcills. Generally, these items are partially manufactured off site with significant work on site to cut, shape and fit.

Cabinet-makers produce finely manufactured timber items including furniture and kitchen units, and are workshop-based, although they will often come to site to fit their work, if necessary.

Of course, there are overlaps between the trades, and these definitions are fairly generalised. An on-site carpenter, for example, will be more than happy doing second fix skirting boards, joists and rafters. A joinery workshop that usually makes window frames may revel in the opportunity to make a specialist piece.

⌃ Internal glazed screen. *This living/dining space is separated from the kitchen by a glazed screen. The American white oak frame was made off site in a workshop, and incorporates a sliding door to the right-hand side.*

‹›Built in wardrobes. *These drawings illustrate the detail design of built-in wardrobes made with walnut-veneered MDF. Notice the dimensions shown on the drawing, and the handle and hanging rail specification. The level of detail you include at this stage depends on just how much control you want. If you want a wardrobe door to open in a particular way, then you will need a drawing that illustrates that level of detail. If, on the other hand, you simply say that you want hinged doors, the drawings will be quicker (and cheaper) to produce, and a joiner will work such specifics out to his own design.*

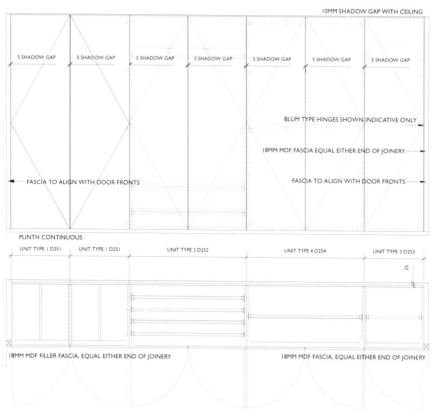

10MM SHADOW GAP WITH CEILING

5 SHADOW GAP · 5 SHADOW GAP · 5 SHADOW GAP · 5 SHADOW GAP · 5 SHADOW GAP · 5 SHADOW GAP · 5 SHADOW GAP

BLUM TYPE HINGES SHOWN INDICATIVE ONLY

18MM MDF FASCIA EQUAL EITHER END OF JOINERY

FASCIA TO ALIGN WITH DOOR FRONTS

FASCIA TO ALIGN WITH DOOR FRONTS

PLINTH CONTINUOUS

UNIT TYPE 1 D251 · UNIT TYPE 1 D251 · UNIT TYPE 2 D252 · UNIT TYPE 4 D254 · UNIT TYPE 3 D253

18MM MDF FILLER FASCIA, EQUAL EITHER END OF JOINERY

18MM MDF FASCIA, EQUAL EITHER END OF JOINERY

- ALL CUT EDGES TO BE SANDED TO SMOOTH FINISH TO REMOVE CUT MARKS
- ALL DOORS TO BE WHITE SPRAY FINISHED OFF SITE.
- ALL VISABLE JOINERY I.E. SHELVES, ENDPANELS, AND COVER PANELS TO BE CUT FROM MDF PRE-SPRAYED WHITE OFF-SITE.
- ALL FRONT EDGES TO BE PRE-SPRAYED, ALLCUTS TO REAR.
- FOR INTERNAL/LESS VISIBLE JOINERY I.E CUPBOARD CARCASSES, PAINT FINISH ON-SITE

Since joinery is so apparent in most properties, the detailed design of the joinery is very important. Whether you ask your architect to produce detailed design drawings, or you work out what you want with your builder or joiner on site, consider the following points.

Note the precise dimensions and aesthetic proportions of what you want. Will new items look right in the room, and will they all work together? Remember to think about ergonomics (for example, can you reach the shelves?).

The materials and finishes involved need to be considered. Joinery items that will be painted can be made from softwood, such as spruce, and any imperfections filled before painting. If you want to see the timber grain, choose a more attractive timber, such as oak. The joints will need to be carefully produced, as they will be visible through the varnish or lacquer. Consider any practical issues – for instance, what sheet size or length the chosen material is available in.

Bear in mind practicality. Do you need to allow space for pipe work (for example, in a bathroom cupboard) or cables (for an office desk)? You may be planning a stone surface: does the joiner need to build a base for it?

What drawers, doors or handles are you going to use? Hinges, catches, runners and sliding mechanisms need to be chosen, as they will have an impact on the design of any joinery. For example, different types of hinge allow a cupboard door to sit, either within, or in front of, the cupboard carcass.

Choose practical finishes for your joinery. Items that will be regularly handled, such as cupboard doors, need a very durable finish to avoid them getting grubby over time.

For best results have as much joinery made (and painted or sprayed) off site as possible, with only the fitting needing to be done in situ. The controlled conditions of a workshop will generally be more conducive to producing high-quality finishes.

Where joinery is exposed to the elements, such as external windowcills, you may be advised to use a hardwood. Be careful to choose a sustainable timber that has not been taken from a tropical rainforest.

Joinery that is to be painted is quicker and cheaper to make than joinery where the grain is to be exposed. Imperfections can be filled and sanded before painting, so less care (and time) needs to be taken during manufacture.

Where fire-rated internal doors are required, remember to include smoke seals around the edge. Do not recess handles into the doors as this could undermine the fire rating.

The level of detail that joinery drawings go into can get very pedantic and involved. Ensure that you have the appropriate level of detail for your requirements. Balance the desire for control against the cost of producing the drawings.

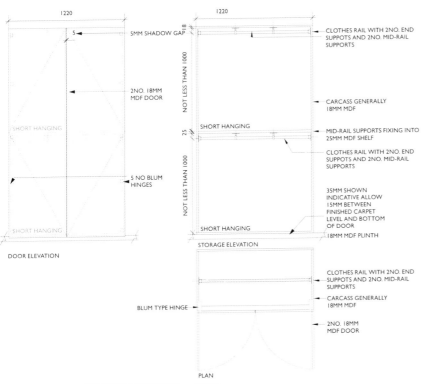

DOOR ELEVATION

STORAGE ELEVATION

PLAN

NOTES
FITTING SHOWN INDICATIVE ONLY. TO BE INSTALLED TO MANUFACTURERS GUIDELINES.
DRAWINGS ANRE INDICATIVE ONLY. DO NOT SCALE

FINISHING
- ALL CUT EDGES TO BE SANDED TO SMOOTH FINISH TO REMOVE CUT MARKS
- ALL DOORS TO BE WHITE SPRAY FINISHED OFF SITE.
- ALL VISABLE JOINERY I.E. SHELVES, ENDPANELS, AND COVER PANELS TO BE CUT FROM MDF PRE-SPRAYED WHITE OFF-SITE.
- ALL FRONT EDGES TO BE PRE-SPRAYED, ALLCUTS TO REAR.
- FOR INTERNAL/LESS VISIBLE JOINERY I.E CUPBOARD CARCASSES. PAINT FINISH ON-SITE

QUANT	CAT NO.	DESCRIPTION
10	322.11.530	BLUM TYPE HINGES. 5 PER DOOR
10	322.85.750	HINGE MOUNTING PLATE
2		HANDLES TBC
1	801.11.741	25MM NICKEL PLATED RAIL.
10	803.51.757	NICKEL PLATED RAIL END SUPPORTS
2	805.02.250	RAIL CENTRE SUPPORT
4	322.67.190	SOFT CLOSE

Creating storage solutions in joinery

This relatively small project to refurbish three rooms in a house included joinery as a significant part of the work.

The bedroom required new built-in wardrobes, a built-in unit in the bay window for drawers, and small recessed shelves in the wall above the headboard. The wardrobes were designed to maximise hanging space – there was enough height to include double-decker hanging rails. The unit in the window was manufactured in cherry wood to match the bed frame, which the customer already had. The stone top was designed to go into each window recess so as to maximise the feeling of generosity.

In the living/dining room downstairs, the two areas required different units to suit each situation. In the dining area, full-height cupboards, with minimal-style doors, were designed to conceal the old chimney breast and form a new clean wall plane, while providing plenty of storage for crockery and other items.

In the living area, a low unit, with doors and a stone top, was designed to be multi-functional. The storage beneath is a great place to hide DVD players and other equipment, and a cable hole allows just the TV to sit on the stone top. The top, however, doubles as additional seating when the sofas are not enough, and the stone also acts as a hearth beneath the new gas fire.

︽ **Dining room.** *In the dining area, we built full-height cupboards to conceal the old chimney breast, and to provide storage for crockery and other items.*

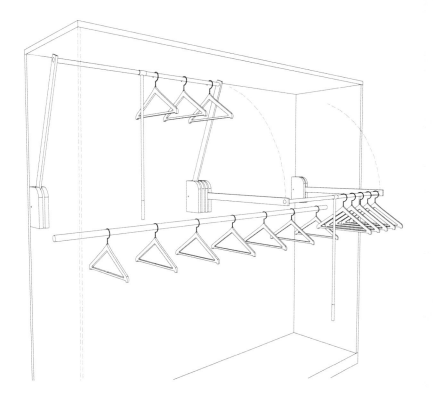

◁ High-level hanging rails.
*The hanging rails used for the wardrobes
in this project, cleverly allow garments
to be hung at the top of tall wardrobes.
They are accessed by being pulled down
to a reachable level.*

Pull-down hanging rails are a wonderful
way to provide practical and easy access
to high-level storage spaces. Very often
the top of tall wardrobes are only for
seldom used items, as they are so
difficult to reach.

Taking the stone top of the bedroom unit
right into the window recesses was
difficult and required a considerable
amount of work, but the simple luxurious
effect was deemed well worth the effort.

Reusing existing building fabric can be
much more environmentally responsible
than replacing with new. The floorboards
in this living/dining room have been
salvaged, sanded and sealed to provide a
warm, softening effect.

All of the joinery units were manufactured
in a workshop and brought to site for
installation. The stone was cut off site from
a template, and handles and fittings were
fitted last of all. The on-site time required
for joinery was kept to a minimum.

The gas fire used in this project is
'flueless', which avoided a great deal of
cost in opening up a redundant chimney.
There are, however, important regulations
relating to the ventilation of the room to
avoid carbon monoxide build-up.

⋀ Bedroom unit. *The six-drawer unit in the bedroom bay window was manufactured in
cherry wood to match an existing bed frame. A stone top was designed to spread into each
window recess to give a more complete appearance.*

◁ Living room. *This room required storage and occasional seating. We built a low unit to
hide TV equipment, and a stone top for the TV, additional seating and fireplace.*

Good detailed drawings, combined with
templates cut on site, meant that all of
the joinery on this project could be made
in a workshop off site. Generally, a better
finish is possible this way.

The building regulations

Understandably, many people get confused between planning permission and the building regulations. Both are statutory requirements, both are approvals that generally need to be gained before building work can start, and both are (usually) administered by the local authority. Nonetheless, it is vital to understand that they are completely separate.

Planning permission ➤see also **Planning permissions** pp.104–19 is all about the use of a building, and the effect it has on its environment. This includes its visual impact, occupancy, the relationship to other buildings and the space around it, traffic use, privacy, trees and green space.

The building regulations are based on the notion that buildings have to be built to minimum quality standards. The first incarnation of building regulations was introduced after the Great Plague of 1665 and the Great Fire of London that followed it, in 1666. It was determined that buildings should be built to minimum standards of fire safety and hygiene to prevent such catastrophes happening again.

Their scope has extended from just fire safety and hygiene to include both public and private health and safety in and around buildings, disabled access, pollution and noise control, ventilation, energy conservation and more.

What are you allowed to do?

If the building regulations had to set out exact requirements for every type of construction and every eventuality, they would be impossibly large and complex. The requirements are, in fact, cleverly made clear, as they set standards, then give examples of how those standards can be met. You do not have to follow their examples, but if you deviate from them, you may be required to demonstrate that you have achieved at least the same minimum standard as if you had. Sometimes this can mean expensive testing to prove your point, although, in the main part, a reasonable assessment can be agreed.

In England and Wales the building regulations are broken down into 14 parts, each of which has an 'Approved Document' that sets out example details and diagrams, which explain minimum compliance. In Northern Ireland there is a slightly different system, and in Scotland there is the 'Building Warrant' system, which sets out seven sections and three appendices. Speaking in broad terms, however, the systems are the same.

Here follows a brief list of each of the 14 sections of the building regulations for England and Wales. This is not intended to be a comprehensive summary of all the areas covered, but rather a list with some notes as to the subjects that seem to occur frequently. I have paid more attention to parts A, B, L and M, as these are the ones that, more than any others, tend to need special attention in the design stages of home owner projects.

A lecturer at college once explained that the Approved Documents were arranged in the order of the speed with which failure to comply might kill you! The regulations start with structure, because if a building falls on you it will be quick, followed by fire, then through various levels of hygiene, through to fuel conservation and disabled access.

Approved Documents

A: Structure

It is a cornerstone of the regulations that the structure of buildings should be sound, safe and suitable for their purpose. Even if you have no need for the full plans application ➤ see also **Building regulations approval** pp.200–1, you will have to provide a set of written calculations to prove that the structural proposals have been worked out correctly. I always recommend that a fully qualified structural engineer be engaged to provide these calculations, even if the job is relatively simple.

B: Fire safety

This part of the building regulations was set out to prevent buildings from spreading fires from one house to the next. One of the areas that often trips people up is the part relating to the 'means of escape in case of fire'.

The regulations require that any habitable room, with a floor more than 4.5m (15sq ft) above ground level (second floor and above, generally), must have a direct protected route to the exit (usually the front door) without passing through any other habitable rooms. A 'habitable room' includes a bedroom or living room, whereas a storage area or bathroom is not counted. If you plan to convert your loft, and you have an open-plan ground floor leading to the front door, you may find that you need to think again. There are ways to solve this situation, such as installing a sprinkler system or an automatic fire shutter, but it is usually better to design around a problem than to have to solve one.

C: Site preparation – Resistance to contaminants and moisture

This section rarely causes problems for home owner projects, but comes under close scrutiny with basement projects. There are several very different ways of going about the tanking and waterproofing of a basement, and different specialists can often give conflicting advice. I would always suggest consultation with your building inspector about your proposed tanking method at an early stage.

D: Toxic substances

This section covers a whole range of items but asbestos tends to be the headline issue. People have become paranoid about asbestos. It is vital that dealing with it and disposing of it is taken seriously, but there are companies who will take advantage of the paranoia and turn a minor removal procedure into an elaborate, costly affair.

E: Resistance to the passage of sound

This section can become a major issue for new-build flats, terraced and semi-detached houses, and for conversions of buildings where two or more dwellings are created. The regulations now require that the building should be sound tested on completion to prove compliance. This often encourages people to overdo the sound insulation, just in case.

Most of the requirements of the building regulations are common sense and good building practice. Attempts to swerve the rules usually backfire or leave you vulnerable to danger.

Note that part K states that guardings and balustrades should not be climbable. The horizontal bars, used extensively in the 1920s and 1930s, would not be deemed safe today.

Part L of the regulations covers the installation of boilers. It now sets a higher minimum standard of efficiency, thus helping to reduce carbon emissions.

People often complain about the cost of meeting the standards set by the building regulations, but many of the standards help to save the home owner money in the long run.

You do not have to apply for approval for the replacement of a roof covering, as long as the new covering is the same type as the one it replaces. Similarly, most like-for-like repairs do not need approval.

The approved documents illustrate some means of achieving the necessary standard. While it is usually easier to follow these approved methods, you are free to use any system you choose, so long as you can demonstrate that you will meet the standard.

F: Ventilation

Habitable rooms, such as bedrooms, need a slot in the windowframe to allow trickle ventilation. Bathrooms, shower-rooms and WCs that do not have a window must have suitable mechanical ventilation that extracts air at a minimum number of litres per second and achieves a certain number of air changes per hour.

Construction also needs ventilation, with spaces being required between layers of roofs, to prevent the build-up of condensation, and below raised floors to keep damp at bay.

G: Hygiene

For home owner projects this section is really about common sense. If basic methods and fixtures are used in the standard way, there are very rarely any issues of compliance under section G. The most pertinent part deals with the requirements for hot water storage in a dwelling, and the arrangements for venting.

H: Drainage and waste disposal

The big issues here tend to be about the horizontal distances and gradients of waste pipes and drains, both above and below ground. Clearly the healthy condition of a drain is vital for the health and hygiene of the occupants and the neighbourhood.

If you are connecting to an existing drain, it is not unusual for the building inspector to require a survey. This can be done using a specialist CCTV camera in the drain to see if there are any cracks or imperfections.

J: Combustion appliances and fuel storage

The correct ventilation for gas appliances is vital to ensure that poisonous carbon monoxide gas, and other such pollutants, do not build up in a way that could be dangerous. This part of the regulations also deals with chimneys and flues, hearths, aperture sizes for fireplaces, the storage of heating oil and other such matters.

K: Protection from falling, collision and impact

The design of staircases, guardings, balustrades and handrails are all covered in this section of the regulations. There are very helpful diagrams to explain the minimum standards of what can be quite complicated requirements. In particular the regulations explain what must be done with tapering treads on a spiral stair, or the winding treads on a turn of a staircase.

This section also sets out provisions to prevent collisions by preventing windows from projecting into the path of pedestrians, and ensuring that doors that swing both ways have vision panels.

L: Conservation of fuel and power

The amendment to part L of the regulations that came into force in April 2006 has caused great consternation and confusion ever since. The reason for the consternation is that it threatened to prevent people from doing precisely what so many people want to do, which is to extend their house, with lots of glass in the walls and roof. The reason for the confusion is that there are three different ways to calculate what you might be allowed to do. These calculations are fiendishly difficult, leaving many people not knowing what they can and cannot do.

Glass area is generally the most thermally inefficient part of the exterior of a building. However, glass area also promotes solar gain, which can be used – up to a point – as a positive to offset the downside of the heat loss. Often the best way through this matter is to engage a specialist surveyor who can undertake a complex process called a 'SAP calculation'. This provides a mathematical assessment of the energy efficiency of the building before and after the proposed changes.

M: Access and facilities for disabled people

While people expect part M to apply to public buildings and understand why it does, most people are quite shocked and sometimes resentful that their home may have to comply with regulations for access for disabled persons. 'But no one in my family is disabled – so why on earth do we have to do this?' is a common complaint.

In truth, the requirements are not generally onerous. New works must have level access to the entry level of the building, and must have a suitable WC facility on that level too. Suitable usually means suitable for an ambulant disabled person rather than a wheelchair-bound person (who would require more space). Staircases may have to comply with regulations for ambulant disabled people, with regard to the amount of risers, gradient and stair nosings (stair treads that project beyond risers).

N: Glazing – Impact, opening and cleaning safety

There have been many tragic accidents involving people who have smashed into glass doors that they thought were not there. This section introduces requirements for 'manifestation', which involves markings on the surface of the glass so that people will realise that the doors are shut. This part also outlines the need for specially strengthened glass in doors and areas adjacent to them, and also minimum standards for the consideration of how glass may be cleaned safely.

P: Electrical safety

The most recent additional section to the regulations, part P was brought in to combat the dangers of DIY electrical work in people's homes. Now, anything more than the simplest repairs must be done by a qualified electrician who can certify that the work has been done to the necessary standard.

The Approved Documents do not spell out exactly what you must do, but the guidance is very practical and it is generally a good idea to follow it. If you do want to pursue an alternative, you may need to prove compliance.

Sometimes people become so focused on meeting regulations that they forget the original design intent of the project. If you have to implement changes as a result of regulations that you have not foreseen, do not lose sight of your original design.

Part L of the regulations, and its focus on energy efficiency, is the headline-grabbing section regarding green issues. However, many parts of the building regulations contain important controls for the protection of the environment.

RIBA bookshops sell the Approved Documents in hard copy at a price around £10 each, but you can download any of them for free from the planning portal website: www.planningportal.gov.uk

Failure to comply with the building regulations is a criminal offence, and ongoing noncompliance can incur severe fines. However, if the work has been complete for 12 months or more it is very difficult for the local authority to fine you.

Most building inspectors who visit building sites are very helpful. It is their duty to be pedantic about the regulations and they will not appreciate attempts to hide things from them.

Building regulations approval

Many people confuse building regulations approval with planning permission ➤ see also **Planning permission** pp.104–7. The issue is further confused by the number of alternative methods for applying for building regulations approval, and the different bodies to apply to!

For all large-scale projects, a full plans method is the only option, but for small, private residential projects you may be able to use the building notice method.

The full plans method

In many ways similar to making a planning application, you need to submit a full set of drawings of your design proposals for examination and approval. The drawings need to contain more detail than planning drawings, because they need to demonstrate compliance with the building regulations. For example, building regulations stipulate that a WC without a window needs to have an extractor fan that extracts air at a certain number of litres per second, achieving a certain number of air changes per hour. This information will need to appear on the drawings.

Due to the amount of detail required, it is very common for plans to be rejected on the first attempt. They can be sent back with a list explaining where additional detail is required. Do not be alarmed if this happens; you simply need to add the extra information and send the drawings back.

Once your drawings have been approved (plans approval) you know that, as long as you build entirely as per the drawings, your building will comply. When you are ready to start work, you need to submit a building notice that tells the inspector that work is about to commence. Periodically through the development, the inspector will visit to confirm that everything has been done correctly.

This process usually requires two fees: a fee for the plans approval and a fee for the on-site inspection.

The building notice method

For smaller, private residential projects it is possible to do your development without a full plans application. You simply submit a building notice a minimum of 48 hours before the works commence. A building inspector will visit your development and agree everything on site with your builder.

The good thing about this method is that you avoid the expense of having detailed drawings prepared. You also avoid waiting for approval and the extra cost of the plans fee. For simple works, where there is nothing particularly difficult or controversial, this can be ideal.

The potential downside with a building notice application is that if your proposal does not comply with the regulations, you will not find out until work is about to start. For example, if you plan to open up the ground floor, have you considered whether this will undermine the fire escape route from loft bedrooms? Such fundamental matters cannot be accommodated easily on the day.

Who to apply to for approval

Each local authority has a building control department, and it used to be the case that the department administered all local applications. While they still deal with the majority of local applications, deregulation means that this is no longer the only option.

The government allows private licensed organisations to process applications, commonly known as Approved Inspectors. One well-known organisation is the NHBC, but many small, local chartered surveyors' offices are beginning to get approved status. Therefore, you can opt to have your full plans application considered by an Approved Inspector, instead of by your local authority.

As local authority building control departments now have to compete with private firms, they are beginning to act in a much more commercial way, generally offering a more helpful and proactive service than before deregulation. In some cases, you can ask a different local authority area to administer an application; this is useful if you have already created a good working relationship with a particular office.

This may sound complicated, but once the complexity is understood, there is no question that deregulation has made a significant improvement to the application process.

People often see the building regulations as the enemy, but it is worth remembering that they are there to ensure our safety and sanitation and that buildings are constructed responsibly in relation to people and the environment.

Trying to accommodate regulations in a design that was prepared without early consideration of their requirements can ruin the proportions and appearance of the proposals. For example, adding fire doors or vent pipes at a late stage can look dreadful.

The building regulations are the government's most effective tool in trying to improve the energy efficiency of the nation's homes. However, they have no effect upon existing homes that are not undertaking building work.

The building notice method is a great deal cheaper to follow than the full plans method, because the application fees are less, and there is no need for special drawings. However, the full plans method gives much more certainty.

The building regulations apply to all new buildings, structural alterations, extended or altered drains, electrical or gas appliance installations, cavity insulation and unvented hot water storage. They do not apply only to small and specific types of project.

The deregulation that has allowed private approved inspectors, as well as local authorities, to administer the building regulations has led to much better consultation all round.

Case study

4. Detail design

We return to our case study, and this time look at the detail design drawings that were used in the project. The full set of drawings included many detail elements, from the masonry construction to the location of drawer runners.

On the next few pages is a selection of some of the detailed drawings alongside photographs of the elements that were built from them.

When working with an architect and commissioning detail design drawings, it is important to strike a balance between having enough detail to control the project, and having so much detail that the cost of design and drawing work becomes disproportionate to the cost of the work. There is no easy solution, as each project is different and every home owner will have a different point of view.

Opposite, one of the detailed drawings for the staircase is shown including an enlarged detail of the tread and riser construction.

Separate detail drawings were prepared for the tension cables and turnbuckles that adjust and control the tension, and the special fittings that hold the glass together and support it on the cables.

On the following pages are examples of the details for the kitchen, the bathroom, with the floor drain, and the timber-clad recess in the external wall.

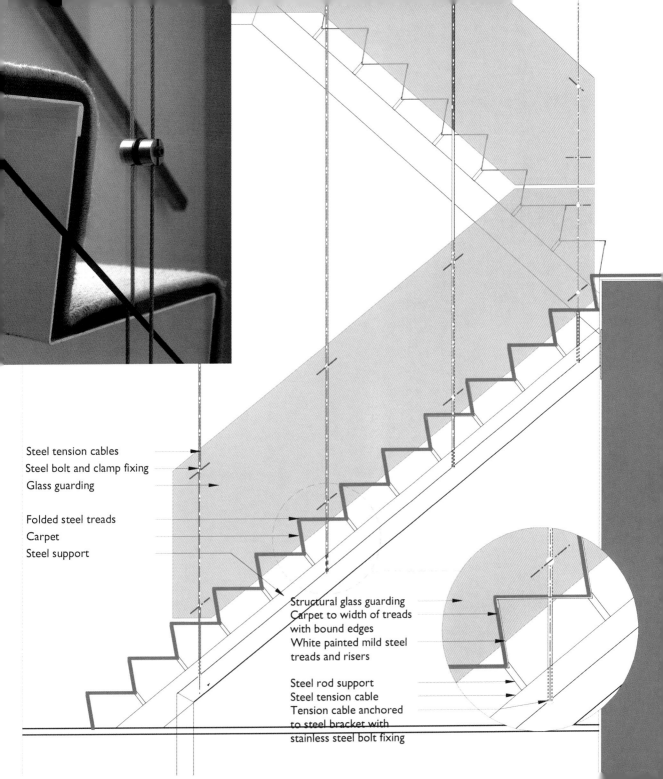

Steel tension cables
Steel bolt and clamp fixing
Glass guarding

Folded steel treads
Carpet
Steel support

Structural glass guarding
Carpet to width of treads
with bound edges
White painted mild steel
treads and risers

Steel rod support
Steel tension cable
Tension cable anchored
to steel bracket with
stainless steel bolt fixing

▽ Co-ordinating different elements.

The detailed drawings of the kitchen are the means by which the units, worktops, appliances, electrics, gas supply, lighting and finishes, all sourced from separate suppliers, can be co-ordinated.

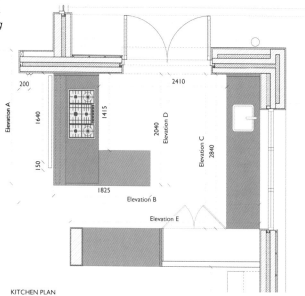

KITCHEN PLAN

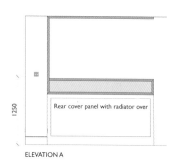

Rear cover panel with radiator over

1250

ELEVATION A

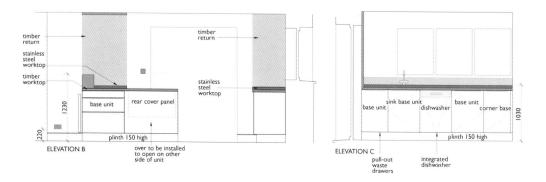

timber return
stainless steel worktop
timber worktop
1230
base unit   rear cover panel
220
plinth 150 high
ELEVATION B
over to be installed to open on other side of unit

timber return
stainless steel worktop

base unit   sink base unit   dishwasher   base unit   corner base
1030
plinth 150 high
ELEVATION C
pull-out waste drawers   integrated dishwasher

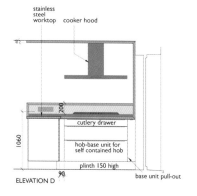

stainless steel worktop   cooker hood
200
cutlery drawer
1060
hob-base unit for self contained hob
plinth 150 high
90
ELEVATION D
base unit pull-out

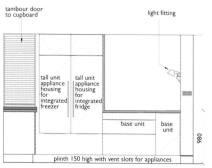

tambour door to cupboard   light fitting

tall unit appliance housing for integrated freezer   tall unit appliance housing for integrated fridge
base unit   base unit
980
plinth 150 high with vent slots for appliances
ELEVATION E

Blue rubber bathroom. A fun, splash-proof family bathroom, with a linear drain in the floor and rubber tiles on the walls and floor, needed careful detailing to ensure that everything lined up simply and evenly.

Timber-clad external recess. The external recess feature on the wall facing the garden was achieved by cutting away part of the original outer skin, which was then clad with timber, and building a whole new inner skin of thermal blockwork.

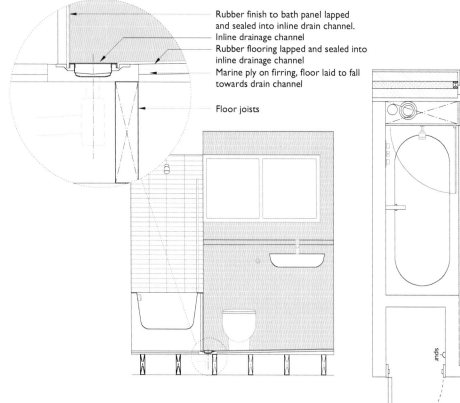

Rubber finish to bath panel lapped and sealed into inline drain channel.
Inline drainage channel
Rubber flooring lapped and sealed into inline drainage channel
Marine ply on firring, floor laid to fall towards drain channel

Floor joists

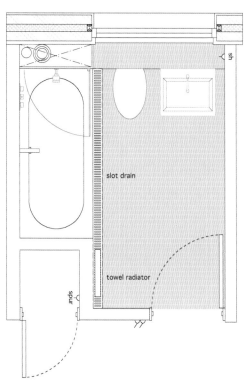

slot drain

towel radiator

spur

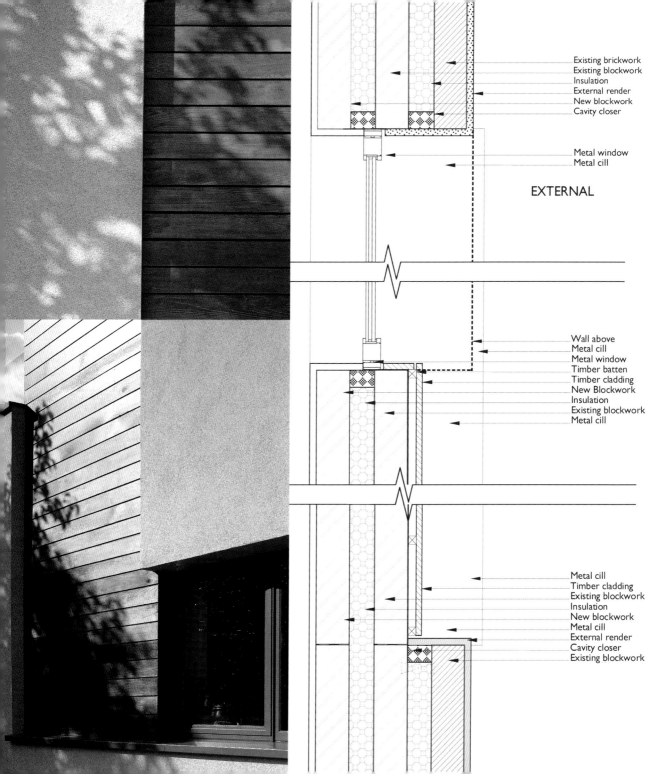

Existing brickwork
Existing blockwork
Insulation
External render
New blockwork
Cavity closer

Metal window
Metal cill

EXTERNAL

Wall above
Metal cill
Metal window
Timber batten
Timber cladding
New Blockwork
Insulation
Existing blockwork
Metal cill

Metal cill
Timber cladding
Existing blockwork
Insulation
New blockwork
Metal cill
External render
Cavity closer
Existing blockwork

5 Specification

Specification is the process of choosing and deciding exactly what materials, fittings and finishes are to be used in your project. You may also need to specify who supplies them, or where products come from, and these decisions need to be communicated to those responsible for the building work.

The choice of fixtures, fittings and finishes used in your project will not only have a huge effect upon the eventual result, but will also have a profound effect on the eventual budget, as the cost variations between the highest quality and the most utilitarian choice are so significant.

practicality

aesthetic

environment

cost/value

regulations

communication

What is specification?

Every **component** *used in a project will need to be* **chosen** *by someone. The* **extent** *to which you make those decisions will* **influence** *the success and cost of the project, and depends upon your* **knowledge** *and self-discipline.*

Many of your material choices will have been made, as the design has developed through the outline, scheme and detail stages. But where a wall may have been identified as simply 'brick' up until now, the question of precisely which type and colour of brick needs to be made.

The problem that many people face when it comes to specification is that they often do not know whether or not a particular choice will be suitable for the task in question. Secondly, because people often do not know where to look for certain items, they will often choose from what they can find easily. In both of these cases an architect will be able to help. An architect will be able to source and present a range of choices to the home owner, all of which should be plausible.

Why do you need to specify?

In any particular given case, if you know exactly what you want, and want to ensure that you end up with just that, a specification is really the most comprehensive mechanism to help you achieve your goal. For example, if you have seen a door handle that you like, you will need to find out where that precise handle can be bought and specify the exact one. If you skip the bother of specification, and simply try to describe to your builder the sort of handle that you are after, you may end up with something similar (if you are lucky!).

How far to specify?

While there may be particular items that you want to specify, it is likely that you do not have strong feelings about everything that is needed, as long as they do their job. For example, I do not know many people who really care about the exact make, model and specification of their boiler, so long as they have hot water when they want it.

Most people are happy with a general requirement for many of the items within their home, but will have key items that they want incorporated specifically. Some people become obsessed with controlling every detail, whereas others are more relaxed. In short, control gives you much more certainty, but the additional time, energy and cost of the administration necessary to achieve that level of control needs to be factored in.

Specifying construction materials

It is possible to specify every component part of a building project, and there are ways to specify the exact level and quality of workmanship wanted. However, this would be too time-consuming and costly to be feasible for most home owner projects.

It is usual to specify particular items, such as those that people generally care about and that they can see and use in their finished home, while the rest are covered by a general requirement for suitability and workmanship. For example, people usually want to choose their wall tiles and the type of bath they have, but the specification of construction materials, such as the grade of timber used for the floor joists, or the thickness of roofing felt, is generally left to the architect, other consultants or the builders.

Specialist input

Sometimes you need a specialist to advise on specification. For example, it is vital that any concrete that forms part of a structure is mixed properly, otherwise it may not be strong enough for the job in hand. There are all sorts of standard recipes for concrete mix, but usually, along with structural calculations, a structural engineer will supply a mix specification.

Best practice

To standardise the process of specifying construction materials, and make it more efficient, there are many references you can use. The British Standards Institute (BSI) has a huge library of standards that are based upon years of testing. These allow you to quote the relevant BSI number and then the builder can reference the specification. There are also bodies, such as the Building Research Establishment (BRE), who research products and establish standards. Some organisations focus on specific product groups – for example, TRADA (Timber Research and Development Association).

Performance specification

Another common approach is to state what standard is required as an end result, but leave the precise solution up to the contractor. For example, you may choose to set a performance specification for a central heating and hot water system. This would state the required level of hot water storage, control, adjustability and power rating, but leave the choice of boiler and tank up to the contractor.

Has your specification been met?

Finally, it is worth thinking about the extent to which you are able to verify that your specifications have been met. Clearly, if the bath that you chose is not the one that has been installed, you will notice, but if the concrete mix is wrong, or the wall ties used are different from those specified, who is going to point this out? It is important to be realistic about the time you allow checking and changing these things and, like everything else, balance it out for your particular purposes.

Rather than dictating the choice of everything, it may be more pragmatic to outline your key requirements, and ask your consultants and/or contractors to choose accordingly.

The evidence of thorough specification can be seen most clearly in the small details. For example, does the silver finish on the light switch plates match that on the door furniture?

If you want environmentally friendly materials to be used, you will need to specify them. Sheep's wool insulation, for example, will need to be specified, otherwise you will probably be provided with mineral wool.

If you allow yourself to get carried away at the specification stage, costs can soar. A high-quality item can cost ten times that of a basic item.

Make sure that your choices take any regulations that might apply into account. This includes everything, from matching materials on a listed building, to the fire-resistance rating of fabrics, and the energy efficiency of a light fitting.

While the system of British Standards is comprehensive, if you want to understand a particular one before specifying it, you will need to purchase each individual standard document. These cost about £75.

Bricks

Available in a range of colours including yellow, blue, brown and red, bricks vary in texture; they can be consistent and smooth-sided, or mottled and full of individual character. Bricks also have different constructional qualities, strengths and levels of absorption, and vary hugely in price.

Many people want to match the brickwork of an extension to the original brickwork of their house. This can be difficult, even if you get the same clay from the same brickworks, because age and weathering will have changed and added tremendous character to the existing brickwork. The only really effective way to match is to find a source of reclaimed bricks that have aged on another building. Because these have been taken from a demolition site, separated, and had the old mortar cleaned off, they tend to be very expensive.

Handmade bricks

Traditional, handmade bricks are made from clay and baked in a kiln. The clay mix is thrown by hand into a brick-shaped mould to form the shape and then baked. As a result, each brick has an individual pattern of creases on the surface of the brick, giving it additional character. Still available today, handmade bricks are expensive.

⌄ *Different bricks and patterns.*

1. Mixing in a few reclaimed yellow stock bricks with new bricks is cheaper than using all reclaimed, and breaks up the uniformity.

2. A low garden wall built with reclaimed yellow London stock bricks.

3. Uniformly red bricks, with fine joints and alternate ends/sides (headers and stretchers) in a late Victorian house.

4. The same bond (pattern) in an old brick that is generally yellowish brown but contains blues, reds and purples too.

People often refer to a simple brick wall as one of the basics of building work, but fail to understand that there is huge variation, not just in the choice of bricks and mortar, but also in the skill of the bricklayer.

Yellow London stock bricks

Most of the Victorian housing in London was built with yellow London stock bricks. These are available as new, but the majority of brick Victorian buildings are anything but yellow. The effect of the city for 150 years has turned them a grimy grey/brown colour. While this sounds unattractive, it does have a certain weathered charm, and new yellow stock bricks built against originals jar. You can find reclaimed bricks that will match better, but the price is twice that of new bricks.

If you want a brick wall to have a traditional beauty, consider using a traditional pattern like Flemish bond. People will not notice exactly what makes it appealing, but it will just feel more human.

Engineering bricks

Hard, strong and almost impervious to water, engineering bricks are a completely different product. Generally available in red or 'blue' (a very cool and sombre dark purple), they are excellent in areas where the load of a beam needs to be spread, and also at the base of walls as an effective damp-proof course. They are machine-made and, unlike their handmade cousins, their beauty is in their uniformity.

The idea of using reclaimed bricks is not often thought of as recycling, but that is just what it is. It may be expensive, but reclaimed bricks tend to be more beautiful than new, and save both energy and landfill if used again.

Machine-made bricks

Modern machine-made bricks have a regular appearance, but this can make them a bit soulless. A lot of machine-made bricks are extruded like toothpaste through a rectangular opening, cut to brick depth, and then baked. Some cheaper bricks have a secondary 'sand-face' added to imitate a more attractive brick.

Flettons, a type of machine-made brick, are a pale terracotta colour and are used mainly when walls or buildings need to be rendered or plastered. To a great extent they have been superseded by concrete blocks, which are cheaper and quicker to lay.

Bricks vary in price from under 20p to over £1 per brick. Where a lot of brickwork is needed, your choice of brick specification will have a significant effect on your budget.

Brickwork needs to be able to expand and contract and the building regulations set out maximum horizontal expanses of brickwork. If a wall needs to exceed this distance, an expansion joint will have to be designed into the wall.

Brickwork bonds (patterns)

The other important thing to think about with brickwork is the pattern that they are laid to. With the advent of cavity walls, bricks are almost universally laid end-to-end in half-staggered courses, but when walls were thicker, bricks were often laid across the width, showing the end of the brick. Patterns such as English bond and Flemish bond, were popular and can be made using half-bricks, even with cavity construction.

The end of a brick is known as the header and the side is the stretcher. A wall built to the thickness of the width of a brick is known as 'half-a-brick-thick', and to the length as 'one-brick-thick'.

Stone and stone products

Most of the oldest buildings still standing are made from stone. Stone was used because it was available, and it has lasted because it is incredibly hard wearing. It was always a luxury building material and remains so today, but natural stone has incredible beauty as well as durability, and will probably still be being used in the future for as long as it has been used in the past.

The most obvious use of stone is in walls. Wonderful, thick solid stone walls, with deep recessed window openings, are synonymous with charming old cottages set deep in the countryside, but stone was used for much more than just walls. Roofs were often tiled with slices of stone. Slate (which lends itself to thin slicing) is one of the great roofing materials of our heritage. Even in buildings with walls of brick, or other materials, stone was often used for the 'important bits', such as corners, lintels over windows and doors, cills and doorsteps. Stone was also used for hearths (to stop sparks from the fireplace setting light to the floor).

One of the joys of looking at stone buildings is the relationship with the locality. In Bath, most of the city is built with the local pale honey-coloured stone. In Wales, the blue-grey slate of the mountains is almost universally used for roofs, and in chalky areas, such as Sussex, flints were crafted into walls as a fantastically durable material. When thinking about stone for your home, it is worth giving some consideration to local stone before choosing something that has been imported from India or China.

Pathways and streets traditionally used flagstones or cobbles, which are still very desirable. Granite setts (small 100mm/4in cubes of granite) give a wonderfully muscular and durable finish externally, and are not too expensive to purchase, but will be expensive to lay as the work is time consuming.

Some of the more common types of stone used for buildings are:

Granite

The formation of granite from slow-cooling volcanic lava results in a wide variety of colours and grain patterns, but the common characteristic is great strength and low porosity. This strength makes granite very durable but also relatively hard to work. The surface of granite can be treated in all sorts of different ways from the very raw, through various hammered, flame-textured and honed finishes, to the high gloss polished finish often seen on kitchen worktops.

Sandstone

Granular sedimentary stone, extensively used across the North of England as a building material, sandstone can be found in a range of colours from white, grey and buff to various pinks and reds. Traditional use of sandstone often saw it beautifully carved. When sandstone is used correctly it can be extraordinarily durable and weather resistant. Sandstone also changes appearance dramatically when wet.

Slate

Like granite, slate has great strength and low porosity, but metamorphosed from sedimentary rather than volcanic rock, slate has the unique layering quality that allows it to be split or riven. Slate has been used for centuries as a building material for cills, flooring, plaques, copings and, most of all, in very thin slices as a roofing material. Most slate is blue/grey or green/silver/grey, but there are black and even red types available.

Old stone and new materials. *The visual softness and weight of an old stone wall can sit beautifully in contrast with sharp, modern materials, such as this glass roof.*

Flint houses. *Flint is very hard and, typically, found as fairly small stones amongst chalk. The stones can be laid with their rounded faces out or 'knapped' to give a sharper, flat finish. Flint does not cope with corners and edges, so stone or brick (both visible here) is used to frame the flint work.*

Limestone

Probably the most widely used building stone of all is limestone, a sedimentary rock that occurs naturally in a swathe across the UK from the southwest up through Oxford to the east coast near the Humber. Typically less granular than sandstone, some limestones such as Purbeck can be polished like marble. Colours and textures range from the almost white Portland stone to the warm honey-coloured Bath stone.

Marble

True marble is metamorphosed limestone and in its pure form is white. Impurities, however, mean that marble is available in a brilliant array of dazzling colours and patterns. Marble is a very hard stone and most commonly is given a polished finish to show off its patterns and colours. Care must be taken with the detailing of marble because acids can affect it, and underlying materials, particularly some metals, can taint and stain marble.

Flint

Flints are very hard stones that occur naturally in chalk. Typically, they are small and therefore cannot be cut into large blocks or slabs like other stone materials. However, the hardness, availability and ease of working with small stones has made flint a popular choice for facing walls of houses in many parts of Britain, particularly Surrey and Sussex where chalk (and flint) is plentiful. Flints can be set into a wall with their natural rounded surface out, to give a 'cobbled' effect, or be 'knapped' to provide a sharp, roughly flat surface.

The great strength and durability of natural stone makes it one of the most practical materials available to build with. However, if not detailed properly, stone can suffer from weathering or staining.

Stone can give almost any visual effect from a riot of colour, pattern and texture to a pure solid strength. Stone can be plain or decorative, carved or polished, mighty or delicate.

Stone is an entirely natural material. While the excavation of stone marks the landscape and moving such weight requires energy, there is no processing, as with metals, or pollutants. Stone can be – and often is – recycled.

While many old buildings are made from large blocks of stone, the high cost and weight mean that most new stone buildings only have a thin stone veneer covering, held on with a metal clip system. This is often detectable on the corners of buildings.

Significant health and safety regulations apply to men working with heavy materials, such as stone blocks. The risk of back injuries incurred through heavy lifting needs to be mitigated and managed by your builder.

If you want a random arrangement of stone, it is sometimes necessary to be very specific as to how you want this done, even to the extent of drawing the exact arrangement for a builder to follow.

⋀ Knapped and squared.
This detail from the house opposite shows how the flints have been individually cut so that neat courses can be laid. This would have been very labour intensive.

⋀ Rough and random.
In contrast, this flint wall has been laid with randomly shaped stones in a jumble of sizes, with no continuous level courses, other than one band of brick.

⋀ Granite setts. Setts are rough cubes of granite that can be laid to form attractive and hard-wearing pathways outside. When wet they become darker and shinier.

Stone for interiors

Durability, strength and low porosity make stone a practical material for use inside the home. The natural beauty and variety of stone adds an exceptional aesthetic, and is a popular choice for flooring, worktops and other features.

Stone items from old buildings, including floors, walls and cills, are often salvaged and sold for reuse. Decorative and carved reclaimed stone items can reach high prices and large, worn flagstones for flooring are very sought after. Because stone is so heavy and expensive to extract, modern use of stone tends to be thin and precise, whereas the appeal of much salvaged stone is its great size and weight.

Floors and walls

Limestone, both as slabs of stone and as tiles, is a popular choice for bathroom flooring. The off-white colour of a natural limestone is set off by the pure white of an enamelled bath or porcelain washbasin. It can be used throughout a property, but remember to factor in the practicality of keeping it clean.

Slate is a very popular flooring material, in particular with a riven finish, which gives a natural texture with good grip. One of the common dislikes of stone floors is that they are cold to walk on, but this can be countered by installing underfloor heating. The stone floor will retain heat and act as a heat store in itself.

Exposed stone walls were common in old properties, but they can make an interior feel cold. Previous generations often used wall hangings and tapestries to warm things up. Used sparingly as a feature, stone walls can add texture and interest to a design, although the cost of the stone itself and its installation will be high.

Fireplaces

One of the useful qualities of stone is its resistance to heat and flame. Fireplaces have traditionally been made from stone and continue to be so today. The building regulations require minimum dimensions for a hearth (the area of fire-resistant material in front of the base of a fireplace). Even in very contemporary designs, stone is often used for this purpose. Limestone and sandstone are particularly popular materials for fire surrounds as they can be carved and worked so readily.

Worktops

Stone is a good choice for kitchen surfaces and bathroom units. Strong and impervious, granite is usually polished to a mirror-like surface, but can also look beautiful if given a matt, honed or even textured (hammered) finish. Slate is another beautiful choice for kitchen surfaces, especially when honed to a very flat matt finish, but will scratch more easily than granite. Marble and limestone can react to acids, such as lemon juice, so can get easily stained when used in a kitchen. They are more often used for bathrooms.

It is vital that the right surface treatment be applied to a stone floor. Many stone surfaces need a sealant to prevent staining and avoid dust and grit damaging the surface.

When choosing a stone from a small sample, be aware that the colour and texture may vary dramatically in the product that you receive, and also that the effect of one small sample will often not convey that of a large stone surface.

While old stone-walled buildings may seem cold on the surface, the mass of the stone offers a fantastic natural heat store, which will often keep the interior warm in winter and cool in summer.

While natural stone is often fiercely expensive, there are many types of reconstituted stone products that offer a lower cost alternative, with many of the qualities of natural stone.

Where stone needs to be matched with existing old stone for repairs to features within listed buildings, make sure that you have samples approved by the conservation officer before placing an order.

Stone worktops usually need to be cut from a template so that they will fit exactly. Working from a kitchen drawing will not allow for any irregularities in the profile of a wall, or anything out of square.

< **On the beach.** *Natural finishes have broadened the use of stone in interiors. This shower-room floor is laid with pebbles like a mosaic (they come prearranged and stuck to a flexible backing sheet), and the wall is made from wedge-shaped, green limestone slips.*

Ceramic and porcelain tiles

Made from clay and kiln-fired, ceramic tiles can be used on all sorts of surfaces including floors, walls, worktops and swimming pools. Standard ceramic tiles vary in size, price and quality enormously, from basic white wall tiles to handmade tiles costing £300 per metre.

The development in production methods of ceramic and porcelain tiles means that there are now a great variety of tile patterns and textures available. Porcelain tiles made to look like natural stone are available at a fraction of the price of natural stone, and are easier and quicker to lay. They also suffer less from the dangers of staining or imperfections. Limestone-effect porcelain tiles have led to a reduction in the use of natural limestone in bathrooms; for most projects, porcelain tiles are cheaper, more practical, and just as appealing.

Tile size

Very large and very small tiles look effective because they get away from the visual prompt of the standard tile. Very large sizes can look strong and simple, and small mosaics become a texture rather than a set of clear units. This is particularly effective when several complicated surfaces are to be tiled.

Porcelain tiles are now available in very large sizes. We recently installed a floor using 900 x 900mm (35 x 35in) square tiles and the scale is very impressive. Since this project, the same tile company has added an amazing 1200 x 1200mm (47 x 47in) tile size to their range.

A mosaic tile is simply a term for very small tiles and covers another huge range of options. Most mosaic tiles come already stuck to a backing sheet, which means that tiles can be set as a group rather than individually. Even so, the labour time involved in laying mosaics is considerably longer than for larger tile sizes. Mosaics are available in coloured glass, ceramic, porcelain and hand-cut stone, and in a variety of shapes, from long thin strips to tiny squares and circles.

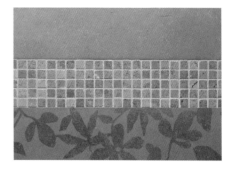

Printed decorative tile. *The leaf pattern on the lower tile matches nicely with the top, plain tile and slightly warmer mosaics.*

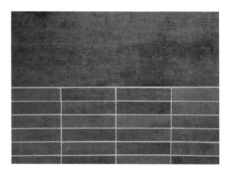

Breaking up scale. *This rust-coloured porcelain tile is available in a large format (top) and has a matching strip mosaic (bottom) that can be used to subtly highlight certain areas.*

All white. *Tiles need not be rectangular. These white tiles are circular and give a lovely textured effect without any added colour. If in doubt, always go for something simple. You can always add splashes of colour with towels and bath mats, but a recipe of glass, white tiles and chrome fittings is unlikely to tire.*

Mosaic tiles on a bathroom floor. *Here, mosaic tiles have been laid across a bathroom floor, and brought up the wall a short way, like a skirting. The small size of the tiles creates an overall texture, and provides good grip in the wet shower area.*

Fitting ceramic tiles

Although ceramic tiles are waterproof, they are often very brittle, and it is vital to ensure that the surface onto which they are applied is very stable and cannot flex. Any flexing will lead to cracking in the tiles or grout, or both. Usually, joints are neatly filled with grout that complements the tile colour, sometimes as a contrasting tone and other times to blend, depending upon the effect required.

Underfloor heating

Ceramic tiles convey heat just as well as real stone, so they can be used over an electric underfloor heating system set into the tile adhesive layer. Some underfloor heating simply takes the chill off the floor, making it more comfortable to walk on. Other systems can also fully heat the room with an even temperature.

∨ **Tiles, mosaics and mirror.** This loft bathroom has pale, large-format tiles on the walls and a darker tone on the floor. A large, rectangular mirror is tiled in, and mosaics add highlight texture around the bath and above the WC.

If the sub-base is stable, and the tiles are laid correctly, a tiled surface can be very durable and practical. However, the grouted joints can trap dirt, and if stagnant water is allowed to collect, the joints can develop mould growth.

A tiled wall or floor can be a fantastic statement within a room. While tiled walls are expected in bathrooms and kitchens, a striking decorative tiled surface within a living room or bedroom can create impact.

The durability of tiles means that they offer long life for their manufacture. However, the more they become a fashion item, the more often they will be stripped off and replaced with new.

Be very careful to identify the total cost of tiling. Budget for the price of the tiles, adhesive, grout and labour.

Slip resistance is an important factor when choosing floor tiles, particularly in areas that may get wet. Most manufacturers give each of their products a slip resistance rating, which relates to recommended areas of use.

Choosing and setting out the proposed arrangement of tiles on a wall, so that a certain number fit exactly along a length, takes time and trouble, and needs to be clearly shown on a drawing.

Timber and timber products

Timber has always been a versatile material in home construction, from the structural use in roofs and floors, to practical and decorative dado rails and skirting boards. Timber can be cut and fixed with relative ease and can be sanded, painted, waxed or oiled to get the look you want.

One of the most wonderful things about timber is that it is sustainable, as long as it comes from a managed source. European and North American forests tend to be well managed and there are many approved sources of sustainable hardwoods from all over the world. However, there is still a great deal of illicit rainforest logging, which is causing environmental damage, so always check the source of your timber.

Choosing timber for joinery

Most standard on-site joinery – for instance, architraves and skirting boards – are made from soft wood, that does not have a particularly attractive grain pattern, such as European spruce. Blemishes, nail holes and knots are filled, sanded and painted (usually with an undercoat and then two or three coats of tough gloss, eggshell or satin finish paint). European spruce is an ideal choice as it is cheap, stable, easy to work and sustainable.

If you want to see the grain and colour of your joinery you have a wide choice. As well as appearance, check the hardness, stability and absorption qualities of the timber, and whether it is fit for purpose. When you find a wood you like, you also

⋀ Parquet flooring. Rectangular blocks of oak, with tongues and grooves that slot together, have been laid in a chevron pattern, and waxed to give a wonderfully soft, clean appearance.

〈 Black American Walnut. In this exciting space, veneered panels of Black American Walnut have been used very effectively in the kitchen, with solid flooring of the same timber. The variation of tone and direction of grain pattern are cleverly used to set off the very dark dining furniture and lightweight staircase beautifully.

Oak-framed glass screen. *This elegant screen, incorporating a sliding doorway, has been beautifully made in oak, with stainless steel details.*

have to identify the colour tone and grain pattern you want. The joinery must be done with much more care and attention (which means more time and cost), because there will be very little scope for blemishes to be filled.

Matching timbers

People often become slightly obsessed with the idea of matching all of the timber within their home. I don't think this is always necessary. Blending different timbers can give a beautiful effect as long as you use timbers from the same family:

- Deciduous trees, such as oak, cherry, beech and walnut
- Evergreen softwoods, such as cedar, Douglas fir and pine
- Tropical or Australian timber, such as jarrah, iroko or teak.

Practicality

One limitation of most timbers is their deterioration if they are left damp over a period of time. Western Red Cedar copes well with the weather and will turn a silver shade, but many timbers, including oak, will twist and swell if left untreated. This leaves them vulnerable to fungal attack, such as dry rot, so it is important that the right timber and the right treatment is chosen for each application.

Timber products

Timber can be processed and made into other products such as ply, MDF (medium-density fibreboard) and chipboard, all of which have hugely increased the ease and effective use of timber in many applications. Timber veneers (thin slices of beautiful timber) can be cut and applied to sheet materials, such as MDF, to great effect. Sheet timber products have the added benefit that they use off-cuts and small branches, which may otherwise be wasted. Veneers require beautiful timber, but they are produced with such tremendous efficiency, using only the thinnest layer of wood, that a single tree can spread its beauty across a large number of boards.

You will almost always find something suitable for the job in hand. Timber can be cut to fit and fixed on site, so is hugely versatile for interior tasks.

While timber can add beauty and warmth to an interior, it can be overwhelming. For example, a timber kitchen worktop will look good with white doors, or timber doors with a stone worktop, but timber with timber is often too much.

Timber-based construction is generally seen as the way forward, as long as the timber comes from well-managed, sustainable forests. More information can be found on the Forest Stewardship Council website – www.fsc.org

Timber prices vary tremendously and it is worth shopping around. In many cases the DIY superstores are astronomically more expensive than a builders' merchant.

Although timber is flammable, it can be treated to make it flame retardant. Where timber is used on an escape route or facing a boundary, the building regulations may insist upon flame-retardant certification.

The Timber Research and Development Association (TRADA) is a great source of information about different timbers, their qualities, appearance, sustainability, treatments and best applications.

Timber flooring

Timber flooring has become one of the most popular interior products of the past decade. I remember suggesting a timber floor for a living room in the early 1990s and the clients looked at me as if I was making a radical proposal. Nowadays, it is more often carpet that is considered unusual.

If your home has original floorboards, these may be of sufficient quality to sand and seal. Otherwise, there is a large selection of timber flooring to choose from. The main types are solid timber, engineered boards and laminate flooring.

Solid timber flooring

Solid timber flooring is made from sturdy pieces of wood that fit together with a tongue-and-groove system. Solid timbers tend to give the most character, but do have the tendency to shrink, swell, twist and move, if the humidity in your home is not consistent. Underfloor heating can, in some instances, exacerbate this effect. Many types of timber are suitable for timber flooring, and the image below shows just a small selection of the many choices available. You can also get different results with varnish, staining, and waxing.

∨ *Timber flooring samples. There is a huge range of different timbers available for timber flooring, with different construction, finishes, grain patterns and colour tones. Small samples give an idea, but it is often only when you see an expanse that the overall effect can be appreciated.*

Reclaimed timber flooring. This beautiful antique elm floor was reclaimed from a French country house that was being demolished.

Timber flooring is very practical because it can be cleaned easily, is very durable, works well with underfloor heating, and adds beauty and warmth to an interior.

Pale timber floors, such as maple, allow light to bounce around a room, but can appear hard and cold. Dark timbers, such as wengé, are very classy, but absorb the light. Oak has a lovely mid-tone that has warmth without the heavy feeling of a dark timber.

Bamboo flooring is durable and attractive as well as being sustainable. It grows so fast in tropical countries that there could be an almost inexhaustible supply. On the downside, it needs to be transported long distances.

The price of a particular type of timber flooring is relative to its rarity. Unusual timbers, or reclaimed floors that are in short supply, tend to be very expensive, whereas timbers in plentiful supply can be bought cheaply.

Some apartment buildings have regulations preventing the use of timber floor finishes due to noise transmission. With appropriate sound insulation this effect can be eradicated, but in some instances the rules are the rules.

It is important to be very clear with whoever is laying your floor what detail you want at the edges and thresholds. Have they allowed for removal and refitting of skirtings, or are they proposing a fussy little quadrant to hide the edge?

One increasingly popular product for flooring is bamboo. Bamboo has the benefit of growing extremely fast, so it is eminently sustainable, as well as being very hard-wearing. It also has an attractive pattern and is available in some lovely warm tones.

Engineered boards

This type of flooring is made from a layer of solid timber, usually around 6 or 8mm (¼ or ⅓in) thick, and bonded on top of a cross-ply of timber. This gives the boards stability, and they tend to be able to cope with changes in humidity more evenly. Because the timber layer is fairly thick, the floor appears solid, and there are plenty of types to choose from that have the appeal and character of solid timber.

Laminate flooring

Laminate flooring is made from several layers of material (particle board and resin saturated paper) that are fused together. Beneath the top, transparent layer, is a thin layer to give the board its appearance (typically this is a printed photographic image of wood on cellulose paper, but sometimes it is a very thin layer of 'real' timber veneer). This is generally the cheapest type of 'timber' flooring and most examples have a very artificial appearance, particularly in any expanse. It tends to be very stable, but does not wear well as the top layer is so thin. Sharp objects and stiletto heels can ruin a laminated floor in a very short time.

Reclaimed boards

For a beautiful floor, you could choose reclaimed boards. The boards can have fantastic character, but are usually expensive to purchase. They may also need a huge amount of work to prepare them before being laid. The elm boards shown in the picture above arrived full of nails, and many were tapered and had to be cut parallel before they could be used.

Metals and metal finishes

Metals are used extensively in the construction of most buildings, from steel beams and columns ➤ see also **Structural changes** pp.120–3, to metal studwork ➤ see also **Internal walls** p.152, wall ties and restraining straps ➤ see also **External walls** p.150. However, there are many more uses for metals within a building where the material is visible, and the choice of surface will affect your finished design. Here are some of the most widely used metals.

Iron

You can find plenty of examples of both wrought (or worked) iron and cast iron in Victorian houses, but steel has taken over almost entirely these days. Even railings are commonly manufactured in steel and painted to give a wrought-iron effect. The one still common use for cast iron is for drainpipes and soil pipes. While these are significantly more expensive than the more common PVC pipes, they tend to be much more durable (in certain instances cast-iron drainage pipes *have* to be used).

Mild steel

Mild steel is very strong and relatively low in cost. It can be painted with enamel, powder-coated, chrome-plated (and highly polished), or galvanised (dipped in a tank of zinc), which gives it a silvery surface and a resistance to rust.

The two main drawbacks are the environmental concerns over the amount of energy used to produce and process steel, and the problem of rust. Any structural (floor supporting) steelwork must be protected from fire as the heat of a house fire will cause it to fail, so exposing a steel beam as a feature of your interior design will require the professional application of intumescent paint.

Stainless steel

To many architects, stainless steel is almost holy. It does not rust, has a much more natural silver colour than mild steel and can be polished or given a 'brushed' finish. It is versatile and can be used for structural purposes, as well as for details such as light switch plates. However, it is much more expensive than mild steel, and is also more expensive to work. As a result, stainless steel is mostly used in thin sheet form (for example, as a kitchen worktop), in tubes (for instance, handrails), or in small components for fixings.

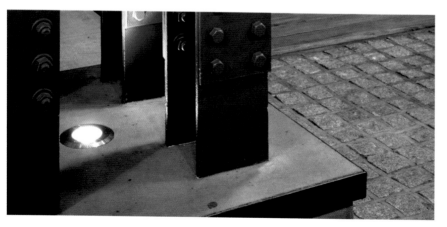

< *Muscular mild-steel columns.*
These massive steel columns in a converted warehouse give a very muscular feel, but as they are structural they have to be fire protected. This would usually mean boxing them in plasterboard, which would have been a great shame in this case. Instead, they have been treated with intumescent paint, so that the form of the steel remains a feature. Note how the concrete, granite setts and timber have been placed alongside the steel to create a very masculine palette of materials.

◁ Metals in interiors. *The kitchen unit doors (far left) are made from MDF and clad with thin sheet stainless steel 'trays' that cover the face and edges of the MDF and are given a directional grained or 'brushed' finish. The polished chrome tap and shower set (left) provides a shiny focal point in this bathroom.*

Try to match the qualities of the different metals with the function of the component under consideration.

Aluminium

While aluminium is a lot less expensive than stainless steel and does not rust like mild steel, it is not nearly as strong as either. Much thicker sections are needed to do the work that steel does, and its surface is much more prone to scratches and becoming dull. It can be powder-coated or anodised for a more even and maintainable finish. SAA (satin anodised aluminium) has a similar appearance to brushed stainless steel, but is much cheaper. It is often used for door handles, hooks and fittings.

Metals seem to look their best when they express their function. Mechanisms, metal fixings and tension buckles can be both functional and beautiful at the same time.

Brass

Brass is considered to be more traditional than stainless steel or chrome. However, in my view there is nothing classic about a brass, antique-style power socket. For many fittings such as taps, brass is used as a base for chrome plating.

Mining for metals harms the environment, and processing them (even recycled scrap metal) uses lots of energy. However, metals can be used very efficiently as they are so strong and can last indefinitely.

Copper

As well as being used for fabulous roofs ➤ see also **Copper roofs** p.159, copper has always had a big part to play inside buildings – for example, for water and gas pipes. While plastic pipe is cheaper to produce and easier to install, copper still has a role to play. Copper is not widely used as an interior finish because it is soft and will oxidise.

Manufactured off site, bespoke items can be very expensive. Mass-produced items can be very cost-effective.

Bronze

Whilst it is relatively expensive, bronze is a very beautiful material that I think is under used. Bronze can be used for both classic and contemporary items and fittings. It is hard wearing, and will not oxidise or decay. Door furniture in old and contemporary buildings can look beautiful in bronze. However, beware of bronze-coloured paint; the depth and variation of bronze cannot be replicated with a paint.

Conservation officers often seem to consider the use of 'authentic' metals in listed buildings important – for example, cast iron and bronze.

Mixing metals

In many cases, two different metals fixed together can react negatively and cause problems such as accelerated oxidisation, so be careful.

If you are unsure about the best way to use a certain metal – for example, whether it would be better to weld or bolt the junctions – speak to a metal worker, whose expertise can really be helpful.

Windows and glazing

The surge in popularity for roof windows, glass roofs, folding and sliding glass doors, combined with new awareness of environmental issues, means that glass companies are developing new products at great speed.

Glass is typically the least efficient part of the outside of a house. It has the worst 'U Value' for thermal efficiency, so the building regulations aim to reduce the total amount of glazed area allowed in houses and extensions. We all have a duty to make our homes energy efficient, and in the UK, more than anything else, that means keeping the heat in. Recent changes in the building regulations have contributed a great deal of confusion over how much glass you can use.

How much glass can you use?

The method for calculating the amount of glazed area you can have is fiendishly complex, and there are three approved methods for calculating what is or is not allowed. One method ➤ see also **SAP calculations** p.199 takes into account the potential heat loss of a glazed area and also the potential warmth that builds up inside (known as 'solar gain'). When offset with additional insulation or other improvements, such as an efficient boiler, this can allow for almost unlimited amounts of glazing to be within the regulations.

The green debate

The environmental issues with glass are not straightforward. More glazing will often mean more natural light, which will save energy on lighting. On the other hand, the energy lost through the glazing during the winter months may (or may not) supersede this. High thermal-efficiency glass can also retain heat. It is now possible to use heated glass in windows, replacing the need for radiators.

Solar-reflecting glass

Many people ask for solar-reflecting glass to cut down the glare and heat of the sun. Whilst this sounds like a good idea, this type of glass can be unattractive from the outside and gloomy on the inside when the sun is not fully out.

Roof windows are very practical because they come with flashings and frames, can be opened for ventilation, and can be turned almost 180 degrees to be cleaned from inside.

A room flooded with natural light feels larger and more airy than a gloomy space with a small window. The quality and intensity of daylight from above is significantly more effective than light from a side window.

The most effective way to shade a room with a glass roof from overpowering sunlight and heat is with external blinds or louvres. Internal blinds help psychologically, but do little to prevent heat build-up.

Roof windows are very cost-effective compared to a full glass roof. The speed and ease with which they can be installed saves a great deal of labour time and cost.

In order to demonstrate that your extension does not exceed the limits on thermal efficiency, you need to have SAP calculations done. Your architect may be able to put you in touch with a specialist, who can calculate these for you.

In order to gain approval and stay within the building regulations, you may often need to do more than just comply. You will often need to produce the calculations to clearly demonstrate that you do comply.

< **Glass roof.** The roof of this kitchen extension is two-thirds glass. Having gained planning and Listed Building Consent, the customer paused for a year before proceeding. During that time the building regulations changed. Additional insulation had to be added, and the French windows had to be triple-glazed to achieve the necessary levels of thermal efficiency.

> **Picture window.** The original brief was for a glass roof. After discussion, it was agreed that this might be overpowering. The solution was a solid roof, with two roof windows to let in light and maximise the glass available for a garden view.

Internal glass

The use of glass in interiors has grown considerably in recent years. Glass is seen as cool and sleek, it also allows physical separation of spaces without blocking out light. It is now used to divide spaces, for flooring, and for stairs and guardings.

Guardings (glass balustrades)

One of the most popular uses for internal glass is as a guarding (commonly known as a glass balustrade) ➤see also **Stairs** p.186. The effect can be stunning but it can take complex engineering to achieve. Even when toughened, glass is strong in some directions, but weak and vulnerable in others. When used as a balustrade, the glass has to be strong enough to withstand the pressure of someone leaning on the top of it. Very often the glass needs to be 12–15mm (½in) thick to be able to cope with the horizontal force.

A simple way to reduce the force on the glass is to use a timber or steel handrail at the top, fixed to something solid at each end. As long as the span is not too great, this will hold the top of the glass panel, and the glass will be under much less pressure. In some instances, however, this compromises the design.

‹ *Simple glass sheet reveals staircase. The glass panel in this interior forms the necessary side barrier (or guarding) for this plain white staircase. It appears to be simply standing in place, as the fixing channels are cleverly concealed within the floor and ceiling.*

∨ *Frameless cantilevered internal balconies. The sheets of glass on this floor edge are held with large steel fixings within the floor, and because they are concealed the glass appears to stand effortlessly in place.*

Flat, pure and easy to clean, glass can be used for table tops, shelves, worktops and cabinets, among other things. It will scratch fairly easily, so a surface or table top that is in constant use will not stay pristine for long.

Standard glass is slightly green and the colour can be seen at the edges of a piece of glass. Where purity of colour transmission is very important, you can choose low-iron glass (often known as optically clear glass), although it is costly.

Waste glass does not have to be thrown away. It can be recycled and turned into new glass items or gravel for roadworks, and has many other applications.

Interior partitions

Glass can also be used to great effect as an interior partition. The art is to make the effect seem as simple and effortless as possible, while the truth is that there is quite a lot of complicated design and engineering involved to achieve this.

Shower enclosures are more common examples of glass internal partitions and it is nice to design something really suitable for a luxury bathroom instead of putting up with proprietary cubicles. In bathrooms with the drain set in the floor, it is good to try to make the glass as frameless as possible. There is an example of this in the bathroom on page 177.

Coloured glass has become a very popular material for splashbacks and worktops in kitchens and bathrooms. It is easy to clean and can be made to the correct size from a template. These can be very beautiful but are often also very expensive.

Stairs and floors

Because glass is known to be so fragile, it gives a really impressive effect when used to carry weight. Glass stair treads and sections of glass floor are extravagant gestures that can allow light to pass vertically as well as create a daring structure. If you are planning something like this though, beware: the glass will need to be very thick and strong, which makes it excessively expensive. Glass also scratches easily and it can be a good idea to have a sacrificial layer of 10mm glass on top that can be replaced regularly at low cost, to protect the expensive thicker layers below.

If you are proposing a glass balustrade, your building inspector may insist upon detailed structural calculations to prove that it is strong enough to resist the required minimum level of horizontal forces upon it.

'Manifestation' is the requirement within the building regulations for some visible device to be put on glass sheets and doors at eye level, to ensure that people do not walk into the glass and hurt themselves.

‹ *Glass wall. This very high-ceilinged room is divided with a low-iron, optically-clear glass wall, a walnut timber base, and a full-height glass sliding door with concealed mechanism.*

Plastic, linoleum and rubber

The use of plastic within buildings is, for the most part, not evident. While we are familiar with using plastic for furniture and product design, within construction the majority of uses are either concealed or the plastic is taking the form of something else.

Almost infinite colour range. *This colour chart for rubber floor tiles sets out the standard range, but any colour can be made to order if required.*

Plastics

There are two main environmental arguments against using plastic. Firstly, it is manufactured as a by-product from oil, which is a finite and diminishing resource. The second objection is that for the most part, it is not biodegradable. In some ways this is exactly why plastic is used. We can lay a damp-proof membrane and rely upon it staying waterproof for decades. Technology must play its part in developing materials that achieve these levels of usefulness, without having a negative environmental impact.

Plastic windows

Perhaps the most visible use of plastic is in uPVC windows and doorframes. These have the benefit of requiring less maintenance than painted timber or steel windows, and they tend to be draught proof and waterproof. The main visual problem with uPVC windows is that the frames have to be very large to be strong enough, and as such, can appear badly proportioned and ugly. This, coupled with the fact that the surface material is unpleasant to the touch, tends to make them unpopular for quality building projects.

Plastic laminates

Laminates are thin, hardwearing sheet materials created by compressing a printed image under high pressure with a transparent plastic top layer. Particularly effective for worktop surfaces and cupboard doors, laminates can be used to create almost any surface effect, including solid colours, patterns and natural materials. Although reasonably expensive, it is now feasible for laminate companies to manufacture small areas with individual images, such as family photographs.

Linoleum and plastic vinyls

Plastic vinyls are used extensively as floor coverings, and are cheap, durable and can be printed with almost any colour or pattern. Vinyl floors have, to a great extent, taken over from linoleum, which was widely used during the mid-twentieth century. Linoleum is a wonderful natural product made from linseed oil and flax, and has raised the question of whether an environmentally damaging material such as vinyl flooring should be used when there is an effective, inexpensive alternative available.

Rubber

Like plastic, rubber is not synonymous with use in the home, although there are more uses than people imagine. Rubber is very effective as a waterproof seal in plumbing and weatherproofing, and is also very effective as a buffer between hard surfaces that may damage, scratch, vibrate or slip against each other. Unlike plastic, however, rubber is an entirely natural and completely sustainable material.

Perhaps the most visible use of rubber is as a sheet flooring material. Available in tile form, it can also be used on walls. There is a huge range of colours and textures available, it is easy to clean, offers surface warmth and good grip. Rubber flooring is becoming increasingly popular.

◁ **Rubber room.** *In this bright ground-floor WC, the cistern, waste and radiator supply pipes have been boxed in. The textured blue rubber surface washes down easily and is trimmed with an oak shelf, which is removable to access the cistern for maintenance.*

Plastics are very practical for many purposes. Electrical sockets and equipment, and plastic pipes and fittings are effective, reliable uses of plastic.

In furniture and product design, plastics are often used in their own right. In construction and interiors, plastics are, generally, either concealed or are pretending to be something else.

Technology has a responsibility to deliver products that achieve what we require without any environmental impact. In turn, we should use natural products where they are viable, such as linoleum and rubber in place of vinyl floor coverings.

Due to production processes, plastic components that are produced in bulk, such as power sockets and light switches, tend to be cheap. Costs dictate that plastic does not generally lend itself to bespoke manufacture.

Where Conservation Area Consent or Listed Building Consent is required for replacement windows, it is rare that uPVC would be considered an acceptable material for window frames.

Some plastic and rubber materials need special adhesives and some will be damaged by the wrong chemicals. Be sure to give all the necessary information from the manufacturer to your builder.

Honest oak and fake plastic.
These two samples of flooring say very different things. The piece of oak has an infinite variety of colour tones, the grain is visible in the thickness of the wood, and the weight and touch is reassuring and familiar. The plastic floor sample has a repeat photograph of wood printed onto it beneath a plastic coating of uniform sheen. As a material it is disconcertingly thin, light and unpleasant to touch.

The honest and the fake

A very dependable principle of good design is legibility and honesty. In short, if things express what they are, they generally work better in design terms than things that are pretending to be something else.

There is a vast range of products available that take their inspiration from natural materials. Vinyl flooring printed to look like wood grain, and laminates printed to look like marble, are popular. There is nothing intrinsically wrong with laminate as a product; the problem occurs when it claims to be something that it is not.

Many 'fake' products are rarely convincing. Once the secret is revealed, they work very much in the same way as a one-line joke – effective once, but disappointing afterwards. It is important to choose the right materials for the task in question and let all materials express themselves for what they are.

Often, fake products are cheaper than the material that they are trying to ape. Consider, however, whether they offer good value. If your budget will not stretch to real stone, don't use fake stone; use something honest that is cheaper.

It is important not to be dogmatic. There are good porcelain tiles available, with a limestone type surface, which are an immensely practical and cheaper alternative to real limestone. In my personal view, this is acceptable and attractive. However, a tile imprinted with pretend fossils is trite and disappointing.

I recently visited a consumer show and witnessed a demonstration of a product that could be sprayed onto the outside wall of a house. It was a thick, sandy-coloured cement product. Once it had been applied, a man went over it drawing grooves into the wet surface to create the effect of a Cotswold stone wall. The salesman claimed that it added insulation and waterproofing to a home, which I do not doubt, but why did it have to pretend to be Cotswold stone? An insulating acrylic render is a useful product, can look good, and is honest in itself.

Laminates and vinyl

You may have the choice between a real timber floor and a laminate or vinyl floor covering that has the exact wood grain printed upon it. When looking at a sample, they might appear to be very similar. Once laid on the floor, however, there is just no comparison. The laminate or vinyl will be too consistent in tone over a large area, have a slightly too perfect texture to be natural, and slightly too much 'give' when you stand on it.

Plastic laminates are available for a wide range of products (flooring, worktops, kitchen units) and can be produced with any type of printed surface. It is a perfectly worthy material in its own right, having many attractive and useful qualities, so if you want to use plastic laminate, let it be what it is.

Glass and acrylic

When working with glass, the weight of the material is often a challenging part of the design task. People often think about using a polycarbonate or acrylic sheet, such as Perspex, instead of glass to reduce the weight. The problem is that these materials do not behave like glass: they scratch more easily, they lose some of their transparency over time, and they are not as hard and cold to the touch as the real thing. There is nothing wrong with clear acrylic sheet, it has great qualities and can be used in many ways, but it is not a substitute for glass.

Do not be swayed by the argument that plastic surfaces are practical as a justification to use a building product, such as laminate flooring, which is pretending to be something else entirely. You will be living with a lie for a long time.

Any truly natural surface is made up of a variety of different tones and shades of colour. Over a large area the variation of tone gives it visual depth.

Printed vinyls and laminate surfaces are not biodegradable. After their useful life in your home, unless some specific recycling programme is developed for such products, they will remain intact in a landfill site.

Many products that pretend to be something else are cheaper than the material they are trying to ape. You need to consider whether they offer good value.

When repairing or extending a listed building, fake materials are generally not acceptable. Listed Building Consent will most likely insist that the materials you use are a true match – looking similar is simply not good enough.

If your specification is not clear, a builder might take it upon himself to substitute a fake product on the grounds of practicality or cost. Clear communication is vital to avoid such things happening.

Fabrics, leather and carpets

Some architects see the limit of their involvement as being any facet of a home that is functional, leaving decorative items outside of their scope. Fabrics and carpets, in my view, have clear functional purposes, as well as a decorative role to play.

There is no clear definition as to where architectural design stops and interior design starts. Like most things, these disciplines do not fit neatly into pigeonholes. Clearly, a great deal of the design that architects do is concerned with the interior of a house. Blinds can help control internal temperatures, curtains can provide insulation and draught-proofing, and carpets can absorb sound better than hard surfaces.

⌄ ***Fabrics from the same family.** This array of cushions in different patterns of black and white are all part of one 'family' within the manufacturer's range, and are designed to be used together.*

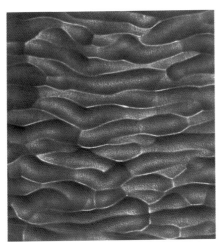

Bonded leather wall panels. *These fabulous panels are machine cut from MDF and the leather is press-bonded to give a remarkable dramatic effect.*

Fabrics

The scope of this book cannot even begin to cover the thousands of fabrics available to the designer. From heavy velvets to gossamer-like voiles, the choices are endless, and the prices can vary enormously. Two important practical tips to bear in mind when considering fabrics are:

- Consider what the fabric will be used for. An upholstery fabric may be too heavy and sag if it is used as a curtain, and a lightweight fabric may wear badly if it is constantly handled. Will you need to clean or wash the fabric and if so, how viable is this? There is always plenty of advice from the fabric supply company, so choose carefully.

- Pay close attention to the fabric width. Fabrics are manufactured in a variety of different widths. If, for example, you want upholstered wall panels, check that the fabric roll is wide enough to cover the full panel with a little spare to wrap around the edges, otherwise unsightly seams may be apparent. This is also important for roller blinds, as vertical seams will, generally, not allow the fabric to roll evenly.

Leather

One material that has become very popular in the home is leather. For years this tough, yet soft, material has been used for upholstery and writing surfaces on desks, but these days it is also available in the form of tiles that can be used on feature walls and, in some circumstances, floors. It is also available bonded to MDF, both flat and textured, which can form interesting wall panels. Most of all, leather is a very real, natural material that is a pleasure to touch. Used where it will be in contact with hands or feet – for example, on handrails – it can give a touch of warmth and luxury.

Carpets

After losing favour to hard floors during the 1990s, carpets have become popular once more. Carpet is easy to clean, absorbs sound and is soft underfoot. It is also very often the cheapest choice for a floor covering in a room that requires more than a basic finish. As with fabrics, there is a wide range of different weaves and constructions of carpet, made from synthetic materials as well as natural fibres such as wool, sea-grass and coir.

Large rooms with hard floors can feel very hollow and uninviting if there is nothing to absorb the sound. Curtains, carpets, upholstered furniture and wall panels absorb sound effectively and can make a space feel more human.

Fabric companies generally produce ranges of fabrics in complementary patterns and colours. When composing a design, using fabrics from the same range is a reliable way to create a sympathetic effect.

The popularity of natural fibres, produced without harmful bleaches and toxic dyes, has grown in relation to people's awareness of the environmental damage that chemicals can do.

Fabrics range in price enormously, so do not be caught out. Always check the roll width and establish whether the price is per linear metre or per square metre. If you calculate wrongly, you can overspend easily.

Many fabrics are given flame-retardant treatments to comply with building regulations. However, do not confuse flame retardant (resistance to burning) with fire resistant (resistance to letting fire through), as they are very different qualities.

Fabrics can be used to express different interior mood and style. With throws, wall hangings, bed-covers and cushions it is often feasible to have different fabrics so that a mood can be changed.

Sanitary ware

The choice of basins, taps, WCs, baths and shower equipment can be mesmerising. Not only are there hundreds of companies, each producing a huge range of choices, but there also seems to be a radical and almost arbitrary range of costs.

A word of caution before you go shopping: beautiful bathrooms are generally beautiful because the space is well designed and the lighting is just right. Expensive sanitary ware cannot make a badly designed bathroom any good on its own, so think about the overall design of a room before you spend any money ➤ see also **Bathroom details** pp.176–7.

Nonetheless, sanitary ware can be very beautiful, both visually and simply as a pleasure to use. You will, up to a point, get what you pay for, and it is worth choosing carefully.

The sources of sanitary ware fall into three categories:

- DIY superstores and builders' merchants offer some very low-cost and, it has to be said, low-quality options. If you are aiming at the budget end of the spectrum there are some very good deals to be had, but look carefully at the items in the flesh – do not rely on an image in a catalogue, as the reality can be flimsy and disappointing.

- Large manufacturers offer a broad range of good quality products and will have excellent websites and sensible prices. For the most part, you will still have to purchase through a dealer, although prices are more carefully controlled as the products are available throughout the UK.

- Designer sanitary ware is the third category and is manufactured by specialist companies, typically in Italy and Spain. These will generally be available through UK bathroom shops. Even if you find the origin of the product on the Internet, most design companies will only sell through dealers and not directly to the customer. The prices for many of these products can be very high, but the quality can also be very special, with some incredibly beautiful and striking designs available. Generally, the attention to detail and manufacture mean that they are made to last.

Washbasins

The type of basin you choose will depend upon the layout of your bathroom. Should it be wall-mounted, or sit on a vanity unit? Should it cantilever off the wall, or stand on a pedestal? If it is part of a unit, should it sit on top like a bowl, or be recessed into the worktop, with or without the rim exposed? Will the taps be mounted on the wall, unit, or on the basin itself? Answering these questions will help to narrow your options, so that you can focus on comparing similar items.

Do not leave the choice of your sanitary ware to the last minute. If it has to come from mainland Europe, it can take up to 12 weeks (especially during August).

The beauty of a quality piece of sanitary ware is not just visual. There is great pleasure to be gained each time you use a well-engineered tap, and each time you lie in a bath that fits your body shape.

On average, showers use much less water than baths, which is good for water conservation and reduces energy usage. However, large showerheads, with torrents of hot water, bring the water consumption of a long shower close to bath usage.

Steel baths (with an enamel surface) are more expensive than acrylic (plastic) baths, but tend to be more pleasing to use and will last longer. If you are buying online it may not be immediately apparent whether the bath you are choosing is steel or plastic.

In shower cubicles, it is important that the shower door opens outwards. In the event of an accident, someone collapsed in a shower would prevent the door from opening.

We all have our own preferences in the bathroom: some people need a mirror and others hate them, some need lots of storage, others need less. Make sure you explain your particular requirements.

< **Simple sanitary ware in good space.** *This pair of semi-recessed washbasins were not expensive and added a beautiful simplicity to this well laid out bathroom.*

Light fittings

Before you choose any light fittings you need to identify the type of luminance you need
➤ see also **Lighting design** pp.182–3. Following this comes the fun part of choosing the light fitting itself. Recessed ceiling lights, wall washers, pendants, concealed halo lights, picture lights and floor lights – there is a great choice available to you. Here are a few of my favourites:

Wire globe cluster pendant

These pendants are handmade in Italy by bending wire into a globe shape, and then weaving strands of small halogen lights throughout the sphere, which gives a beautiful, gentle and yet visually stunning effect. They can be made in different diameters from 300 to 1000mm (12 to 40in). One customer bought three of different diameters, and hung them like planets over her staircase.

Low-voltage halogen spot

These small light fittings are usually recessed into a ceiling, where the transformer that turns the 240v supply into 12v for the light is concealed. This example has a round casing and provides a beam of warm light. It is available either as a fixed (where the beam points straight down), or a directional (where the beam can be angled towards a picture or object) fitting. Square ones are also available and can look very cool.

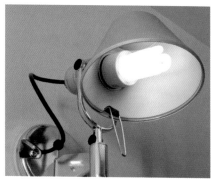

Wall-mounted fitting

This wall-mounted light fitting can take an incandescent light bulb, or a low-energy compact fluorescent lamp. Many people associate low-energy lighting with boring, clunky fittings but this elegant fitting illustrates that even the best lighting can be environmentally responsible. It is part of a range that includes floor-standing and desk-top versions, angle-poise options, and even paper shades in place of the aluminium one shown here. The shade can be turned upward to give uplight.

Feature pendant

This unusual and very striking pendant would be fantastic above a huge dining table or, as here, over the island in a kitchen. The 'wings' incorporate simple fluorescent tubes, which can be dimmed. Both asymmetrical and symmetrical versions of this fitting are available.

Diffused light

Using two simple fluorescent tubes, this fitting hides the direct light, and washes the wall above and below with a beautifully simple and soft light. In this example, the wall covering, which has texture running in two directions, is enhanced by the effect of the light. When using fittings such as this, with concealed light sources, think carefully about positioning, so that you do not catch the source directly from any angle. It is particularly easy to place a fitting on a stairway, for example, only to find that from downstairs you look directly into the light source.

Light switches and power sockets

Essentially functional items, light switches and power sockets can ruin the visual simplicity of an interior if they are not given suitable consideration. In their most basic form, they are available in a white plastic finish. These are eminently suitable for most applications, as they are low cost and do not draw attention to themselves. However, in certain interiors, there is a case for matching the materials of the switch and socket plates with the finish of the wall or door furniture. Switches and sockets can be obtained in coloured, glass and stainless steel finishes.

Dimmer switches are particularly popular, and allow much more control of the mood of the lighting. The choice becomes harder, however, because many lights, particularly most fluorescent sources, cannot be dimmed. Dimmers also require a power rating. This means that if you want to dim a group of lights, you need to ensure that the total power requirement of those lights does not exceed that of the switch.

Lighting control systems are becoming increasingly popular (see below). You can programme combinations of lights at different levels of intensity to create mood settings. For example, you might want to set up one scene for pre-dinner entertaining, a lower variation for dinner itself, and a third brighter scene for clearing up after your guests have left.

If you have an assortment of different light fittings that need different lamps (bulbs) you will need to keep a spare stock of each type. Consider having two or three types only.

The choice of light fittings is important and needs to be considered both in terms of the light they emit and the sculptural role they might play in a particular room.

Do not make the mistake of believing that low-voltage lights are the same as low-energy lights. In fact, low-voltage lights use a great deal of energy and produce a lot of wasted heat.

The total cost of a low-voltage down-light is much more than the purchase price of the fitting itself. You need to budget for the transformer, lamp, wiring and installation, and decorative repairs to the ceiling.

Building regulations require that for new works one-third of the lighting should be low-energy rated. There is some flexibility as to where these lights can be located, and only fittings that can accept low-energy lamps count towards the total.

Lighting control systems, such as those illustrated left, allow you to pre-set different moods of lighting, so that you can have one setting for dinner guests and another for a drinks party.

⌃ *The nerve centre.* This touch-screen panel allows each individual light fitting to be set to a percentage luminance and then grouped so that different combinations can be retrieved.

⌃ *Room by room.* A switch like this one in another room can instruct the system to bring up whichever of the pre-set combinations the touch-screen panel has set up.

Technology

When Bill Gates founded Microsoft, he identified two growth areas for business: the potential for personal computing and the desire for home automation. While he was clearly right on the first point, for some time it looked as though he was wide of the mark with home automation. Now it appears that he was further ahead of his time than he realised.

The ability to light your fire, close your curtains and start the oven from one remote control device, or even from outside the home, is now not just a possibility, but is becoming increasingly popular.

The lighting control system illustrated on page 239 can also be linked to the heating and cooling system, multi-room audio systems, and just about anything that has an electronic control. The control system has a hub, with a touch control screen, which allows levels and settings to be programmed, linked to timers and connected to the Internet.

With Internet shopping becoming ever more popular, there are now fridges with computer screens built into the doors, so that groceries can be ordered directly from the kitchen. Perhaps the most popular recent advances, however, relate to audio and video systems.

Multi-room audio system

The advent of digital audio, stored on a computer or MP3 player, has all but killed off the CD. More and more people are keeping their music collections on a hard disc that can be accessed from several sources at once. The ability to play different music, in different rooms of a house, at different levels, all from one central music library, is impressive to us now, but may well be ordinary and even superseded in years to come. Systems, such as the Sonos player, control the different zones within a house as simply as using an iPod.

Concealed speakers

Aside from the most outlandishly expensive and sculptural varieties, audio speakers have always been something of an eyesore within an interior. This is all set to change, as the new generation of concealed speakers come into general use. These ultra-thin units can be concealed within a painting, ceiling panel, cupboard door, or even built into the thickness of a wall and plastered over.

Home cinema

Many people now require a home cinema – basically, a dedicated TV room, with a giant screen (either a projected system, or a very large, plasma flat screen) and surround-sound. Generally, these are well suited to basements, as the environment is blacked out from daylight and given heavy acoustic insulation.

Home automation can be effective for security purposes. Lights and curtains can follow standard daily patterns, even if the occupants are away. Access control systems can provide a video link to see visitors before letting anyone in.

Comprehensive devices that control all of your equipment from one handset, with a wireless link to a control hub concealed in a cupboard, will mean the end of numerous remote control devices.

It is important to provide plenty of ventilation for any equipment that is hidden in a cupboard, or ceiling void. Computers, DVD players and amplifiers all produce heat, and need to be ventilated.

It is easy to get carried away and spend huge amounts of money on automation systems. Keep the expenditure relative to the rest of the development. Carefully controlled budgets can completely unravel by technology installation.

If you live in a terraced or semi-detached property and you are thinking of in-wall speakers, ensure that you do not undermine the acoustic integrity of the separating wall or ceiling. Cutting in to plasterboard linings may cause unwanted noise transfer.

The Internet is becoming increasingly central to home automation, so that systems can be controlled remotely. For instance, holiday homes can have their heating turned on before you arrive.

◀ *Light-filled living room becomes a home cinema.* Much of the technology used in this home cinema system from the late 1990s has now been superseded. However, the remote-controlled conversion from daylight-flooded living room to darkened cinema space, with the black-out blinds, projector and screen coming down from the ceiling, was at the cutting edge when it was first installed.

Communicating your specification

It is one thing choosing all of the materials, finishes and fittings that you want within your home, but all of those choices are useless unless they are properly and effectively communicated to those responsible for designing and building your vision.

People often think that they can just tell the builder what they want, but trying to work on this basis inevitably leads to mistakes, and more often than not, arguments as to who should foot the bill. To control the process properly, you need to specify your requirements at the time of pricing the project.

Outline Schedule of Works

The most comprehensive way to communicate what you want is with a full specification document to be read alongside the drawings, but for most home owner projects it is not necessary to go into infinitesimal detail. The most common approach is to prepare a document called an Outline Schedule of Works. This is a summary of the work to be done, broken down into chunks, from ground works, external walls and floor construction, through to finishes and decoration. This can include reference to the general standards of workmanship required, as well as specification of particular items, such as door handles or ceramic tiles, that have been chosen.

A good way to set out all the information is with a series of smaller schedules. For example, you may write a door schedule, which is essentially a list of all of the doors within the scope of the project, including the dimensions, materials, finishes and door furniture to be used in each case.

Make sure that your schedules cross-reference to the project drawings in a way that can be clearly understood. If you use codes, such as D1 for door one, make sure that there is no confusion with other references. This can be a very effective way of being specific about the things that you are particular about, without creating unreasonable amounts of paperwork and administration.

Performance Specification

Another method for communication that is often used is a Performance Specification. This involves specifying the standard to which something must perform rather than what it is precisely. For example, rather than specify a particular runner for a set of dressing room drawers, you can say that the contractor can use any drawer runner he likes, as long as it achieves specified levels of smooth running and durability.

Whilst this might seem to be an ideal way to unload the task of choosing the right item for the job, sometimes specifying the performance standard can be even more involved than specifying the item itself. Choose the most sensible approach for your project, and combine both methods when necessary.

< **Different components.** Alongside the detail design drawings, this bathroom needed a clear specification of tiles, bath, concrete bath surround, glass, sliding mechanism and guides for the glass screen, tap and shower controls, cupboard doors and handles.

Not enough detail in specification information can lead to arguments over what should and should not be included in the price. Too much detail can cause unwieldy and expensive administration.

If you lose control of the detail of your project, you may well end up with an end result that you are not happy with. Great detail is the key to making your project really special, but it cannot be achieved without concerted effort and cost.

Even if you choose environmentally responsible materials, your builder may not appreciate the difference and order a less environmentally friendly option. If you feel strongly about something, specify exactly what you want.

One side effect of a detailed specification is that builders will tend to push up the price. You may think that you are making life easier, but a detailed specification can appear complicated and time consuming, so the price will inevitably rise.

The specification will become part of the contract and, if any disputes arise, it may be central to any claim that goes before a court. Make sure you are confident that the information clearly describes what you want.

A simple rule of specification is that if you leave something unclear, it will almost certainly be misinterpreted. Try to be as specific as possible, without creating so much work that it all becomes too complex.

Case study

5. Specification

Returning again to the case study, these pages show some images of a selection of the materials and fittings specified within the project.

Thinking back to the 'starting point' ▶see also **Case study** pp.27–9, we identified a number of aims on the wish list, including 'honest' and 'natural' materials, and durability.

As discussed on pages 232–3, 'honesty' in the choice of materials and fittings does not simply mean natural materials (although most natural materials are 'honest'). Stainless steel, glass, plaster and paint are also 'honest' as they are clearly not trying to be anything other than what they are.

Durability was always an aim, particularly since this is a house for a family with young children, who will inevitably spill paint, overflow the bath, bring in mud and leave grubby hand-prints everywhere. The rubber tiles used in the family bathroom are a good example of how these likely mishaps can be allowed for in advance.

Stainless steel was chosen for the kitchen worktops in the areas where the most wear occurs, around the hob and kitchen sink. However, we felt that if all the surfaces were stainless steel, the kitchen might lack visual warmth, and so cherry-wood worktops were used in areas where there is less wear and tear.

A clear specification is just as important outside the house as inside, and the choices of granite setts, outside lights, the colour and texture of the render, and the timbers for decking and cladding all needed to be carefully considered and specified.

Kitchen worktops. The warmth of cherry-wood worktops combines with the durability of stainless steel in the high-wear areas of the kitchen.

Handrails and fittings. The handrails on the stairs were specified as square stainless steel tube and the fittings made specially from stainless steel.

Blue rubber bathroom. Rubber walls and flooring make a fun bathroom for kids, as well as one that can cope with spills and sponge fights.

Staggered strip mosaic tiles. These ?rcelain tiles in the wet room have been ?anged in a random pattern to give a ?matic horizontal effect. The floor tiles are ? to a fall, so that water will flow to the drain.

A palette of materials. Oak floor and ?lnut-veneered doors blend nicely; granite ?ts on the front pathway; three Artemide ?erior lights for garden illumination.

6 Building your design

A prerequisite for a successful project is to get the design right. If you just charge into the building process without due consideration and planning, the whole project can be a disaster.

Choosing the right contractor to work with, settling upon the right price, making sure that the terms of the contract are all agreed, and sorting out and sticking to the project timetable, all need careful planning.

You also need to think carefully about how the project is going to run. Are you planning to have regular site meetings? If so, how often, and who needs to attend? How much will this cost and at what point is it not worth the money?

practicality

aesthetic

environment

cost/value

regulations

communication

Building your design

You have now reached the stage where the design is finished, the ideas have been developed and turned into detailed drawings, all of the materials and fittings have been specified, and you are ready for the physical work to begin.

Where should you start? How should things be organised? Like many aspects of any building project, people want a simple answer and to know the 'right way' to go about things. Unfortunately, the simple truth is that building is not simple. There are many alternative routes to follow, all of which suit different projects.

The scale of your project, how involved you want to become, the availability of suitable builders and tradesmen, how much you want to spend on administration, and many more factors will determine the best route for you.

The following pages explore ways of running and organising a project, ways of choosing a builder, and different contract arrangements. Your architect can help you decide upon the best route, and can undertake many of the tasks, such as tendering (see opposite) and contract administration ➤ see also **The building contract** pp.252–3 if you decide that is the way to go.

The complexity of any building project means that there are potential pitfalls, whichever route you choose to take. In many cases, the ideal of close control and good organisation has to be balanced against the budget. Like anything else, professional help costs, and while there are many people who are able to advise you, the value judgements can only be yours to make.

Who does the work?

One of the most common dilemmas is whether to use a main contractor, or to sub-contract different tasks directly to tradesmen, plumbers and plasterers, and so on. The idea behind this is to avoid paying the mark-up that the main contractor will put on the cost of his subcontractors (usually between 12 and 20 per cent).

If you decide to take the sub-contractor route, you will need to have a lot of time to dedicate to this task (far more than most people imagine). You will need to understand the building process and know what you are talking about, otherwise you will be taken for a ride at almost every stage. Finally, you need to be tough; if you don't relish confrontation, don't take this on.

Generally, main contractors really do earn their mark-up. They know where to find reliable tradesmen and subcontractors, and they can co-ordinate the work. Suppliers and subcontractors invariably don't turn up when they promise they will, and often try to blame each other for problems. Is this a headache that you really want to take on?

Tender and negotiation

If you are going to use a main contractor, how you choose the right person is vitally important. There is not one way of doing this, and you will need to think through which selection method is right for your circumstances.

The four most common ways of getting to an agreed price for your works with a building contractor are:

1. Tendering. Where different contractors price competitively for a defined package of work.

2. Negotiation. Where the basis for charging is agreed and prices are worked out collaboratively.

3. Fixing a price. Where a fixed price is set for a fixed package of work.

4. Cost-plus price. Where the contractor's time and materials are charged as they add up.

1. Tendering

The traditional approach to choosing a main contractor is to put the drawings and specification information together into a 'tender' package. This package is then sent out to five or six builders who will cost the work in detail and submit their proposals, including price, timescale and start date. The idea is that the pressure of a competitive tender will drive the price down to give the best deal possible.

The main problem with tendering is that it can set up a confrontational contractual situation from the start. Builders are encouraged to make their price look as cheap as possible, so that they will win the work. You may find that they present their tender with half-hidden caveats, which enable them to come back later for additional money.

If you do follow a tender process, the best way of guarding against this practice is to present a very detailed package of information, and then use a quantity surveyor or architect to check the tenders submitted.

2. Negotiation

The alternative to tendering the project is known as a 'negotiated' process. This term is quite unhelpful because it suggests that you start with one position and haggle to get the best deal. The benefits of a negotiated process, however, are just the opposite. The idea is to choose a builder, based upon recommendation and past examples of work, at a relatively early stage of the process. This can enable genuine teamwork to develop. If you can agree the variables up-front, such as the labour rates and mark-up on materials, the builder can then commit to the project, and assist with planning and price prediction as the designs develop.

3. Fixing a price

It is important to recognise that pricing a job is not only a very expensive and time-consuming task for builders, but it also requires them to take on a great deal of risk. No matter how experienced builders are, it is impossible to know exactly how long each task will take to complete, and what sort of problems they will encounter. By committing to a fixed price, builders risk not charging enough.

Fixed price tenders and contracts will contain a certain amount of 'fat' for builders in case of miscalculation. You should also remember that builders need to make a living, and overheads, administration, insurance and profit need to be represented in the price. The element that usually represents these is called 'preliminaries' or 'prelims'.

A tender process can take a month or longer, so if time is a very important factor for you, a negotiated contract may be the best choice.

High-specification projects that require care and attention in their detail and finishing will require different organisational arrangements compared to basic, low-value works that need to be undertaken quickly and cheaply.

Increasingly, home owners are held responsible for looking after the environment around the building site. Intrusive construction noise, mud on the road and the protection of tree roots has to be controlled and monitored.

If a cost-plus arrangement is followed, it is necessary to have strict controls **> see pp.255–6** ensuring that the builder will not drag his heels, taking longer than planned, and costing more than necessary.

If you choose to follow the 'building notice method' **> see pp.200–1**, it is usual for your builder to submit the building notice. Make sure that doing this is stipulated as part of the duties that he will be required to do, or he may seek additional money.

An experienced architect I know often repeats the phrase, 'the most expensive thing you can do is rush!'. Take the time to get the right arrangement and negotiate the right deal for your circumstances.

4. Cost-plus price

An alternative way for builders to charge for their work is on a basis known as 'cost-plus'. The costs that the builder incurs are charged, plus an agreed percentage mark-up on labour, materials and subcontractors. This arrangement suits the builder very well and leaves the customer exposed, not knowing what the final bill will be. On the upside, however, due to the reduced risk, builders will usually be prepared to work at a much-reduced margin. In theory, this should give the cheapest cost in the end.

The building contract

While many forms of building contract are extremely daunting, it does not have to be complex. However, it is absolutely essential to come to an agreement with your builder, before work starts, about what is to be done and what will be charged.

In very simple terms, a building contract is an agreement made between a client (usually the owner) and a contractor (usually a builder). The contract states that the contractor will undertake the work described (shown in attached drawings and documents) within a set amount of time, while the client will pay the amount of money agreed at the set stages throughout the project.

Why have a contract?

The idea of a contract is that there is a written and agreed procedure to deal with whatever circumstances may arise. A simple exchange of letters will constitute a contract, but it does leave both parties rather exposed as many possible scenarios will have no pre-agreed resolution. Some people try to write their own contracts, which can be very dangerous unless you are a professional contract writer!

You can buy standard forms of contract from various bookshops or the Internet. The best are published by the JCT (Joint Contracts Tribunal). You can buy the contract document and complete the project details in pre-set boxes. Even within the JCT, there is a whole selection of different contract forms and many go into so much detail that they would be too complex for most projects. The options include:

JCT contract for a home owner/occupier Very basic, this is a simple agreement between the home owner and builder and is suitable for small and simple building projects.

JCT minor works contract Suitable for most medium sized home owner projects, this form requires that a 'contract administrator' (CA) be appointed (see below). This would usually be your architect.

JCT intermediate form of contract More complicated and thorough, this would usually only be used on large and complex home owner projects and is more commonly used on commercial projects. Again, a CA is required.

Other forms that are less likely to be relevant for home owner projects include: JCT Standard Building Contract, JCT Major Project Construction Contract, JCT Prime Cost Arrangements Contract, JCT Design and Build Contract, JCT Management Contract.

Clauses for every eventuality

While it may seem unnecessary to agree anything more than what is to be done, and for how much, there are a number of issues that need to be agreed in advance. Insurance, site security, and arrangements for resolving disputes, are important matters that need to be discussed.

A building contract is there to protect the interests of both parties in a fair and even-handed way. Neither a builder nor a client should ever enter into a contract with the feeling that they are being led into a trap.

Take time to go through the detail of what you will be agreeing to, and if necessary, negotiate any points that you feel uncomfortable with.

Bear in mind that certain clauses may seem too onerous to the contractor. For example, if you include a penalty clause for late delivery, a builder may not agree to it, or he may put up his price to protect himself from risk. Although this is a sensible precaution, you need to find an equitable solution you can both agree to.

Keeping to a contract

In all but the very simplest forms of contract, it is necessary for someone to take the role of contract administrator. More often than not the architect of the project will take on this role. The contract administrator is responsible for issuing certificates throughout the progress of the contract. These certificates confirm certain stages of completion and are used as the basis for stage payments. At the end of the works the contract administrator will issue practical completion and final completion certificates > see also **The final stages** pp.256-7.

The building process

While it may seem that you have done nothing but spend money for no tangible result thus far, the really expensive phase starts now. Once work starts on site, the key to success is all about control and communication.

If you have invested in professional expertise, detailed drawings, and have a clear contract covering who does what and when, then you should be able to retain good control of the building process.

The main point of contact

Firstly, it is important to identify who is going to be the main point of contact for each party on a day-to-day basis. It needs to be clear who the contractor should come to with queries. You may want to tackle some of these queries yourself, but are you able to answer the more technical questions that may arise? If you want your architect to answer technical questions, make sure you have discussed which type of questions should be directed at you and which at him or her. If you do answer questions yourself, be careful. What may seem to be an innocuous change to the position of a pipe or joist, for a perfectly valid reason, may have implications to a different part of the design, or to elements to be fitted later that you have not appreciated.

When proposing a sum of money for damages if work is late, it is often a good incentive to propose an equal and opposite sum as a bonus to the contractor for early completion.

While a thorough design process tries to avoid the need for changes on site, sometimes you can only make a decision about something when you see it in the flesh. The contract should be able to cope with changes, so if changes need to be made, you can make them.

The discovery of asbestos under floors or within walls will require that all work stops while specialist removal work is undertaken. This would be considered a legitimate reason for an extension of time to the contract period.

Following the issue of a valuation certificate, it is advisable to make payment to the contractor promptly. Contractors come under significant cash flow pressures during a project, and slow or late payment can bring problems that might impact on your project.

If you are following the 'building notice' method for approval >see pp.200-1, there is a chance that the building inspector may require changes to the works. This could add extra costs and time delays.

In theory, all the terms of a contract must be fully met. However, in the real world, when disputes arise, a value judgement sometimes needs to be made, because the costs of forcing through pedantic issues can outweigh the benefits.

On the contractor's side, the main point of contact may be the owner of the business, especially if he or she works on site. A large building company may have several projects on at one time and your main contact may be a contract manager, with a site foreman working under him.

Site meetings

Whatever structure you do have, it is always a good idea to agree upon regular site meetings from the start of the project. The two main points of contact should attend site meetings, with other parties included when required. Sometimes it can feel that progress is held back by meetings, and there is an urge to 'get on with it', but often the benefits of properly structured meetings are well worth the time investment.

Don't break the lines of communication

Once you have established good points of contact and regular meetings, it is vital that these lines of communication are not broken. It may seem expedient and harmless to speak directly to a subcontractor on site, instead of waiting to see the main contractor, but informal conversations can be problematic. For example, you could ask the electrician to change the location of sockets, but this could lead to time delays in other areas. Once you have set up controls, it is in your interest to keep to them.

Disputes

Disputes during the building process are all too common. While many disputes result from one or other party being in breach of their obligations, it is more often the case that disputes arise due to poor communication.

Building projects are complex, there are often many different parties involved, and there is a great deal of money at stake. The combination of these factors means that when a problem arises, there is all too often a tendency for all parties to become defensive and start pointing blame in every direction.

Avoiding disputes

Behind every problem, which has been allowed to escalate, there is usually a perfectly resolvable solution. Clarity and good communication are the way to try to avoid disputes, and heading off potential disagreements is one of the key responsibilities of whoever is trying to run the project. If the level of quality to which something must be done is clearly communicated and understood from the start, there should be little opportunity for argument as to whether that level of quality has been reached.

The first step in diffusing a dispute that is starting to develop is to meet face-to-face and discuss the problem. E-mail can be a very divisive tool and, in my experience, people tend to be much more pragmatic and reasonable when they have to look each other in the eye.

Resolving differences

Most contracts stipulate that if a dispute develops, the parties should attempt to resolve things through an arbitration or adjudication process. There are set procedures for both processes. Arbitration is where an independent person, with suitable expertise, speaks to both parties and tries to persuade them towards common ground and resolution. Adjudication is different in that an independent expert is presented with the arguments of each side, and then makes a decision that is binding.

Taking legal action

The backstop for all disputes is litigation. Many of the arguments used in arbitration and adjudication procedures revolve around what 'would' happen if the case went to court. In the end, if matters become completely entrenched, the injured party will have to choose between walking away and litigation.

People involved in disputes over building contracts often take these matters very personally, and, in many cases, will pursue a dispute to the courts that they should really just leave alone. The amount of time, stress and money involved in litigation can be horrendous, and, unless you are completely sure of your ground and 'up for the fight', I would strongly recommend you steer clear.

Withholding money

One popular tactic, when people are unhappy with aspects of the work being done, is to withhold payment to the builder. While this can be a very powerful lever, it has three potential negative effects.

Firstly, prompt payment is essential for a builder. Cutting this off will certainly undermine any sense of teamwork, and will cement a confrontational relationship. Secondly, if cash flow issues become critical, you may push the builder out of business, which will almost certainly be disastrous for your project. Finally, if withholding payment could be deemed unreasonable, you will be in breach of your contract. This will weaken your case if the matter goes to adjudication or court.

Keeping on track

However well planned the project is, and regardless of how detailed the design drawings and specification are, there will always be problems that need to be solved, decisions that need to be made, and more often than not, changes that have to be accommodated.

These problems, decisions and changes will test your organisational structure and, more than ever, it is the level of clarity and good communication that will determine how effectively the project can ride out these matters.

Managing changes

At some level, changes to the proposed works of any project are inevitable. Whether these are caused by someone changing their mind, the discovery of unforeseen circumstances (such as dry-rot in the roof timbers), or new input from the builder, there needs to be a way to include them in the contract, and a way to agree the cost and time implications.

A huge amount of time, money and energy can be wasted in disputes between parties under a building contract. Very often the practical solution is to back down over the principle and get on with the job.

One of the hardest things to define in a building contract is quality of workmanship and this can often lead to disputes later on. Workmanship standards and sample finishes are good ways to try to solve this in advance.

If a contractor is required by law to fulfil an environmentally responsible task, such as the proper disposal of contaminated material, that may not have been foreseen in the contract, this would constitute a legitimate additional cost on the contract.

To avoid costly claims or fines, it is good to specify things, such as the conduct of the contractor's operatives on site, requirements for environmental protection, safety hoardings and even times for deliveries to be made in the contract.

General provisions within a building contract that require such things as 'all works to comply with the building regulations' would be difficult to enforce should the drawings propose something that is non-compliant.

The Royal Institute of British Architects (RIBA) publishes set procedures for arbitration and adjudication of disputes. It is important to realise that following these procedures correctly is vital, otherwise your action could backfire.

The most popular way to manage changes is called an 'Architect's Instruction' or 'AI'. This term tends to be used even when there is no architect involved. The AI is usually a very simple sheet of paper that records the details of the change in question, the date, and the addition or reduction in price and timescale that would be appropriate. When signed by the contract administrator, or other key contacts, this form acts as a formal instruction to the contractor of a variation in the works proposed.

Valuations and payments

The JCT Minor Works Contract > see also **The building contract** pp.252–3 uses a system of periodic valuations. After an agreed period (every two weeks is common), a contract administrator will issue a certificate confirming how much of the work is complete. The contractor can then invoice the client for the certified amount, less the retention sum (usually 5 per cent). This system of valuations and payments ensures that the client is not exposed to paying for work that has not been undertaken, while at the same time, the contractor receives regular payments to cover costs incurred.

The 'practical completion' and 'final completion' certificates > see also **The final stages** pp.256–7 are the last of these periodic valuation certificates and they draw the contract and payments to a close.

Keeping on time

Your building contract should also set the agreed timescale for the project. If the works overrun, the contractor will be in breach of the contract, unless this is due to a valid reason.

A contract can stipulate a sum of money payable for each day or week that the work runs late. These are called 'damages for consequential loss'. The amount needs to be set into the contract from the beginning and must be demonstrable as a genuine cost or loss. For example, if you rent a house while works are progressing, the cost of extra rent if you have to stay longer would be appropriate.

While building works are often delivered later than the projected date, it is very common for there to be valid reasons which would trigger an 'extension of time' to the contract period. Valid reasons are generally matters that the contractor could not control, such as changes to the design, or bad weather during a crucial stage of the works. All such matters need to be agreed and recorded by the contract administrator to avoid disputes at the end of the project.

The final stages

The end of a project is a tricky and often anxious time. The client is often worried that the builder will disappear having left all manner of things incomplete, and the builder is often paranoid that the client will not pay the final monies now that the property is habitable.

The final finishing touches of a project tend to be fiddly and require short amounts of time from different trades. This places demands upon the builder, who probably needs to get started on the next project. It is also frustrating for the client, who generally sees these final stages as excruciatingly slow.

Practical completion

The most helpful concept that most building contracts include is that of 'practical completion'. The definition of when this is achieved can be pedantically complex, and is subject to more case law rulings than most of us would care about, but, in essence, practical completion is when the work is fit for its practical purpose.

Fit for its practical purpose does not mean complete in every detail, nor that all imperfections are put right. If light switches, for example, are hanging off the wall leaving wires exposed, then one could argue that a house is not ready for a family to live there.

The importance of practical completion is that if the contractor has agreed to a fixed timescale, this is the end point of that time. If you have been living somewhere else while works have progressed, it is at practical completion stage that you would, generally, take occupation of the property. The contractor would be released from his obligation to secure and insure the premises. Final payment of all money is made to the contractor, less an allowance known as 'retention', which is typically 2.5 per cent of the contract sum.

Defects liability and final completion

After practical completion, there follows a set period of time, usually three or six months, called the 'defects liability period'. During this time, any items that are incomplete or defective within the works can be identified, and a list of defects, known as a 'snagging list' can be prepared. It is important to distinguish between genuine defects in the work, and the wear and tear of living in a house. Typical snagging items would include shrinkage cracks in the plasterwork or poorly finished paintwork.

At the end of the defects liability period, the contractor should be allowed access to the premises to put right all of the snagging items on the list. Once these have been successfully completed, the contract will have reached full completion.

If you have used a contract administrator, a certificate will be issued formally confirming practical completion. A final completion certificate will be issued when all the agreed snagging works have been completed. With the final certificate, the contractor should be paid the retention money.

It is important to understand that just because the contract is complete does not mean that the contractor is no longer responsible for things that might go wrong with the work. In law, builders have a 'duty of care', which makes them responsible for the work they have undertaken. Over and above this, special items, such as damp-proof treatments will carry written guarantees, which need to be passed onto the client to keep.

Practical completion means that the works are essentially fit for purpose and that the owner can take possession of the premises. Safety-related matters are usually the final items that prevent practical completion.

When drawing up a snagging list, it is important to be fair and even-handed. No work is perfect, and when identifying snagging items or judging whether they have been put right satisfactorily, it is necessary to be reasonable.

If certain specified levels of thermal efficiency or acoustic insulation have been required within the contract, these can be tested during the defects liability period to confirm that they have been completed correctly.

During the main part of the contract period it is usual to retain 5 per cent of the money against works completed. Following practical completion this is usually reduced to 2.5 per cent.

The building inspector should make his final inspection during the defects liability period. If work is completed, he or she will issue a certificate confirming approval. Any outstanding items should be dealt with in the snagging list.

As with so many other aspects of building projects, the more control that is required, the more detailed administration will be needed and the more complex the contract document may become. All this will inevitably add to the cost.

Case study

6. The built design

The family house extension and refurbishment project that we have followed through each stage of this book is now complete, and these pages show some images of the finished house.

As with any project, there are items that were on the original wish list that we were not able to incorporate and others that we have allowed for, but will have to wait for.

Although expensive, when budgets allow, the plan is to install solar-thermal panels **>** see also **Solar-thermal systems** pp.172–3 on the top of the roof to reduce dependency on natural gas, and the possibility of covering the extension roof with Sedum to make a 'green' roof is a consideration for the future.

Overall, the project has without doubt been a great success. In financial terms, the value added to the property exceeds the total cost of the project by over £150,000, although this rather depends upon what the property market does going forward.

As a family house it is proving to be practical to live in and the thought given to durability of materials, which was identified from the start as an important aim, seems to have paid off very well.

The external space and the way that the interior links to the outside also works very well. In particular, the relocation of the front door has made for much better circulation, and the deck area at the rear of the house becomes a meaningful outdoor room throughout the summer.

Time will tell us how well the materials chosen last, how the red-cedar cladding weathers and if the family use changes as the children get older. For now however, it is a project to be proud of.

Services menu

Architect Your Home has developed a unique menu that allows home owners to **choose** the services that will add **value** to their project. Every customer, every architect and every project is **different** so make sure that you work in a way that is easy for you. Whether you choose to use it sparingly or as a complete service, this menu should enable you to be in **control** of your project from concept to completion.

What happens first?

The architectural process kicks off with an **initial visit**. *It is* **up to you** *how you would like to use your architect's skills and* **expertise** *during the initial visit, but here is an outline of how it usually works.*

Full-day initial visit If a project has several separate elements, or significantly affects a property on more than one storey, an architect will need to spend a full day visiting your home.

The purpose of this visit is to:

> i. Discuss your thoughts and requirements in order to establish a brief of your objectives

> ii. Take rough measurements and make a sketch of the existing layout

> iii. Using these plans, to sit down with you and draw an outline sketch showing the possible options

> iv. Once prepared, to discuss the plans further with you, and then to amend and revise the sketches as necessary. The aim is that you will have an agreed, sketch-drawn proposal in outline form by the end of the visit.

Half-day initial visit When a project only has one element (for example, a bathroom extension or the remodelling of a kitchen), an architect will spend half a day with you discussing options. As with the full-day consultation, the session involves discussions, sketch survey layouts and design options, with an agreed, drawn proposal in outline form by the end of the session.

Half-day home buyers visit For anyone considering the purchase of a property this service can be very helpful. You can arrange for an architect to meet you at the property and spend time with you discussing your aspirations, ideas and budget, and assessing whether or not the property has the potential to realise your needs. As with the other consultations, the session involves preparing sketch design options to help you see the potential of the property, along with notes as to the feasibility of possible alterations.

Architects help with planning permission, detailed drawings and advice on how to find a good builder.

Further meetings

Very often you or your architect have **new ideas** *and discover information that may affect the design. Alternatively, you might want further* **clarification** *on particular aspects of the* **design**.

If so, it is well worth having a further meeting and sitting round a table with the drawings to discuss the implications of any changes or modifications.

General follow up Throughout your project you will probably need to discuss the progress of works, prices, the design development, or any other queries you may have with your architect, which you can do either by e-mail, phone or at a meeting. Similarly, you may want your architect to attend a meeting with you and your contractor, structural engineer, or other consultant.

Travel to/from meetings as required Travel time may need to be charged depending on where the meeting is held.

Printing and Postage After the first set of drawings additional copies or prints may be charged for.

A project such as this one is the investment of a lifetime. Most home owners are not qualified to put their ideas into practice. An architect can help interpret ideas creatively and expertly.

Moving the design forward

Following the **initial** *visit you may require further drawings,* **information** *or clarification on the sketched scheme previously discussed.*

If you are having difficulty in deciding how to organise the space, consider using an architect who is trained to take your brief, offers expert advice and prepares really good plans.

Outlined below are various steps that will move your project forward. An architect can help to choose which are most suitable for you.

Further development of outline level design Having considered the drawings and ideas from the initial visit, you may want your architect to work on some further ideas and layouts.

Investigate related issues
It is often advisable to get your architect to spend some time investigating issues such as permitted development, and planning or building regulations, which may relate to particular elements of your proposals.

Sketch perspective illustrations
To help you visualise how proposals might appear from a particular point of view, an architect can prepare a line sketch perspective drawing.

Computer rendered perspective views and walk through movies
A more realistic illustration of how proposals might appear can be generated using 3-D computer modelling and rendering. Alternatively, a movie file can actually move you through your proposed extension or conversion.

Why a survey?

To enable your architect to prepare useful drawings of your **proposals**, *it is necessary to have drawings of the existing building in a* **CAD** *(computer-aided drawing) format.*

For some projects precision is vital, for others, less so. An architect can advise you on what is suitable for your project.

Full measured CAD survey
Architects can organise full measured surveys of properties. This includes precise plans, sections and elevations of your home in CAD form. It is important to remember that accurate drawings of the existing structure can help to avoid problems later.

Part measured CAD survey In some cases it is only necessary to measure a particular part of a building, and this is likely to be less costly.

Input to CAD from given survey drawings You may already have some drawings of your home. It is possible to work with these, but your architect will need to allow time to input the information to CAD. This can be less expensive than getting a new survey, but note that the accuracy of such drawings cannot be guaranteed.

Input to CAD from outline survey and photographs For simple projects or when precision is not critical, your architect will produce CAD drawings from the measurements and photographs taken during the initial visit. Such drawings should be approximately accurate, but will not be precise.

Next stage drawings

*In simple terms, the more **information** you have on your drawings, the **easier** your project will be to manage*
➤ see also **Chapter 3: Scheme design** pp.100–45.

Complex buildings need a great deal of specification, whereas simple projects can get by with less. Scheme level drawings provide the backbone of what is needed for most projects.

Scheme level drawings for planning applications This is a set of plans, sections and elevations for general use, and are suitable for an application to the planning department. These are CAD drawings (usually based upon a CAD survey) that show the general layout of the proposals as a whole. While these may include some general building notes, and flag where other consultants or further detail may be needed, they are not intended as construction plans. When an application requires particular information or detail to be included (for example, when the building is listed) it can be included here. Additionally to these drawings all applications require a location plan ➤ see also **Gaining statutory consents** p.270.

Scheme level drawings for building regulations applications
This is a more detailed set of plans, sections and elevations than described above, containing the specific information suitable for a 'full plans' application under the building regulations, which an architect is able to provide ➤ see also **The building regulations** pp.196–201. Alongside these drawings, it is usual that additional information provided by other consultants (such as a structural calculations or thermal performance figures) will be needed to fulfil the building regulations requirements. Your architect can co-ordinate with these consultants for you, (see Co-ordinating with other consultants).

Scheme level drawings with additional information To take the project further, the scheme level drawings described above can be supplemented with additional information – for instance, lighting layouts, external works or power point locations – and discussed with your architect. Such a set of drawings are generally suitable for budget pricing purposes, and can form the backbone of what your builder will need to work from.

NB: Following the production of scheme level drawings, it is always a good idea to have a meeting with your builder and architect together to talk through the design, and agree what level of further technical detail drawings or specification the builder might need ➤ see also **Chapter 4: Detail design** pp.146–207 and **Chapter 5: Specification** pp.208–263.

Amendments to scheme level drawings If changes to the design are required, whether due to a change of mind, planning issues or budget, discussions with your architect and time spent amending the drawings will need to be taken into account.

Outline breakdown of works for pricing Your architect will prepare a summary of the main elements of work proposed, broken down for contractors to price against. This can help you make a like-for-like comparison.

Co-ordinating with other consultants You may well need the input of a specialist consultant such as a structural engineer, a party wall surveyor, a quantity surveyor/estimator, a planning consultant, or a building regulations consultant – particularly for 'U' value and SAP calculations ➤ see also **Approved documents** p.199. Your architect can help find who you need and co-ordinate with them, as required.

Gaining statutory consents

These are the **permissions** *you require from bodies, such as your local council in order to* **carry out** *the* **changes** *you wish to make to your property.*

Permitted development application On your behalf an architect can complete the application form for a certificate of lawful development ➤ see also **Permitted development** pp.106–9, print and collate drawings, prepare volume calculations, as required, draft an accompanying letter and submit these to the local authority.

Planning application Your architect will add any necessary further detail to the scheme level drawings, fill out the application forms for planning permission, print and collate sets of drawings, draft an accompanying letter, package and send off.

Location plan For many applications you will need a 1:1250 location plan (usually an Ordnance Survey extract). If you do not have one, your architect can supply.

Full plans building regulations application If required your architect will submit an application for 'full plans' approval under the building regulations, ➤ see also **Next stage drawings** pp.268–9. Armed with information from other consultants (if necessary) your architect will fill out the forms, print and collate sets of drawings, draft an accompanying letter, package and submit the application for approval.

An alternative to this is the 'building notice' method, which is when your builder submits a simple form to the local council ➤ see also **Building regulations approval** p.200. While this is often the preferred route for simple home owner projects, in some cases the building control department will insist on a full plans application.

Other consents Your architect will prepare and submit other applications for you, as may be required, such as Listed Building Consent, a submission for a landlord's consent and preparing Party Wall Act notices.

Follow-up services Your architect will do the follow-up with the council, structural engineers, consultants etc., answer enquiries, or prepare and submit any further information that may be requested as part of any of the above.

NB: The above services are for the time and work involved. Don't forget that with any application there is usually an application fee, which you would pay for separately.

✱✱✱

Planning permission, Listed Building Consent and the building regulations are legal requirements. An architect can advise you on these matters.

✱✱✱

Details and specifications

The more **detail** *that you have in the way of drawings and information, the more* **control** *you will have over your project both in terms of* **quality** *and* **budget**.

The more detailed the design and drawings are, the more control you will have, but the more you will have to pay for them, so it is important to get the balance right. The best way to establish the right level is to organise a meeting with your architect and builder together and work out just what is required.

Detail level drawings Some elements of the proposals often require additional detail, and these drawings show such elements, illustrating exactly what is proposed, with notes on construction ➤ see also Chapter 4: Detail design pp.146–207.

Schedule of works Your architect will prepare a detailed breakdown of the works proposed for your project (although this is not a full specification). This can be very useful when asking building contractors to tender for the work.

Specification information Your architect will put together a package that describes in precise detail the elements (as required) of the design proposals ➤ see also Chapter 5: Specification pp.208–47.

Sourcing of products and materials If required, your architect will prepare a schedule of the proposed building products, components, or equipment (as required), together with information on where/how to purchase them.

Architects have a fantastic knowledge of the design paradigm itself, as well as knowledge of the building industry and they can provide a confident overview of the project.

Bringing it all together

*While the **work** is going on and throughout the whole process, from **concept** through to **finished** project, your architect will be there to **help** as much or as little as you want.*

Architect Your Home is happy to run the whole contract for you or just attend a few meetings to check on progress. Outlined below are the various levels of involvement, and your architect will help you to choose which is right for you.

Sourcing and checking contractor credentials Your architect will source building contractors that may be suitable for you, meet with them, look at their past works and take references. They can also check out recommendations from your friends or neighbours.

Compilation and distribution of tender package Once you and your architect have selected 3–4 builders that you would like to price the work, your architect can put together a package of drawings to demonstrate the scope and detail of the project, along with a breakdown of works for them to price against ➤ see also **Tender and negotiation** pp.250–1.

Going through tenders When you receive the tenders back from the contractors, your architect will analyse these and report to you.

Prepare contract documents You may wish to have a formal building contract ➤ see also **The building contract** pp.252–3. If so, your architect will suggest a suitable one, and prepare the documentation ready for you to sign.

Site visits and meetings You may want your architect to attend site visits and/or meetings, with yourself, builders or other consultants, to discuss the progress of the project.

Contract administration and valuations If required, your architect will take on the role of 'contract administrator' for you (some contracts require this), and prepare valuation certificates etc ➤ see also **The building contract** pp.252–3.

On-site snagging appraisal At the end of the project your architect can prepare a 'snagging list' of unsatisfactory items for the builder to put right ➤ see also **The final stages** pp.256–6.

Contract completion services When your architect has been acting as contract administrator ➤ see also **The building contract** pp.252–3 there may be a contractual requirement to perform 'post-practical completion services' to formally conclude the contract.

Collaboration between you and your architect, and respect for each other's views, will result in a successful solution to your living needs.

The finishing touches

Your architect can help with any part of the building process that you feel would **benefit** *from a* **professional** *opinion, all the way down to sourcing furniture and* **helping** *you choose your kitchen taps.*

Layout drawings Your architect will prepare drawings for you that illustrate the proposed layout of furniture, fixtures and other fittings within your home.

Sourcing of materials and finishes Your architect will put together a package (with samples, as applicable) of proposed materials to be used, and suggested finishes, together with information on where/how to get them.

Sourcing of furniture and fittings/colour schemes Your architect will also compile a package (with pictures, as applicable) of proposed pieces of furniture and fittings, together with information on where/how to get them. An architect can also prepare a schedule (with swatches and colour codes) of the proposed colour schemes to read alongside the plans for your home.

Kitchen/bathroom design Your architect will prepare detail design drawings for your kitchen and/or bathroom installation, with specification of tiles, units, appliances, worktops and basins etc.

Lighting design If required, your architect will produce plans and reflected ceiling plans that show the proposed positions of light fittings and switches, with a detailed specification ➤ see also **Lighting design** pp.182–5.

Index

Acknowledgements

With special thanks to Jude, Jane, Nina, Tristan, Adrian, Cheryl, Chrysoula, Charlotte and Celia in the Architect Your Home head office, to Katie Mortimer and Clare Conville, to everyone at Anova, in particular Caroline King, Katie Cowan, Kate Ward, Victoria Alers-Hankey, Nina Sharman, Becky Alexander, Barbara Dixon and Polly Powell.

Unlike many books on this subject that are filled with stock photography, all of the projects featured in this book (with the exception of six old buildings* and two small reference images on page 29) are the work of the architects and designers within the Architect Your Home network. The majority of these are projects are the work of the author and his team of architects and designers at Architect Your Home Richmond, however the following is a list of projects by the architects at other Architect Your Home branches:

Architect Your Home Buckingham, page 214 (top); Architect Your Home Clapham, page 40; Architect Your Home Highbury, pages 55 (top), 218 (right) and 219; Architect Your Home Kensington, pages 4–5, 130 and 228 (top); Architect Your Home Marylebone, pages 46 and 218 (left); Architect Your Home Oxford, pages 34 and 35; Architect Your Home Putney, pages 126 (left), 155, 166 and 177; Architect Your Home Somerset, pages 48 and 280; Architect Your Home Stratford, pages 100–1; Architect Your Home Wandsworth, pages 125, 156 and 172; Architect Your Home Wirral, pages 128 and 164 (left).

I would like to thank all of the Architect Your Home customers who have provided support and patronage and especially those whose work is featured in this book: Jon and Judy Astley, Sue Chambers, Kate Close, Pat Close, Sophie Conran, Paul Cossel, Paul Crowther, David Da Silva, Emma and Andy Garrett, Joanna Girling, Barry and Lizzie Grimaldi, John Harrison-Church, Allan Hicks, Sally La Torre, Brenda Lattimer, Gary Love, Paul and Pattie Lau, Tom Mockeridge, Christophe and Trudy Nigond, Seamus and Kathy O'Farrell, Howard Packman, Mike Prettyman, John Robinson, Mark and Alison Rowley, Denise Russell, Andrew Shennan, Christian Sullivan, James Tytko and Adam Wolf.

With gratitude to the many photographers whose work is featured, including Peter Cook, David Churchill, Tim Mitchell and Huw Morris.

Thanks to Bill Amberg for supplying the images of wall panels on page 235.

*St Paul's Cathedral (page 23), the 14th–century bookshop (page 127), the gatehouse at Kew Gardens (page 158), Richmond Theatre (page 159), a small brick-built extension (page 213) and a flint house (page 214) both in Lewes, Sussex.

architectyourhome

For more information on Architect Your Home or to book an initial visit with one of our network of architects, visit **www.architect-yourhome.com** or call us on **0800 849 8505**